AF577048

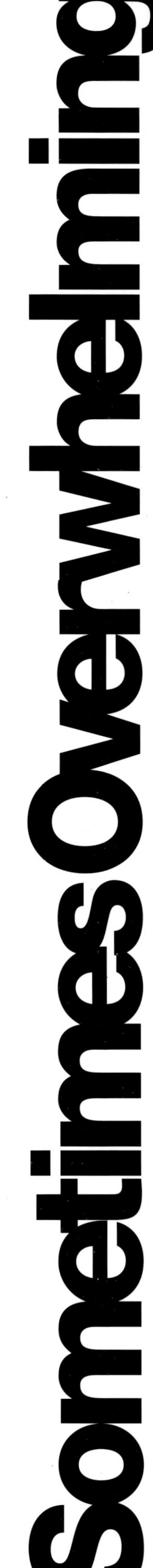
SometimesOverwhelming

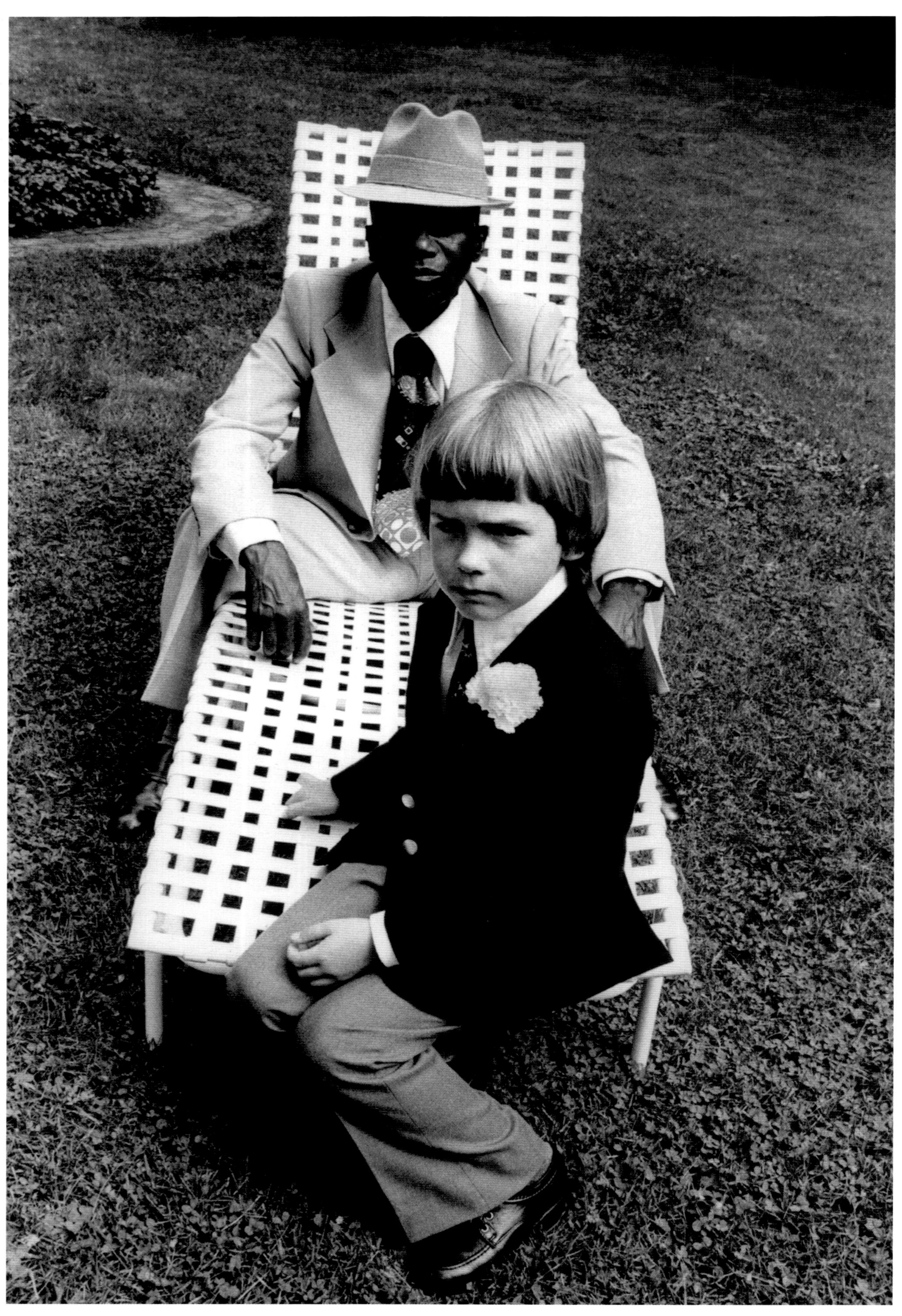

Cover: Hassid and Jewish Bodybuilder, 1980
Left: Wedding Party in Connecticut, 1977

Arlene Gottfried

Sometimes Overwhelming

pH powerHouse Books Brooklyn, NY

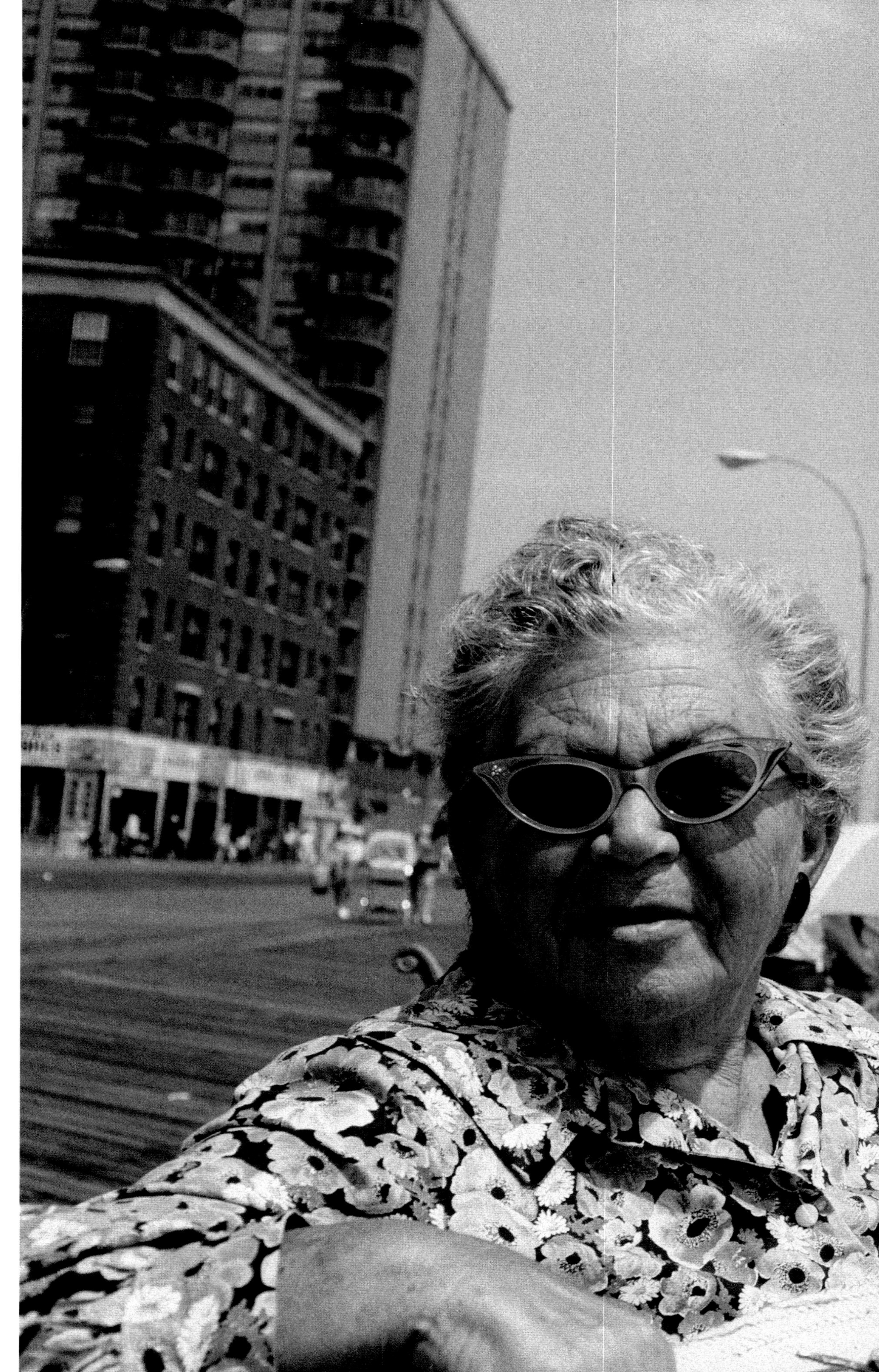

**Angel and Woman on Boardwalk
in Brighton Beach
New York, 1976**

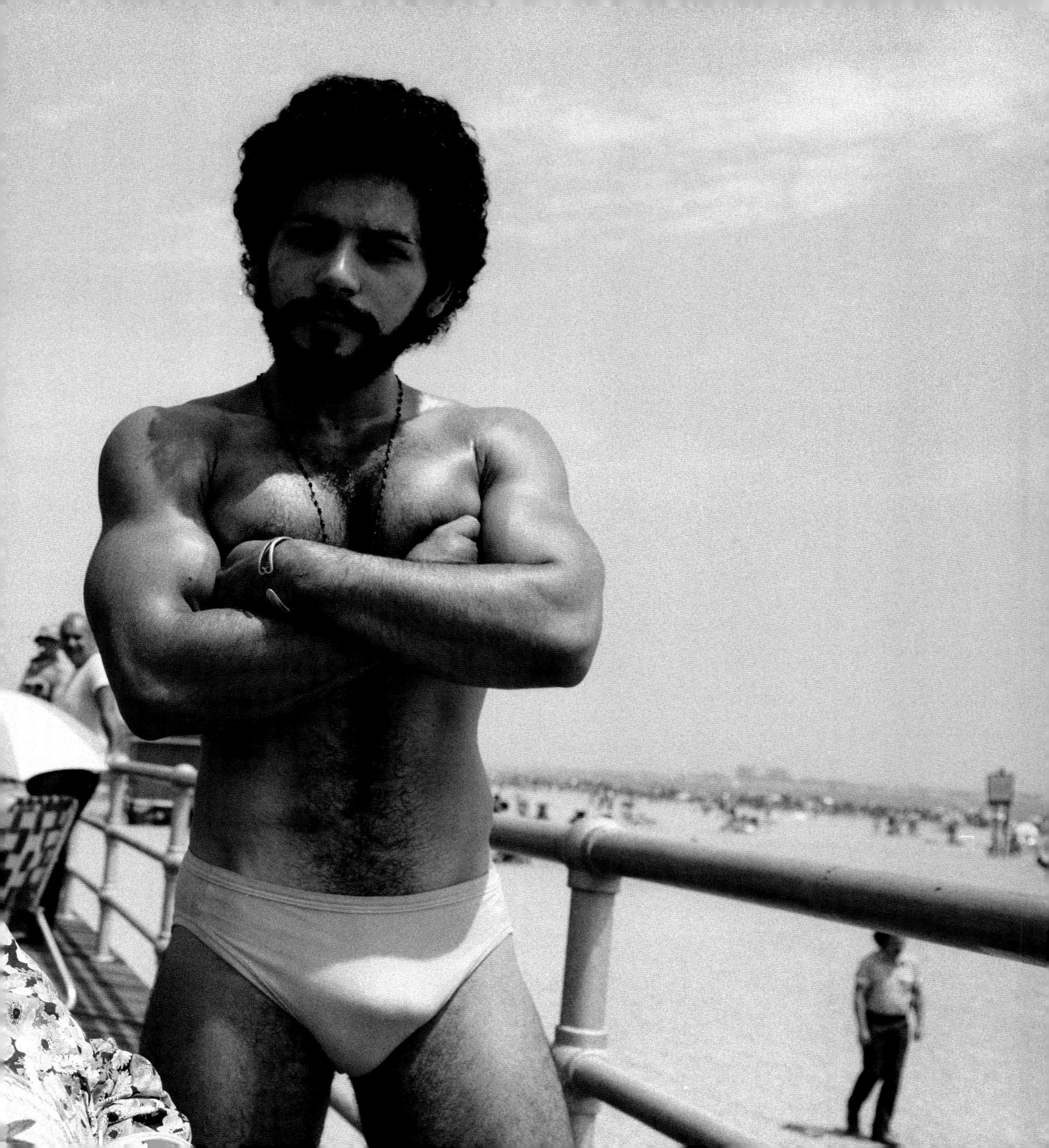

Woman Wearing Sneakers,
Coney Island
New York, 1976

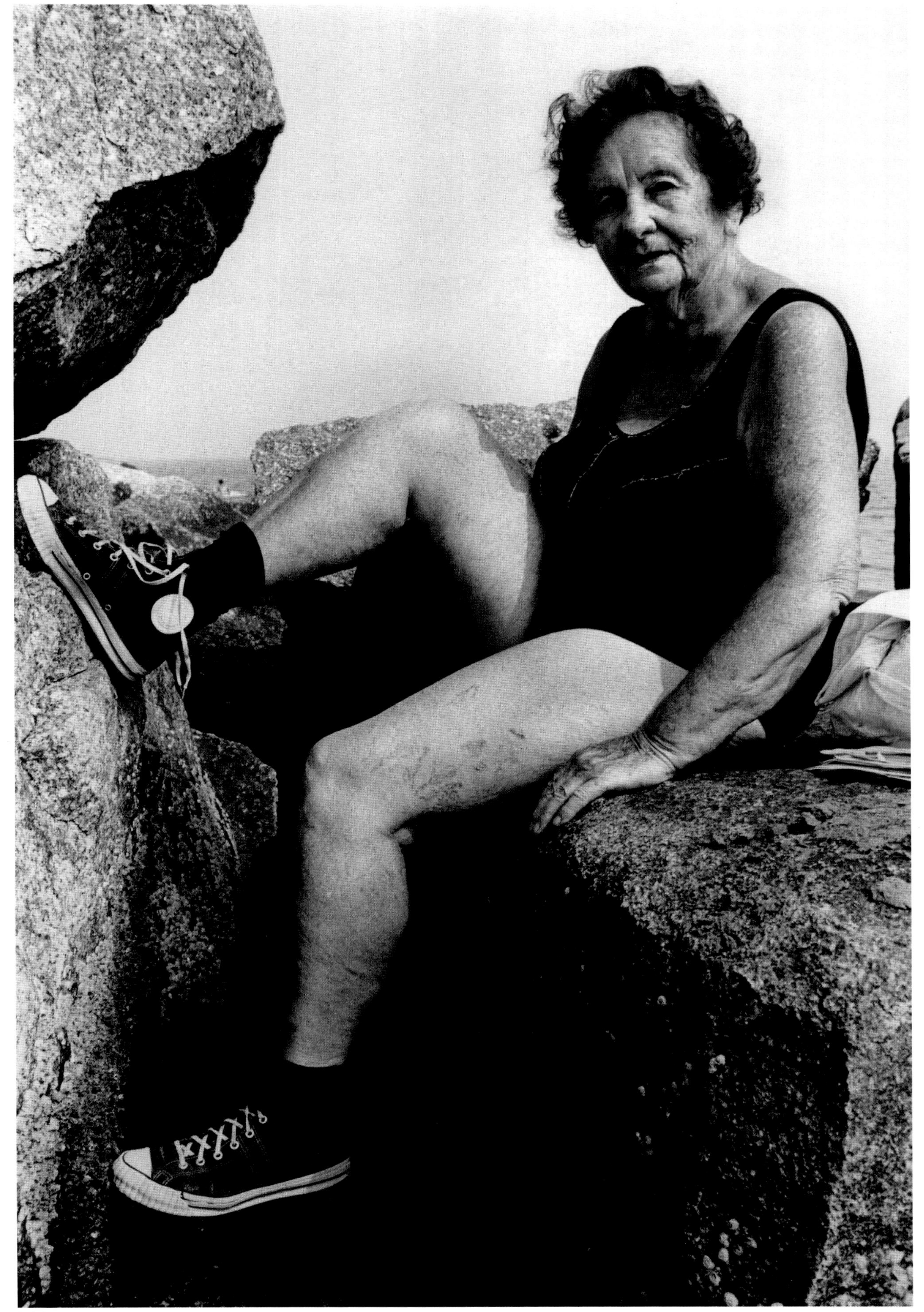

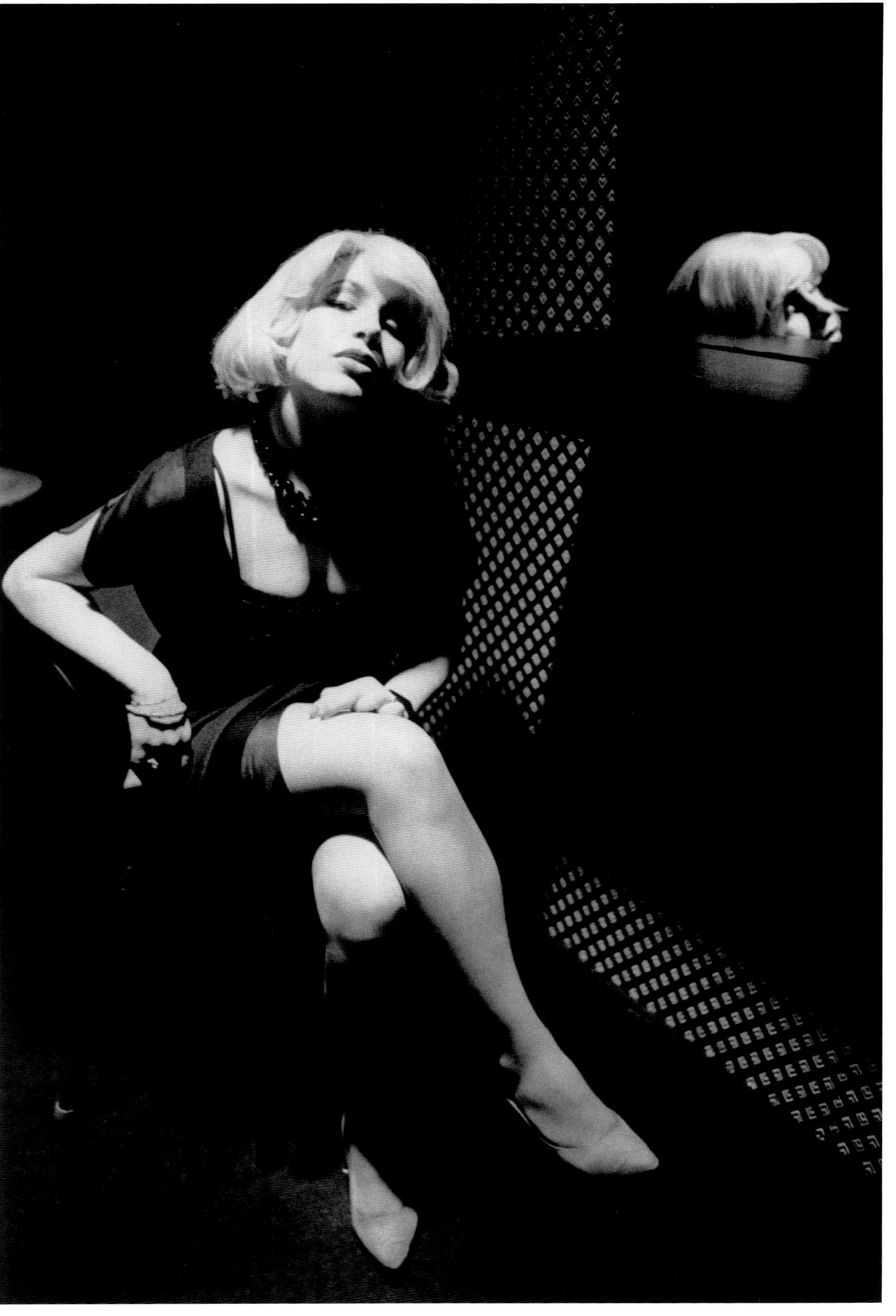

Woman at Marilyn Monroe Look-alike Contest, 1981

Rose Katz on the Pier
at Coney Island
New York, 1976

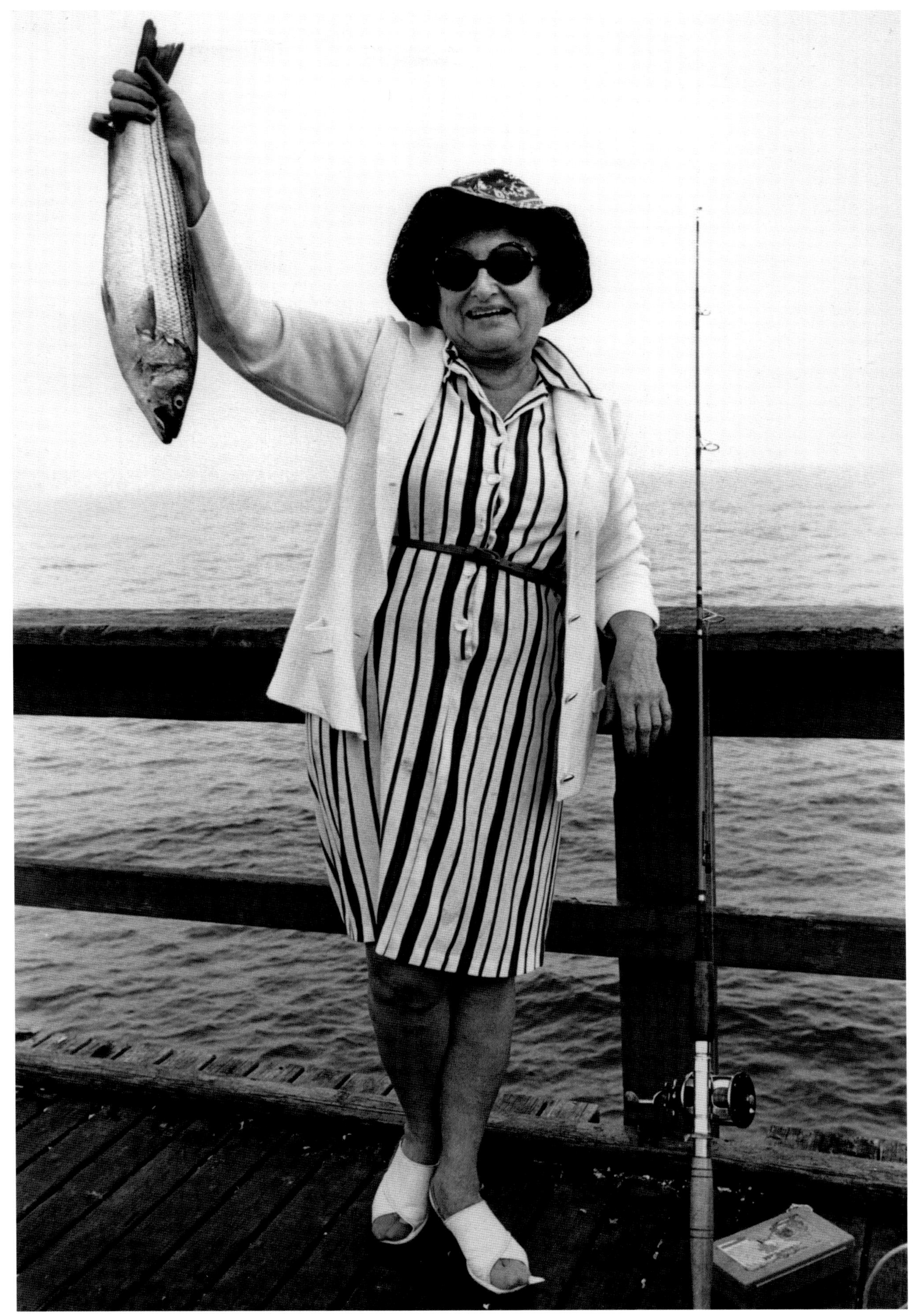

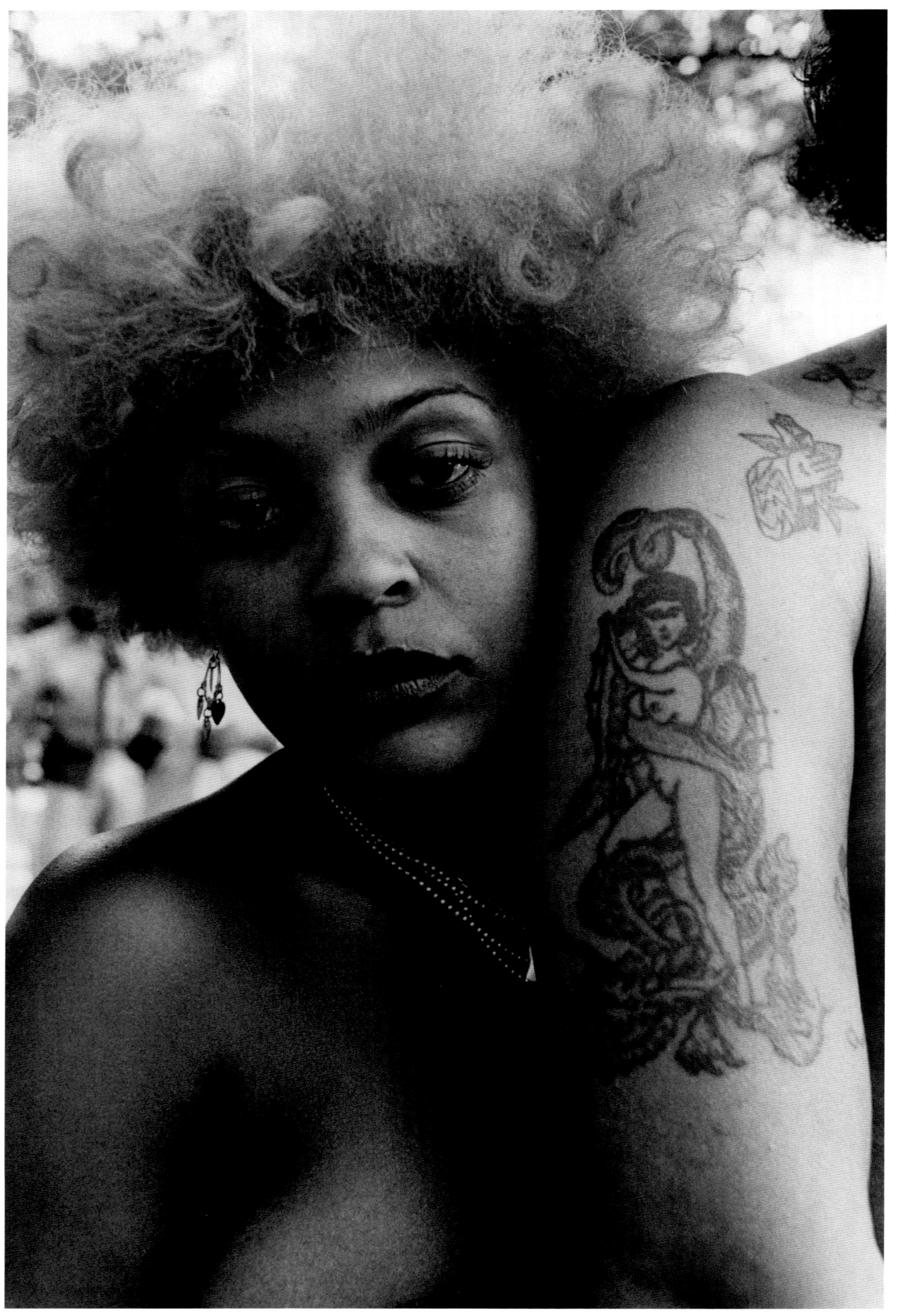

Pituka at Bethesda Fountain,
Central Park
New York, 1977

Elaine Stellar
New York, 1980

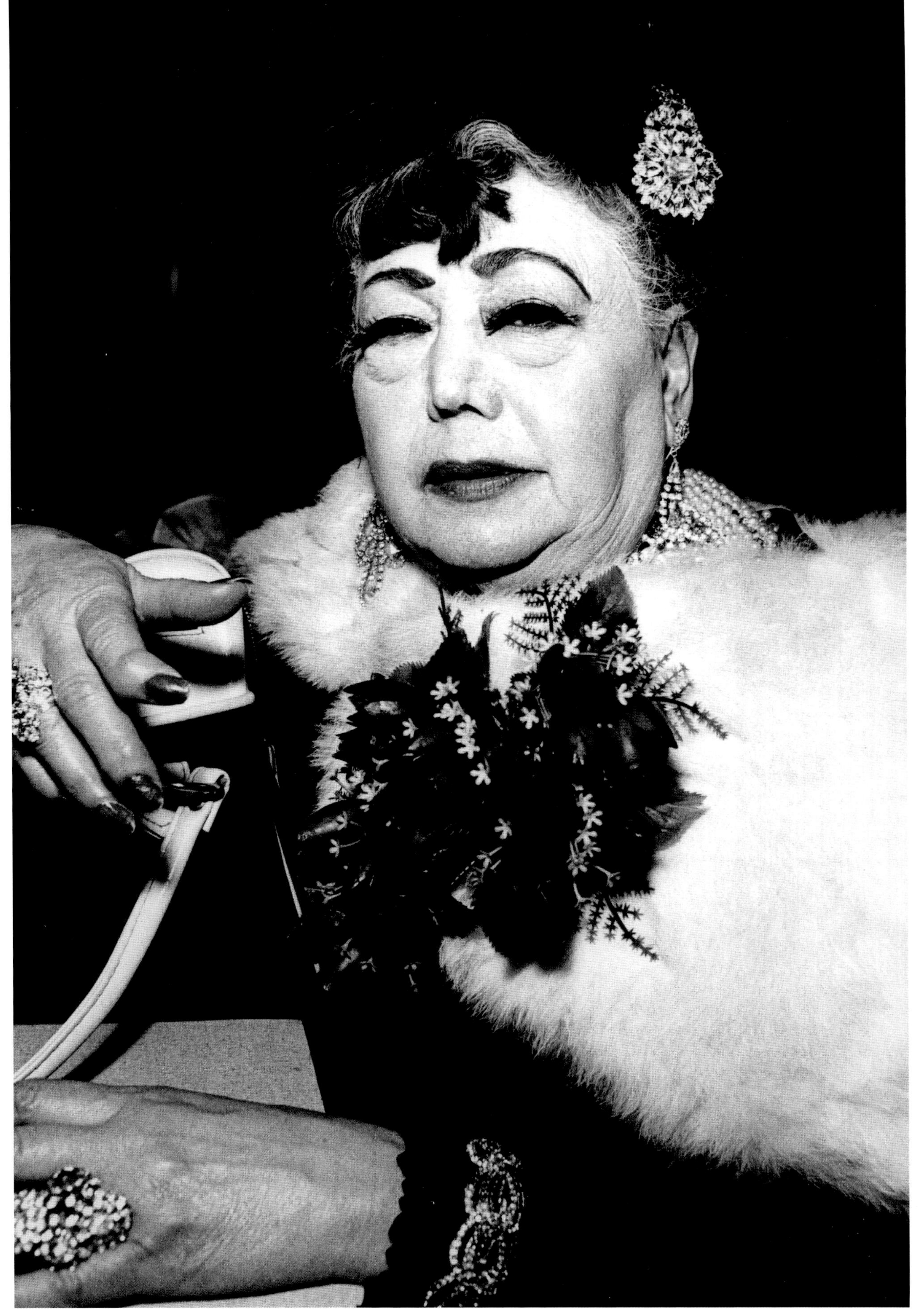

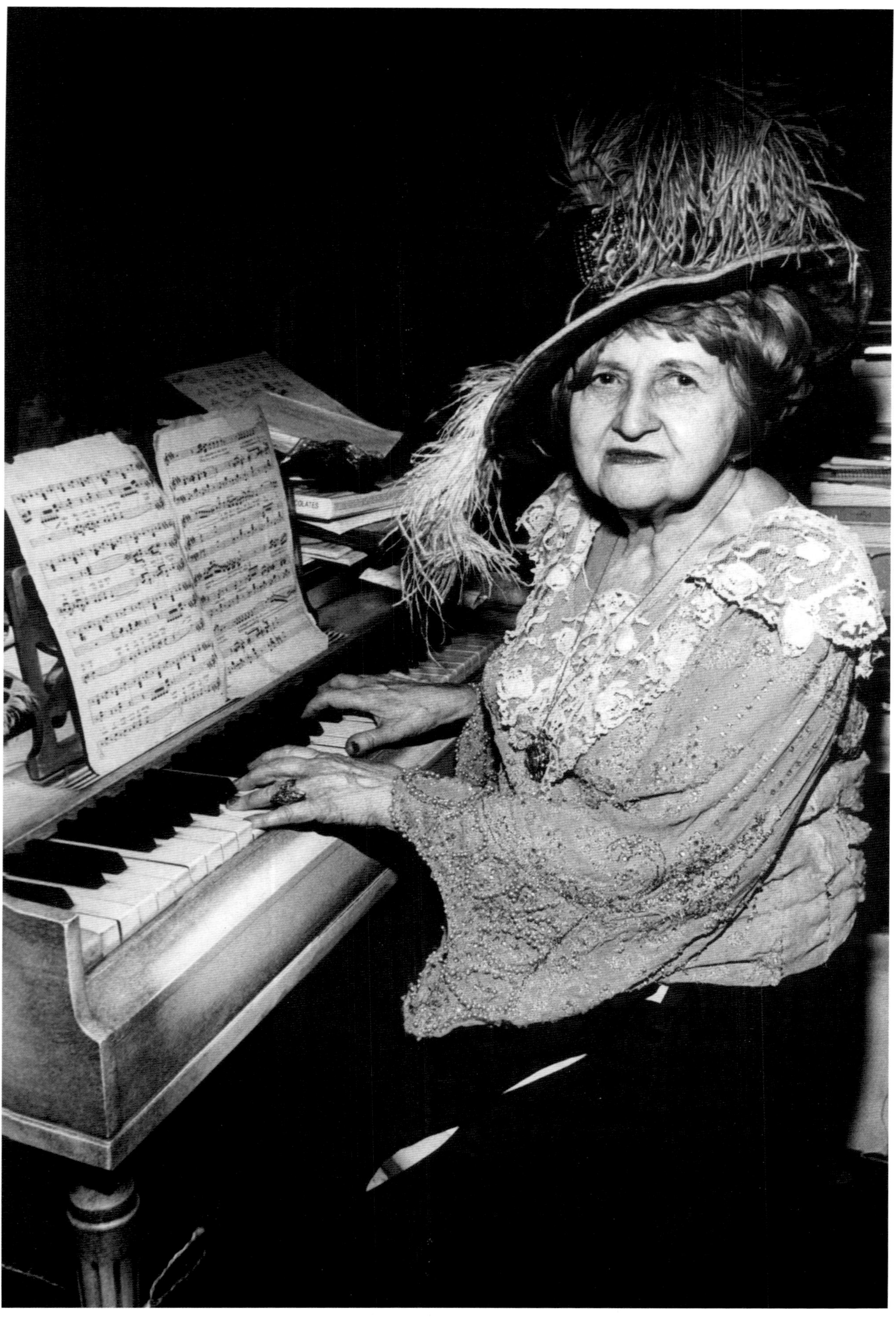

Elaine Roberts Playing Piano at Home in the West Village New York, 1979

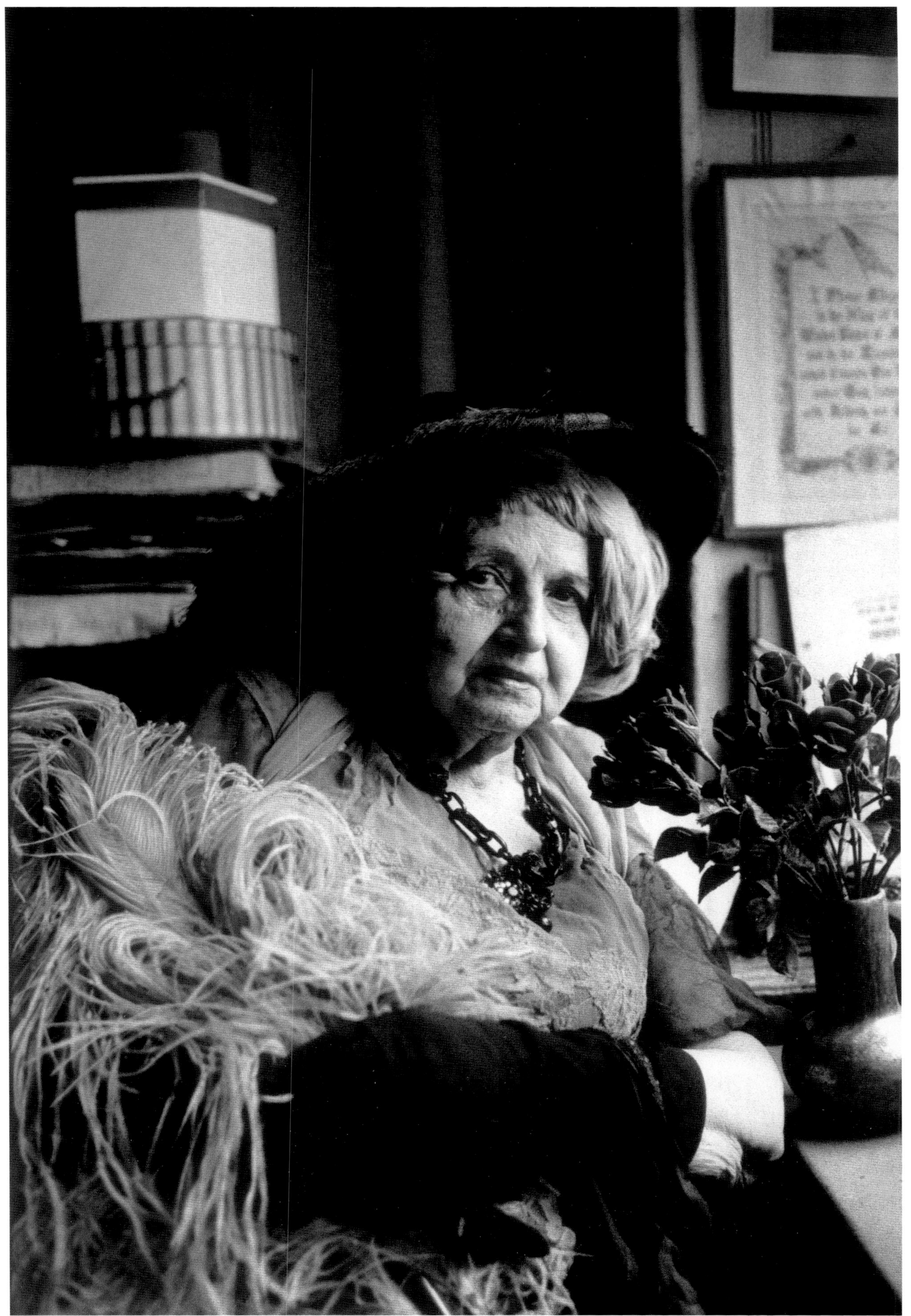

Elaine Roberts in Her Apartment in the West Village
New York, 1979

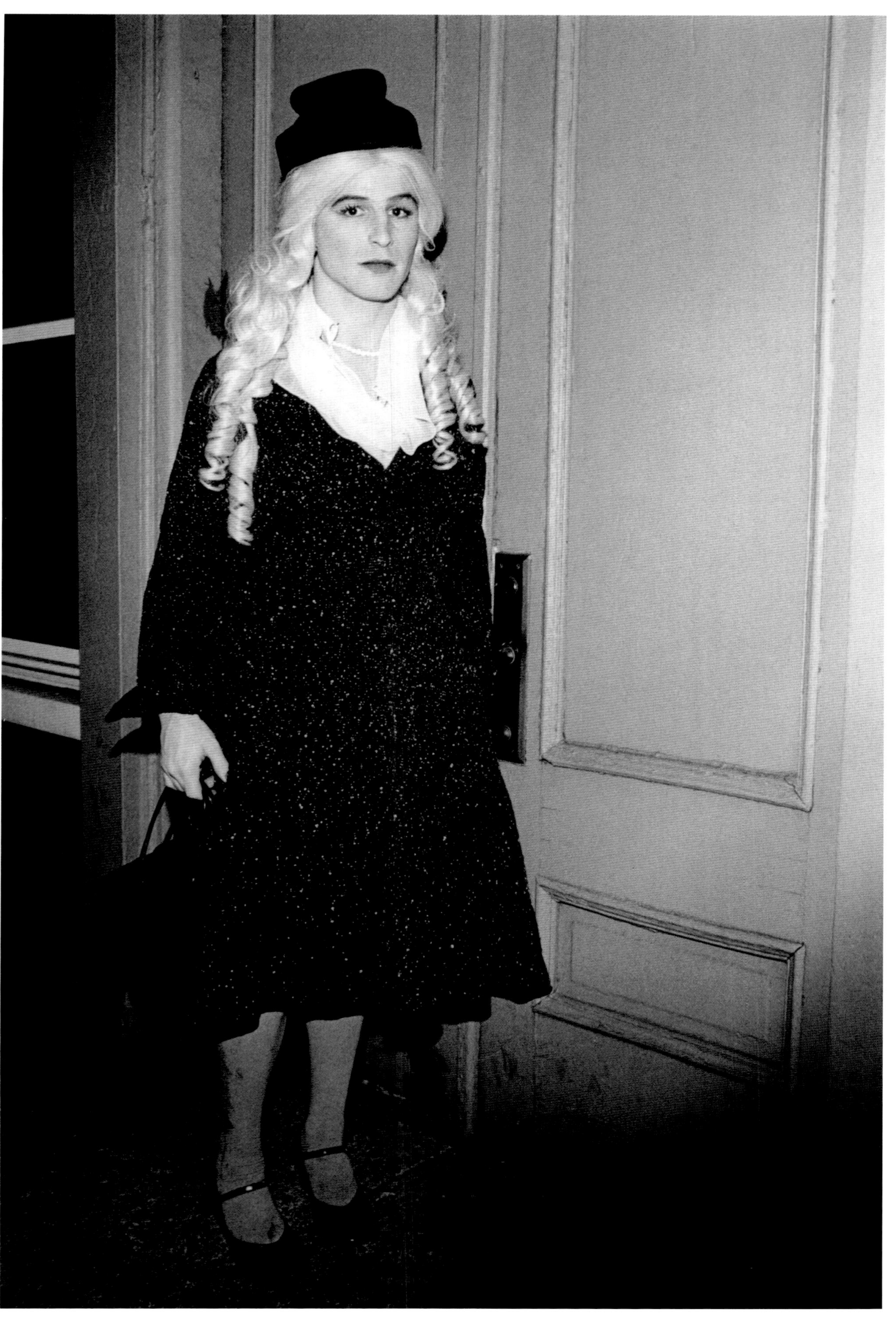

Halloween Parade
in Greenwich Village
New York, 1977

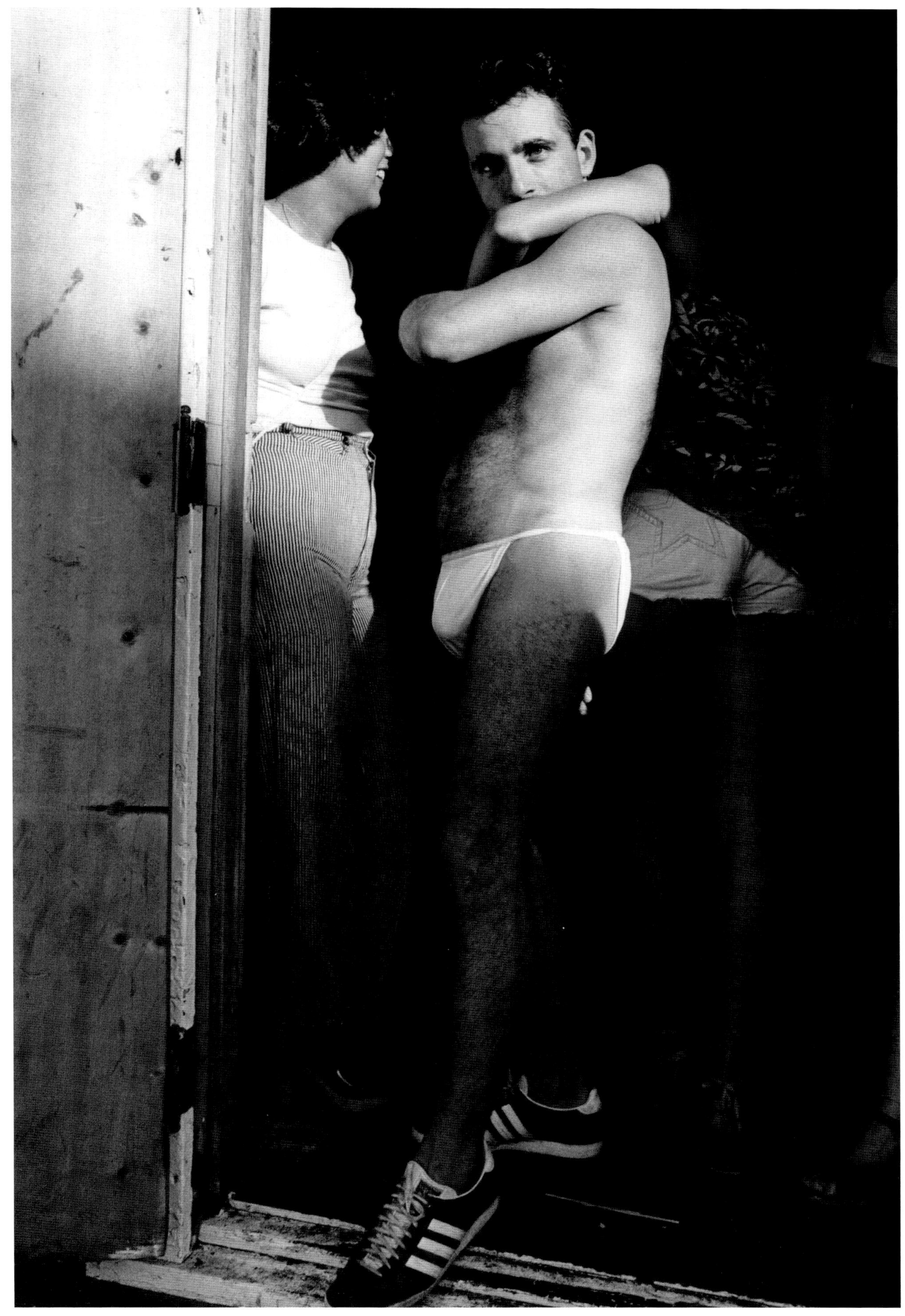

Bar on Fire Island
New York, 1977

Street Photographer, Boro Park
New York, 1979

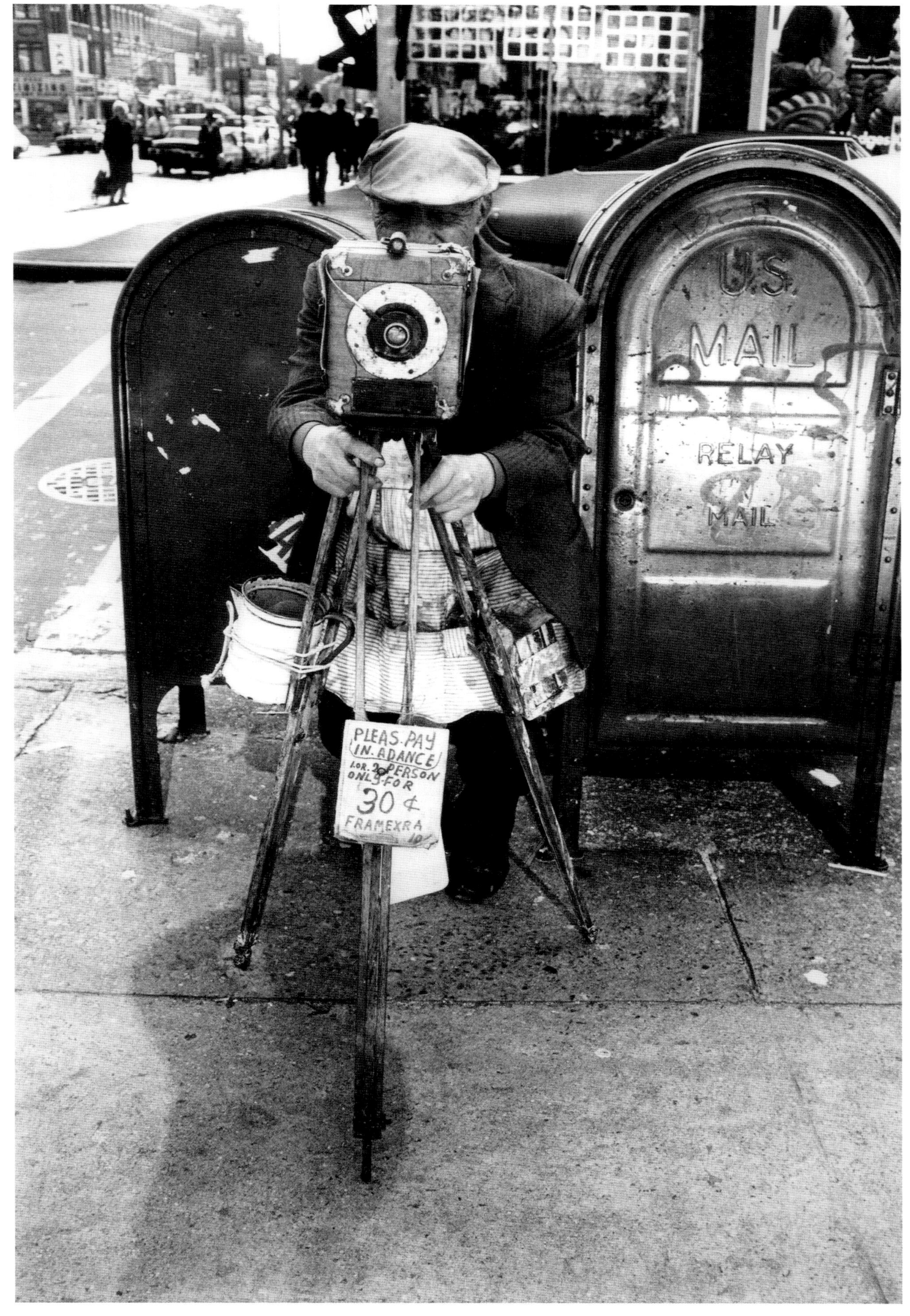
U.S.
MAIL
RELAY
MAIL
PLEAS.PAY
IN.ADANCE
1.OR.2 PERSON
ONLY.FOR
30¢
FRAMEXRA
10

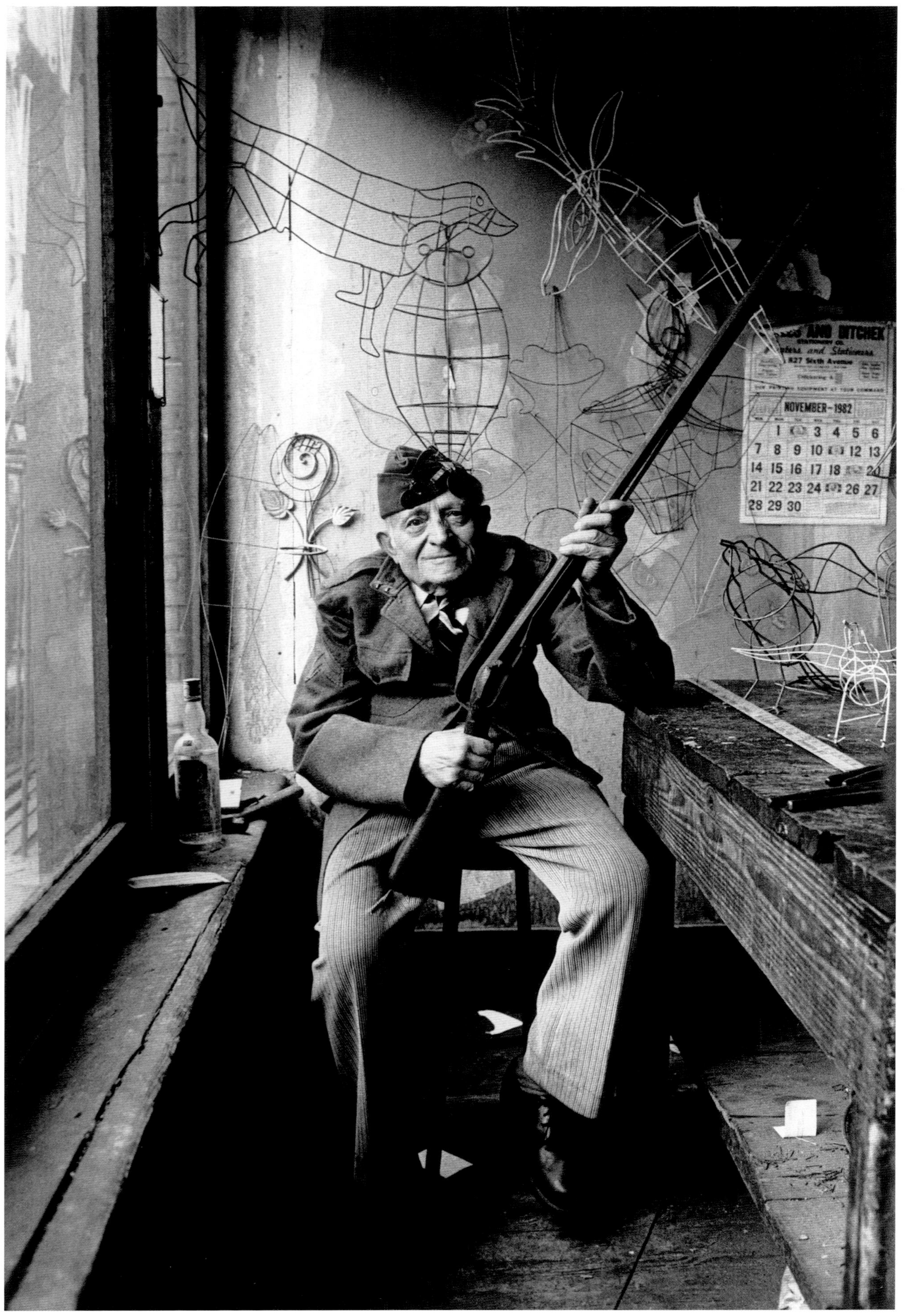

Nick, World War I Soldier
at His Florist Shop
New York, 1982

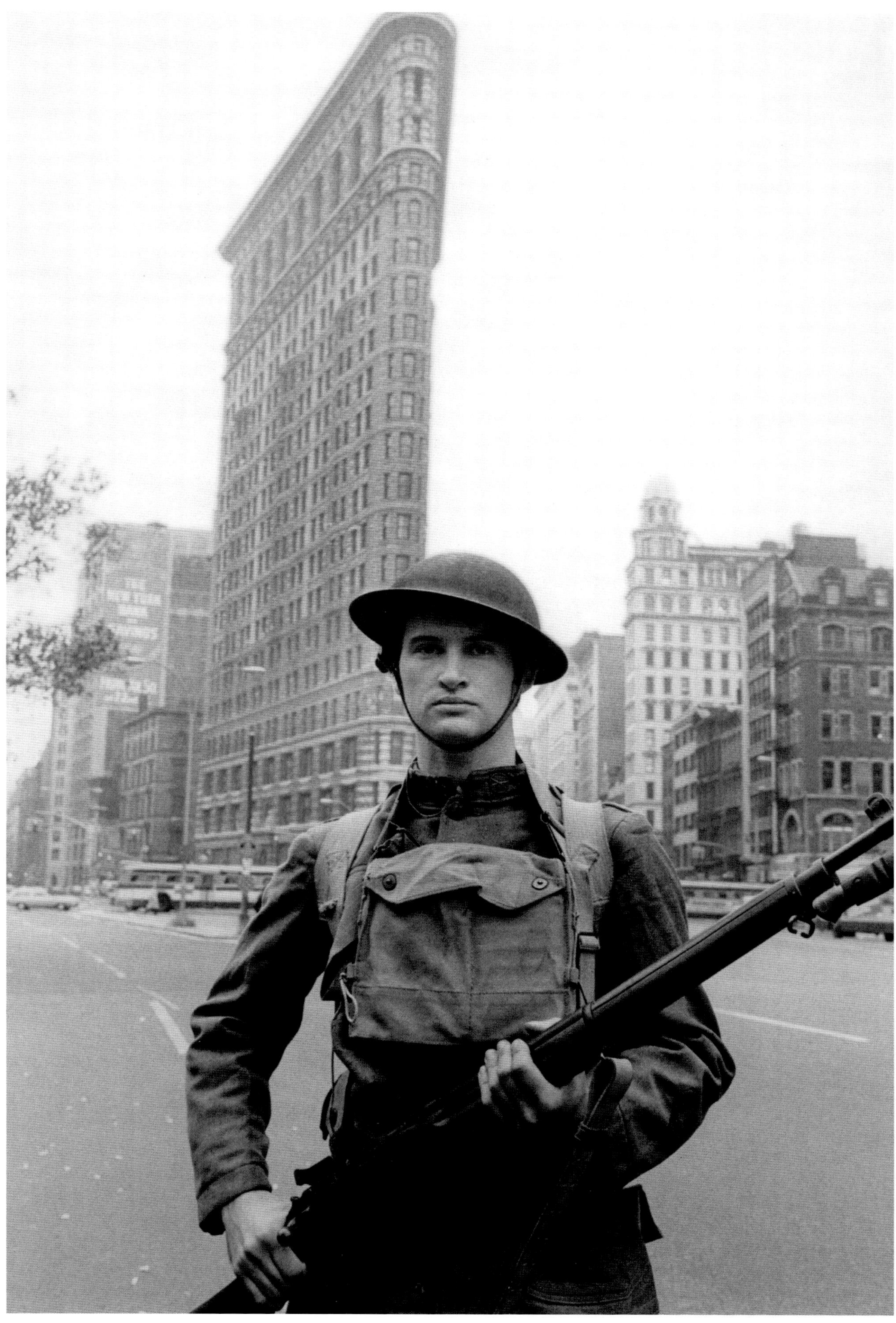

**Veterans Day Parade,
New York, 1978**

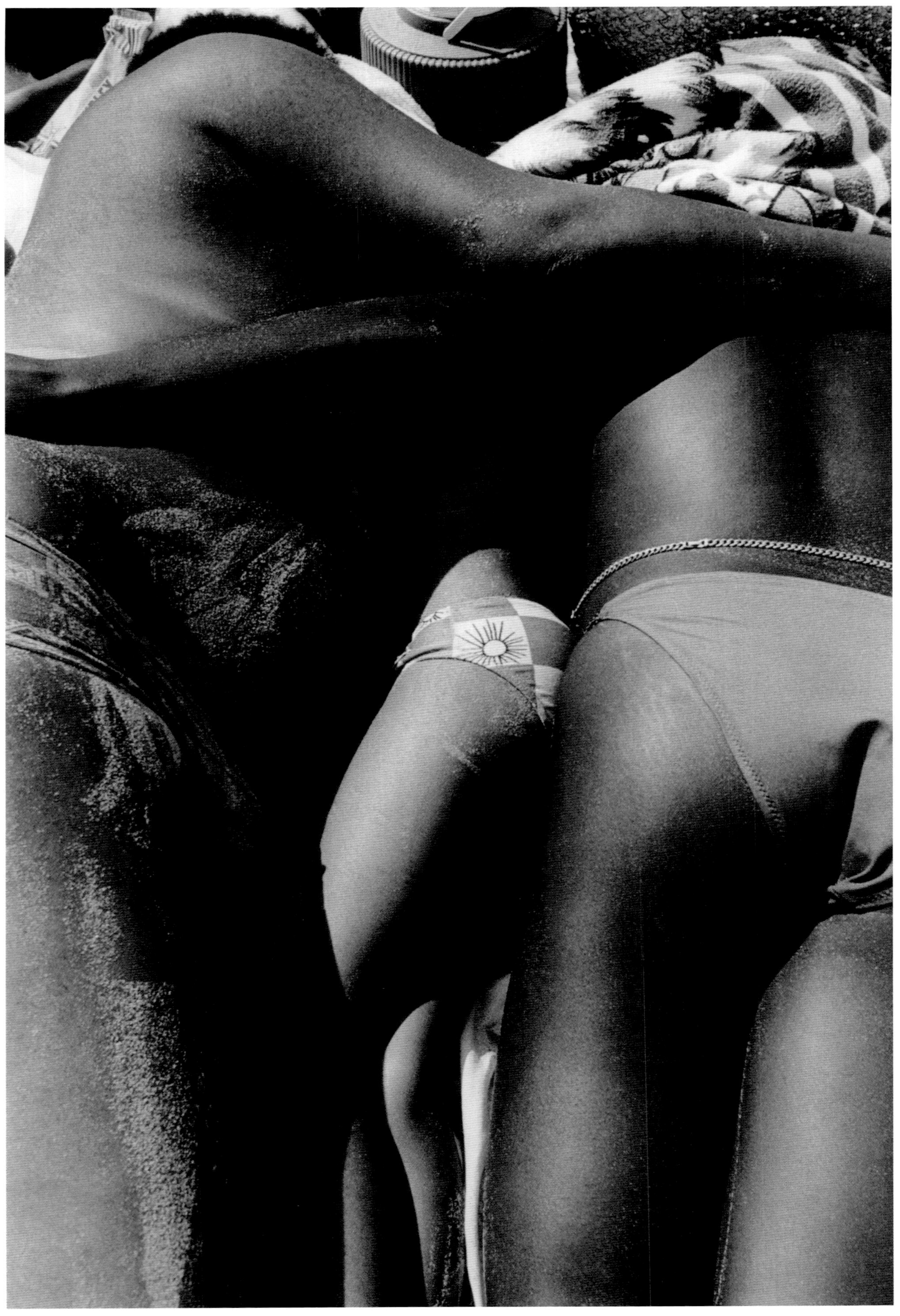

Family on Riis Beach
New York, 1980

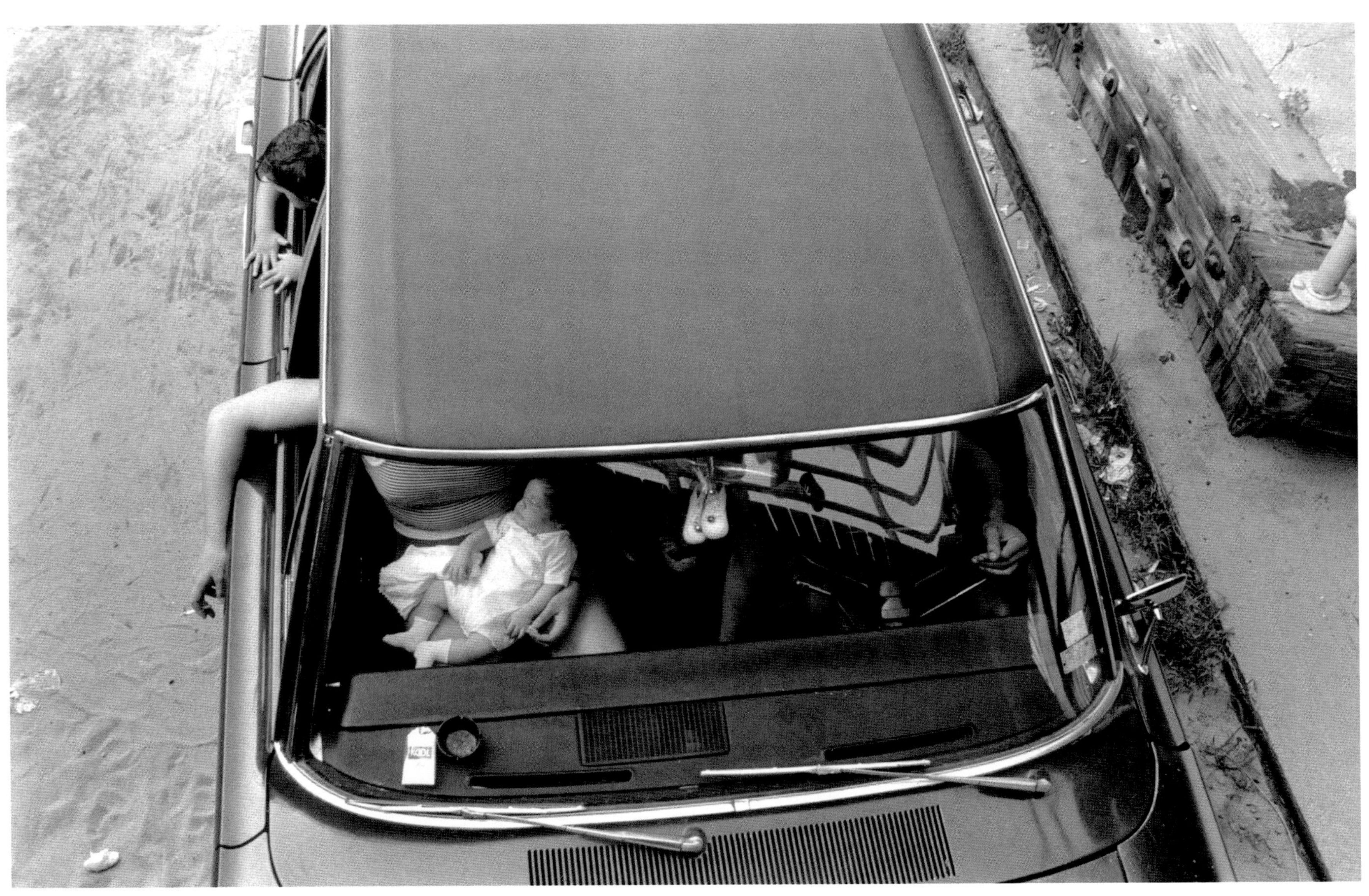

Family in Car, Coney Island
New York, 1976

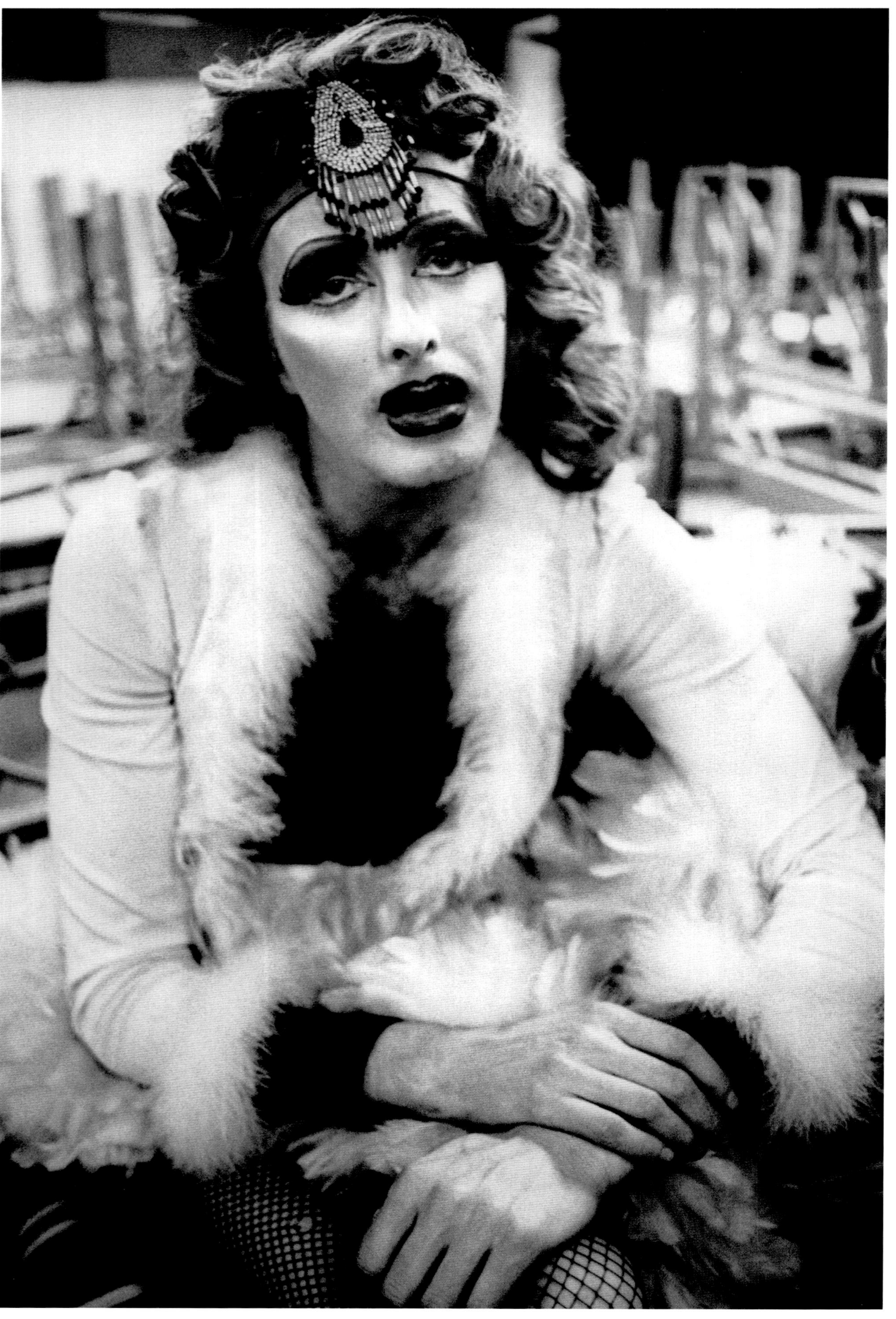

Backstage, Xenon
New York, 1979

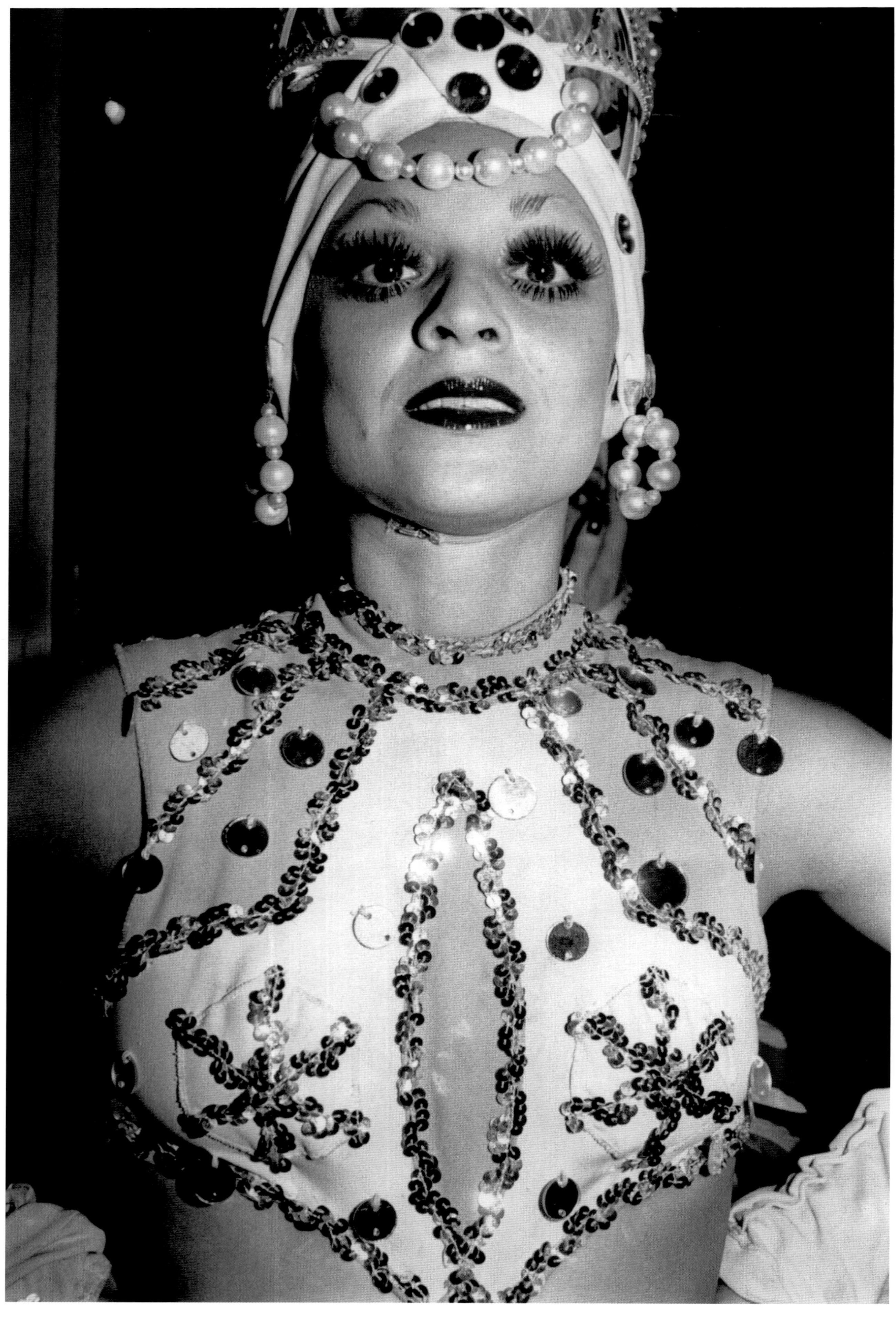

**Rockettes, Radio City Music Hall
New York, 1976**

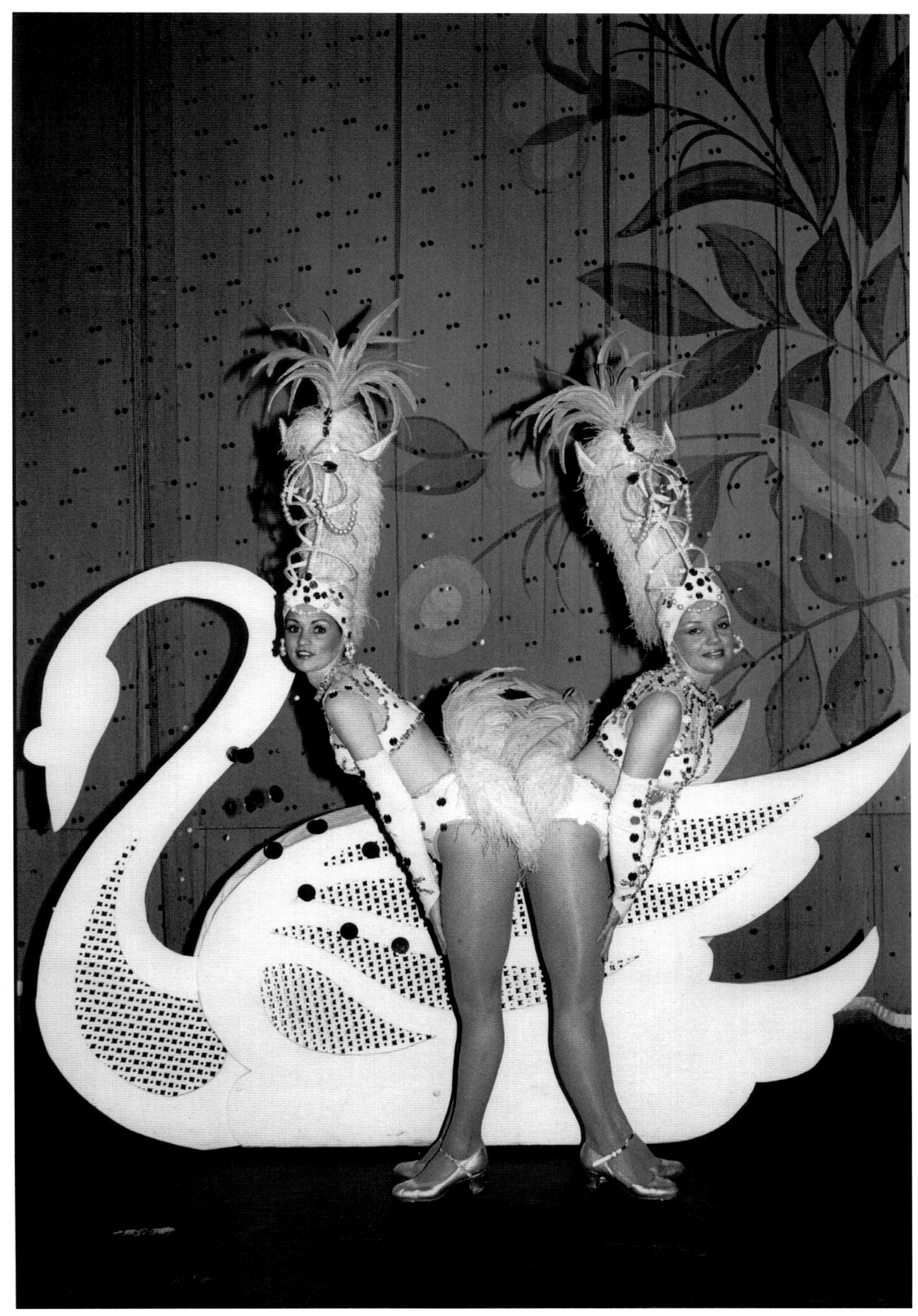

Rockettes, Radio City Music Hall
New York, 1976

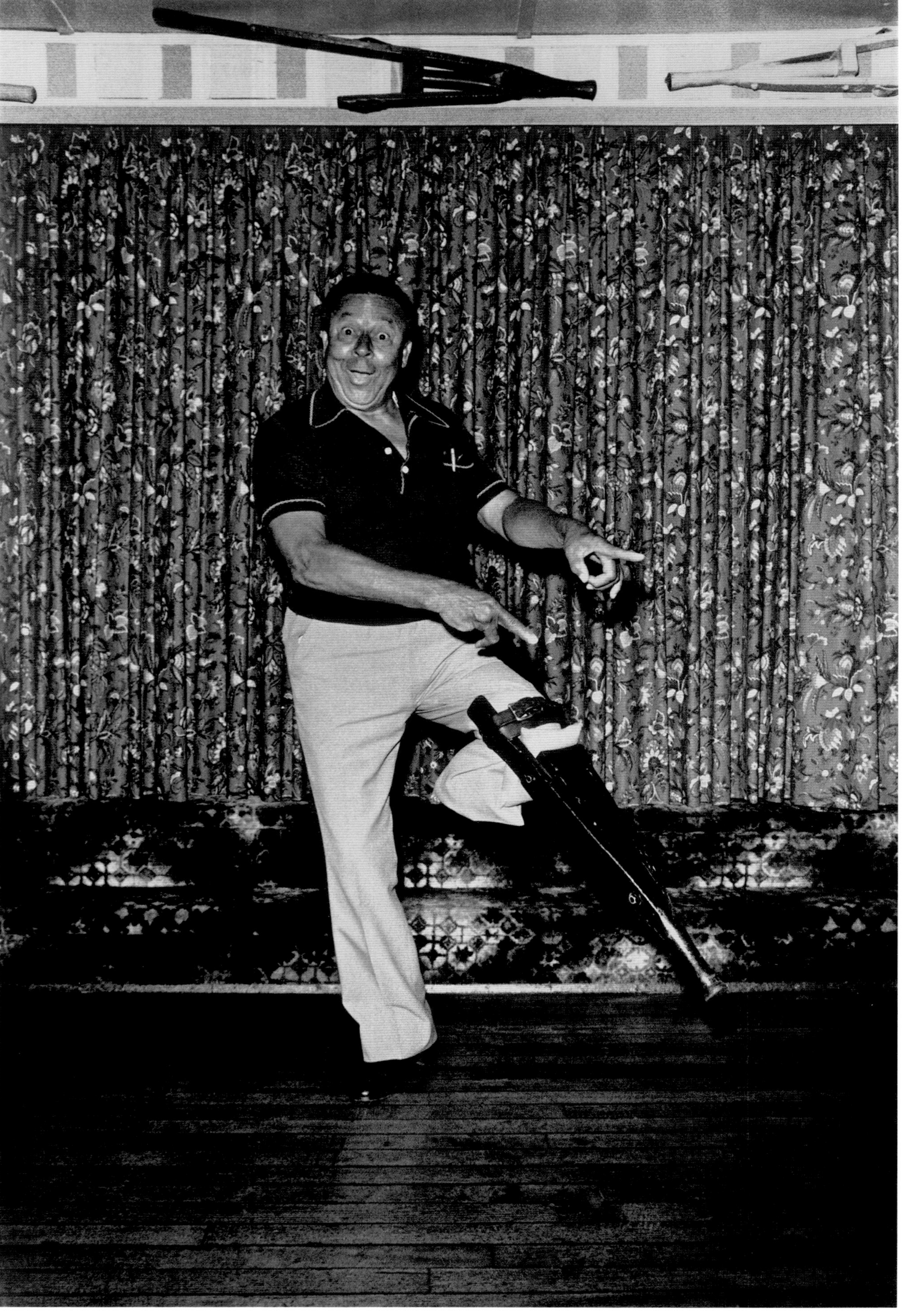

Peg Leg Bates,
Kerhonkson, New York, 1983

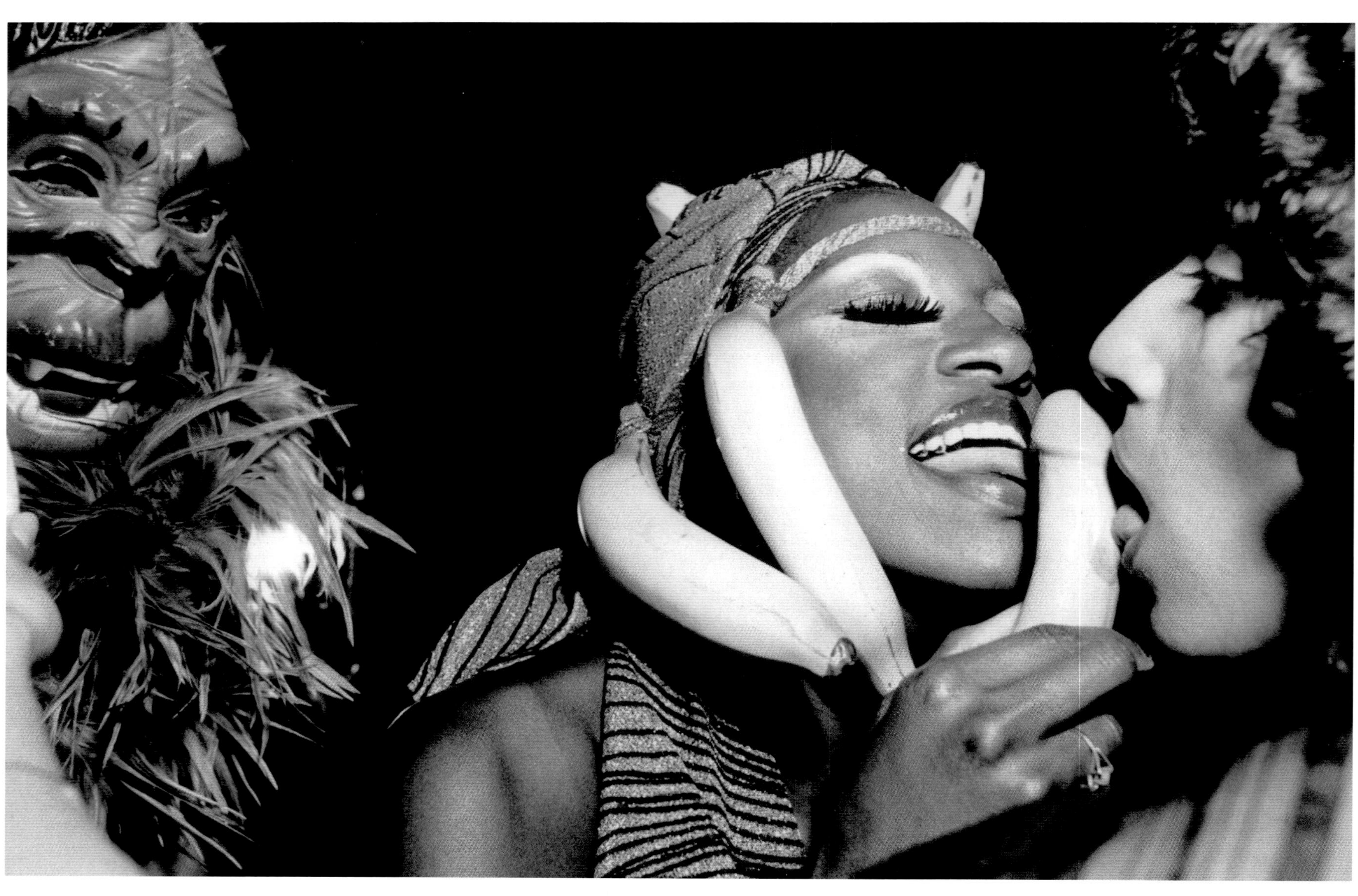

Danger, Woman, Monkey, and Banana at Le Clique New York, 1979

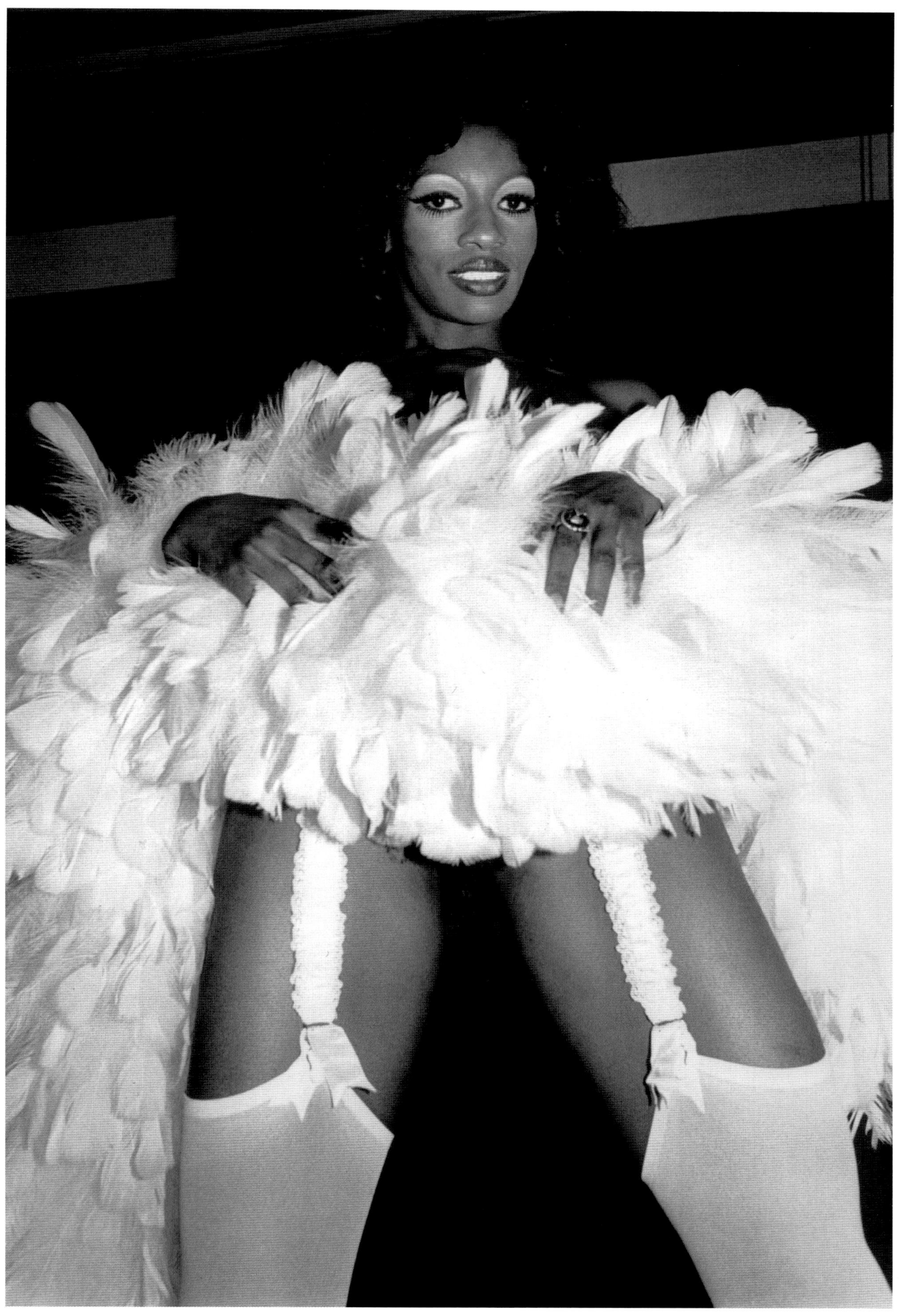

Danger at LeClique
New York, 1979

Whelan's Drug Store, 1976

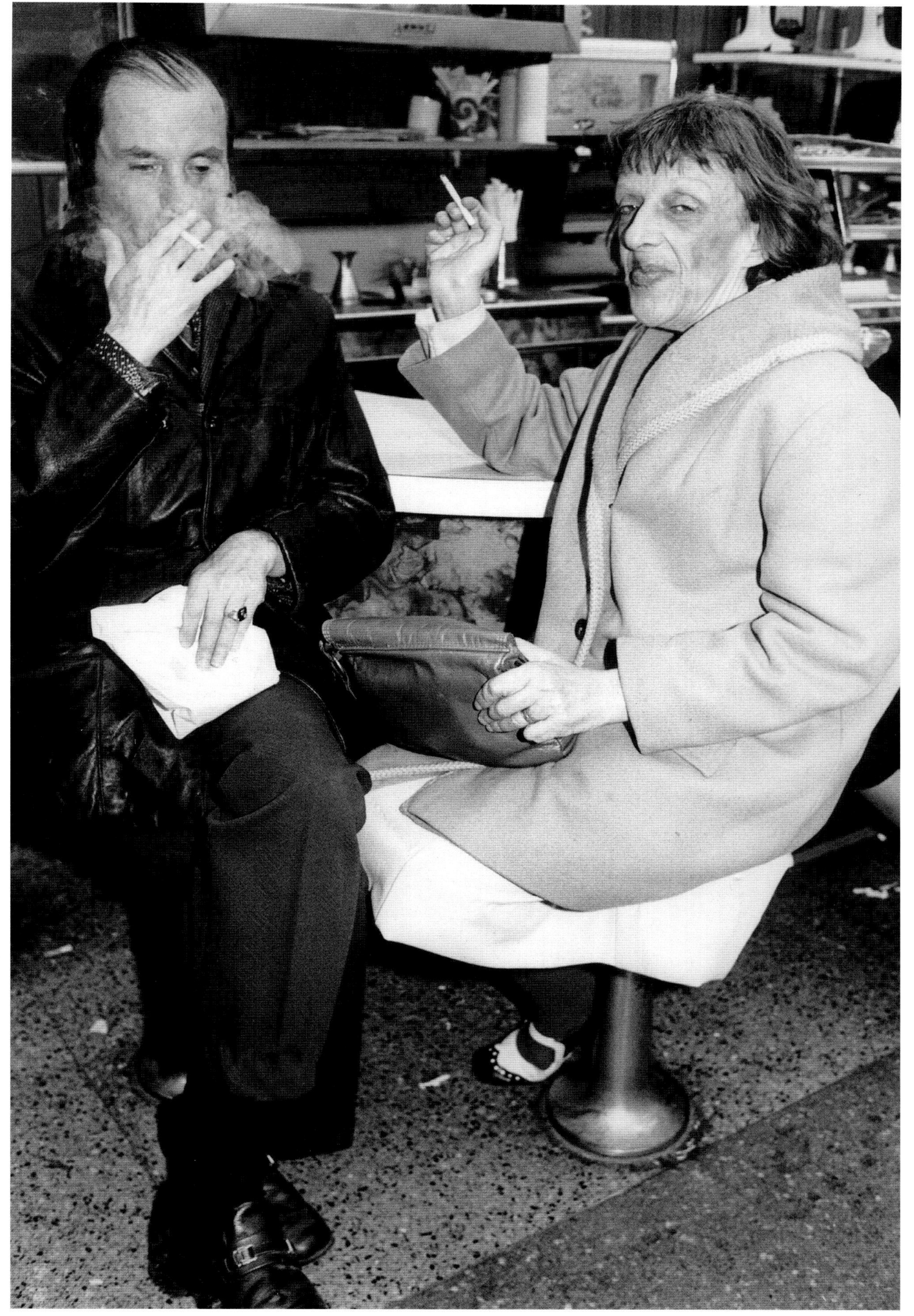

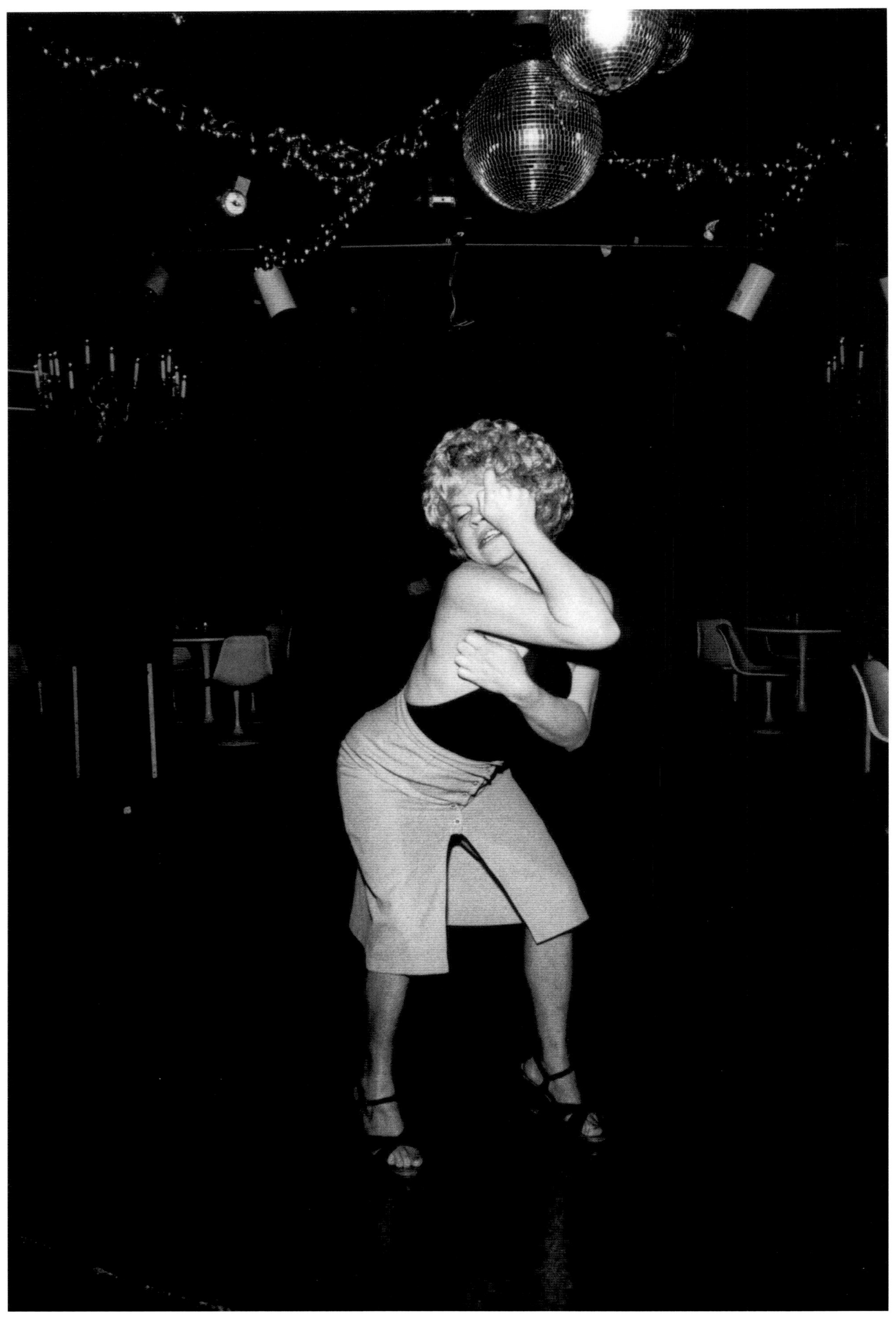

GG's Barnum Room,
Times Square
New York, 1979

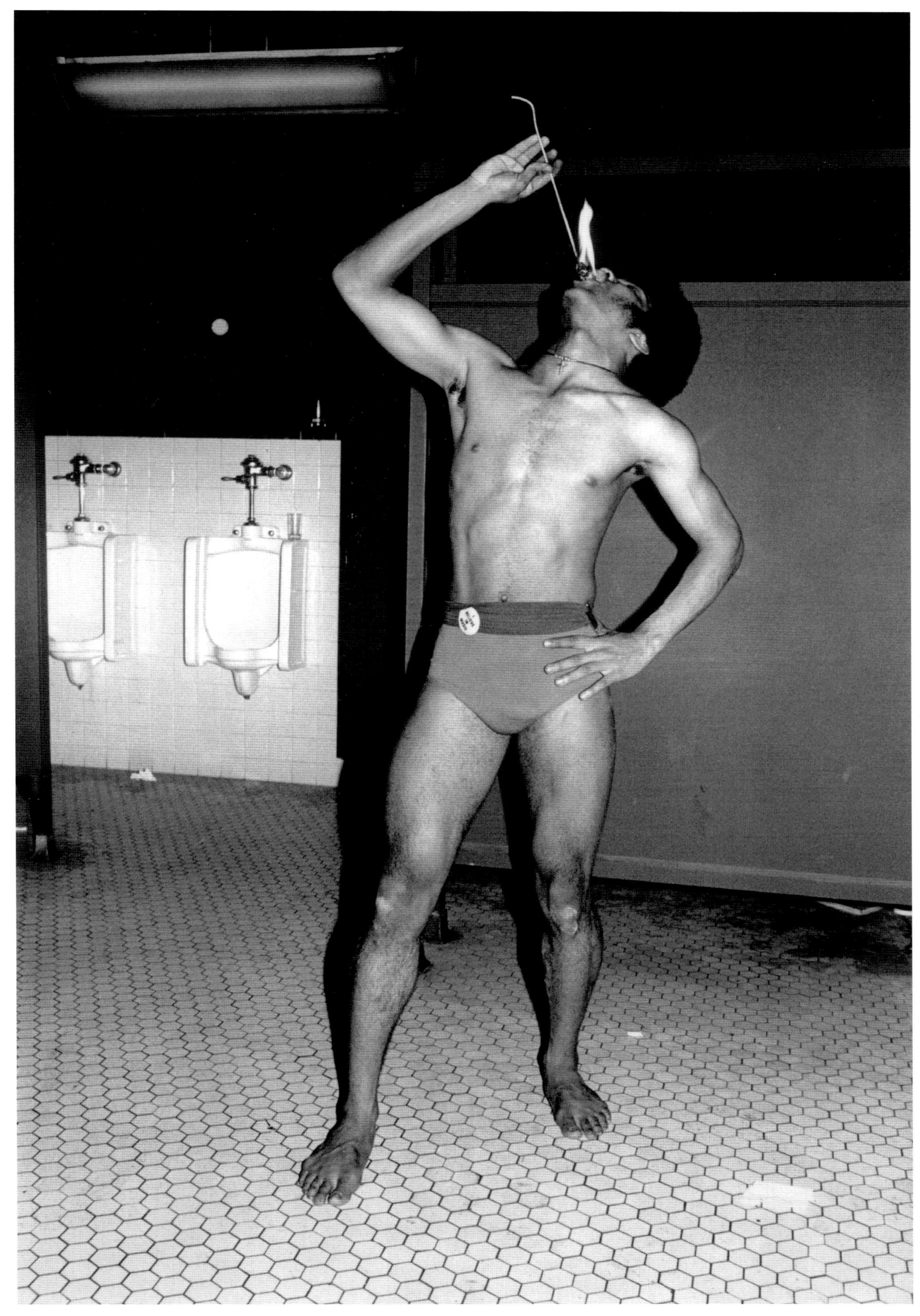

Men's Room at Disco, 1978

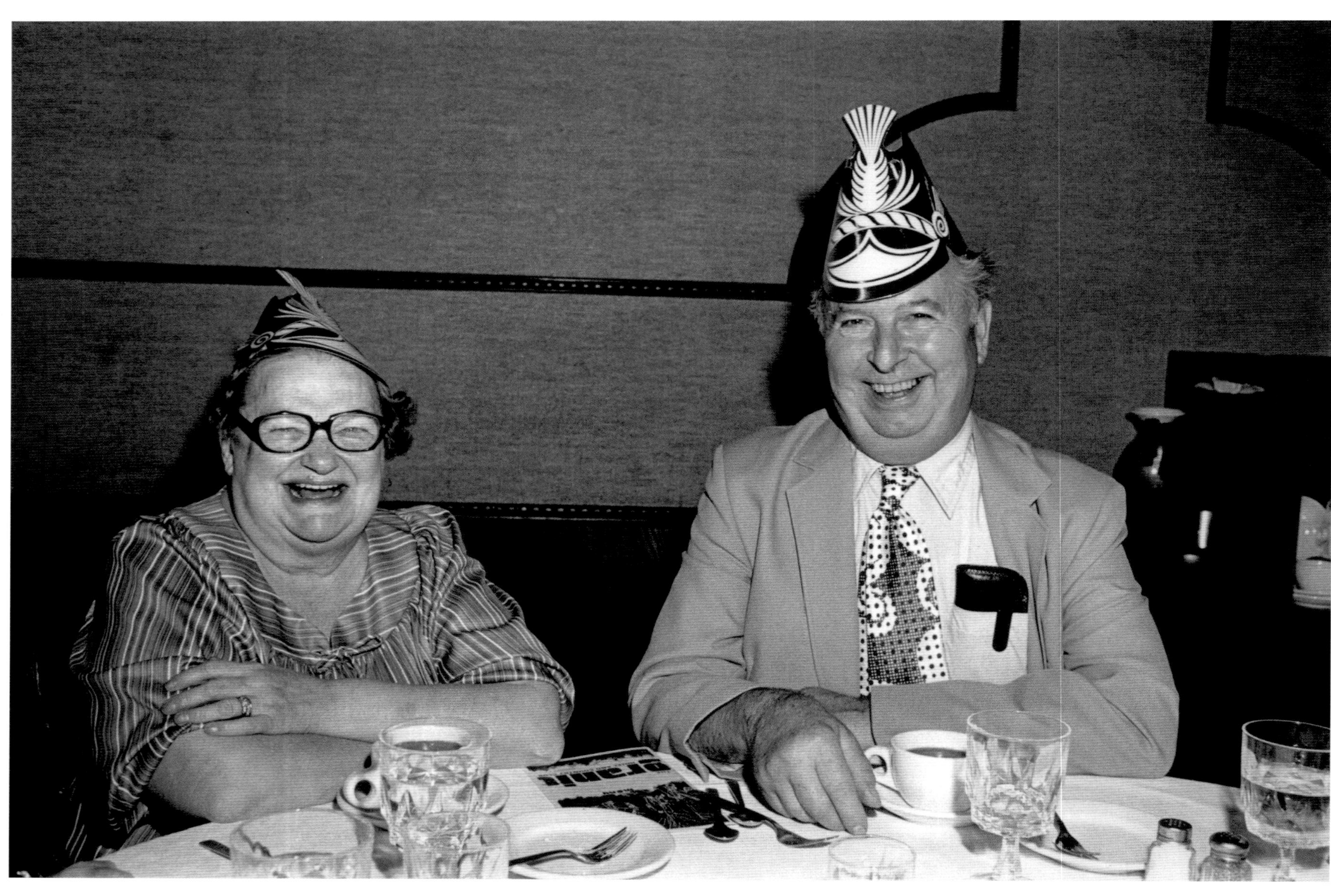

Granit Hotel and Country Club
Kerhonkson, New York, 1983

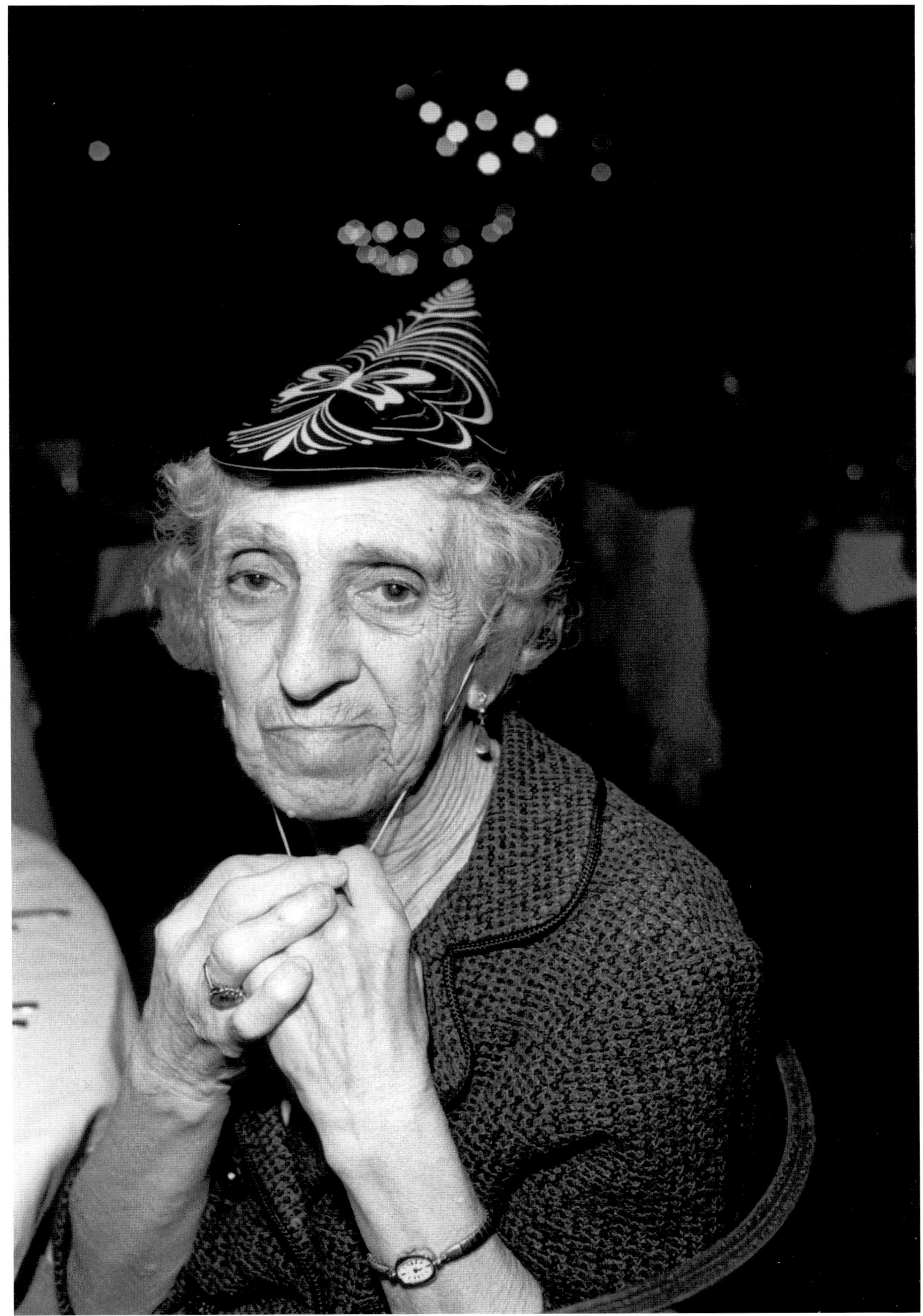

Granit Hotel and Country Club
Kerhonkson, New York, 1983

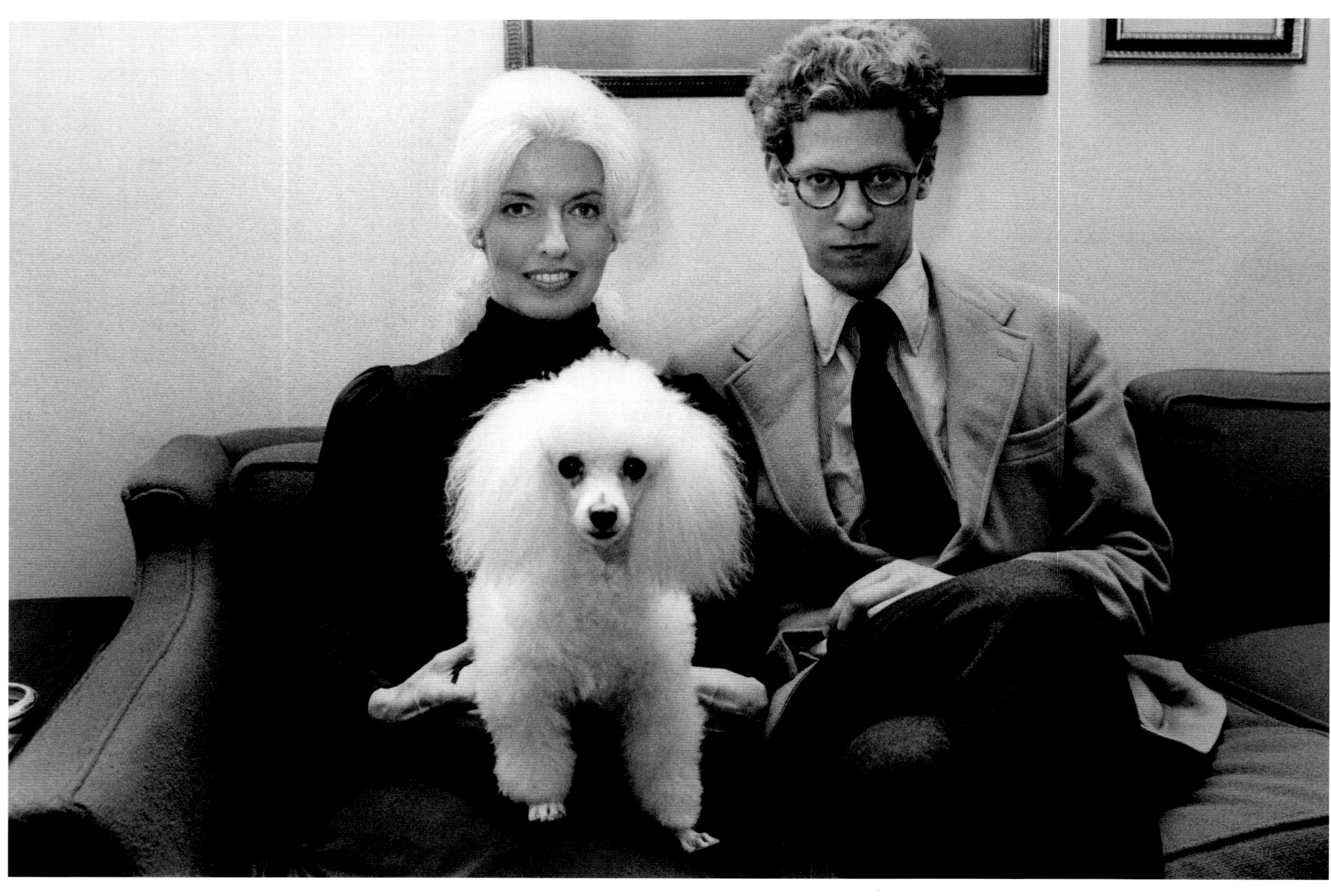

Tim Fine, His Mother, and Her Poodle
New York, 1977

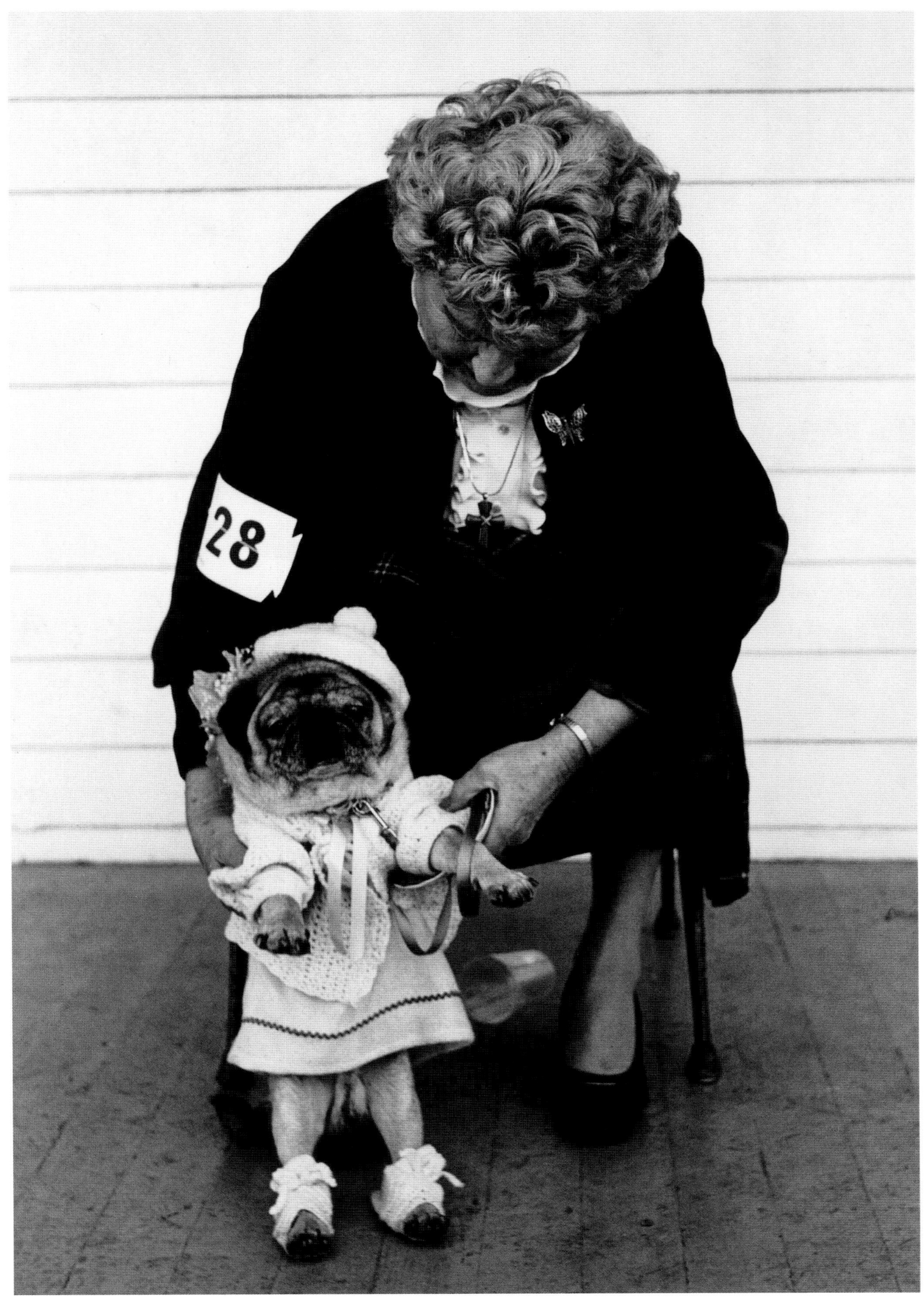

Pug Dog Show at Alice Austen's House, Staten Island New York, 1986

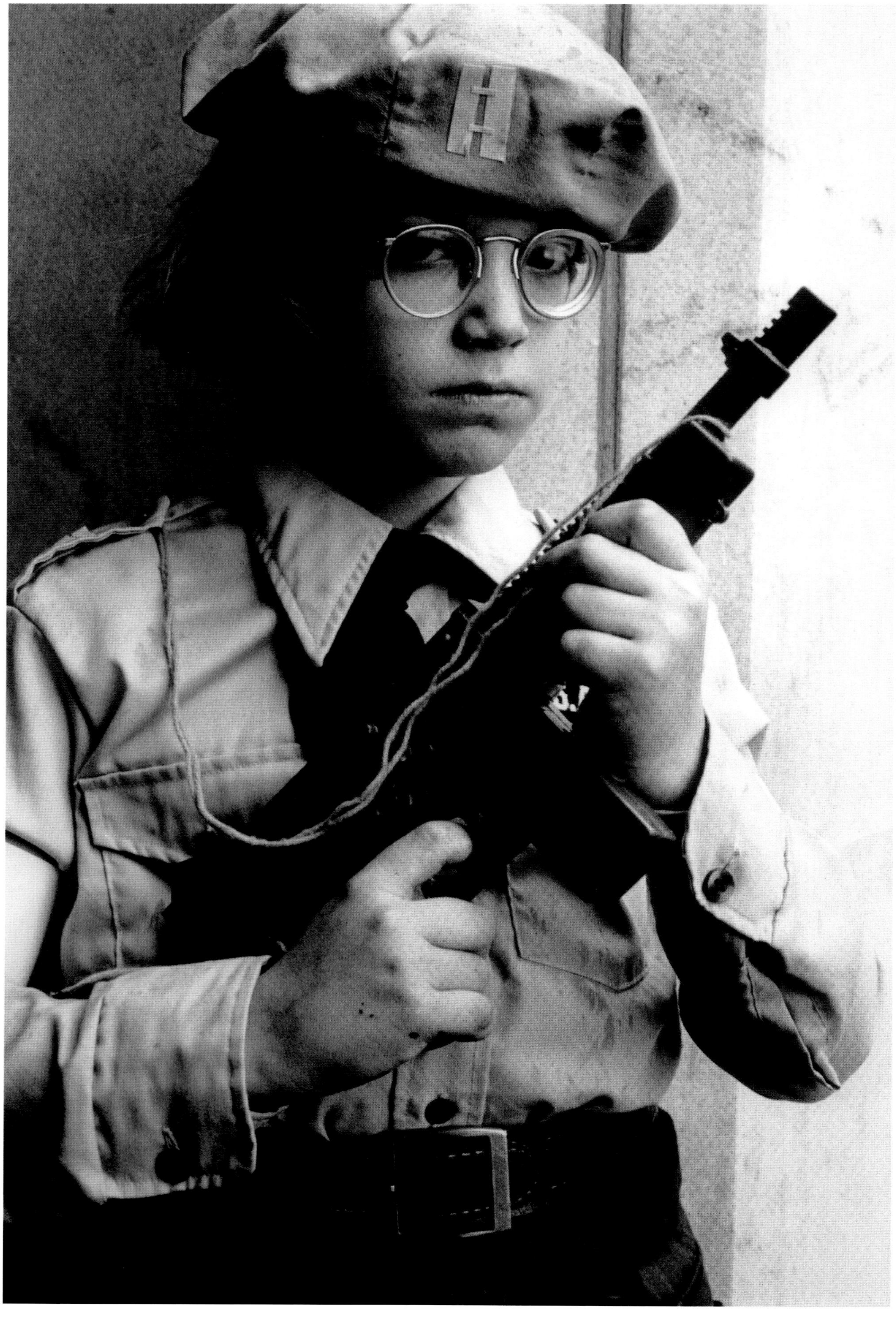

Luke Silverman, 1977

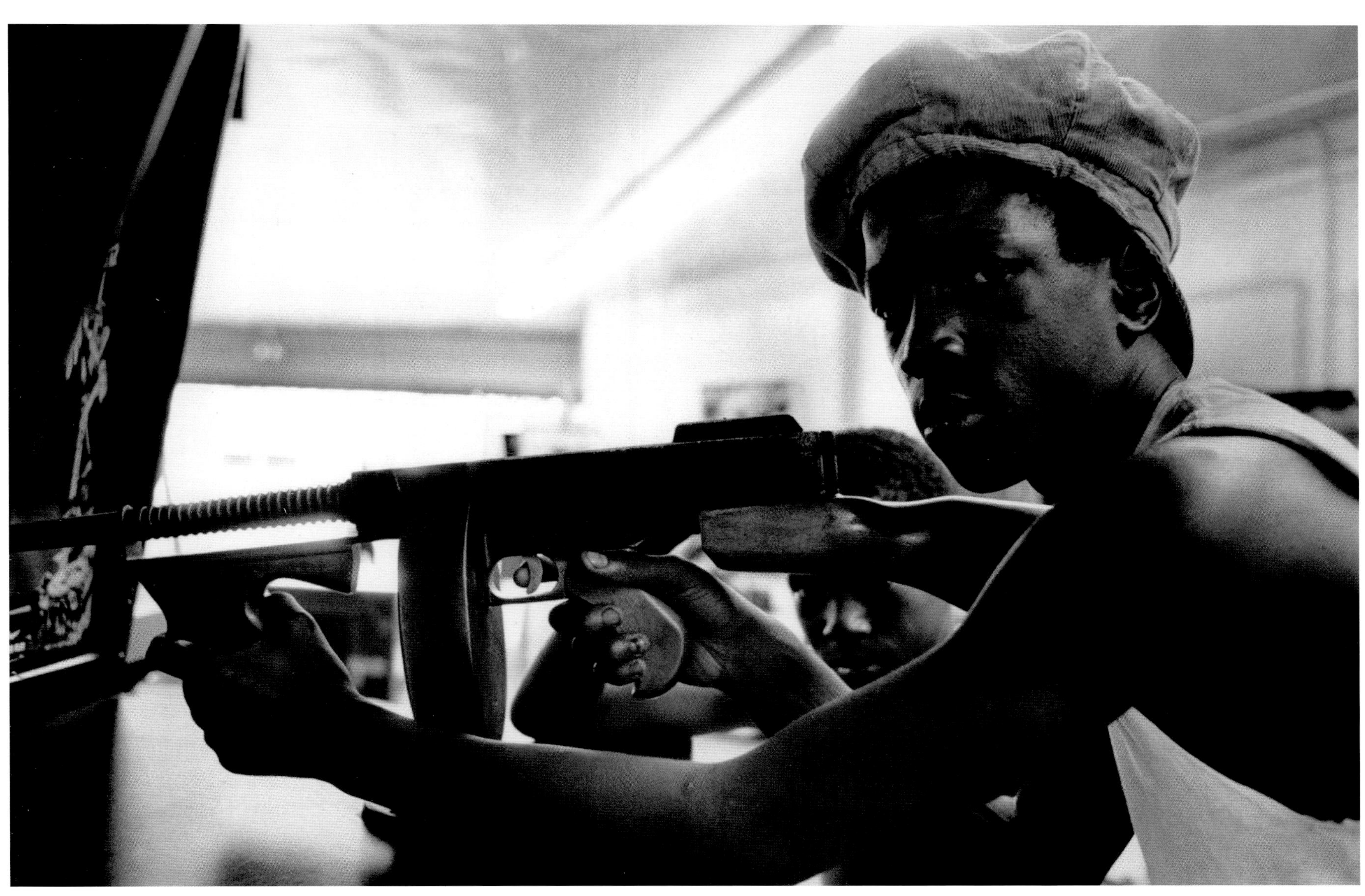

Machine Gun, Coney Island
New York, 1976

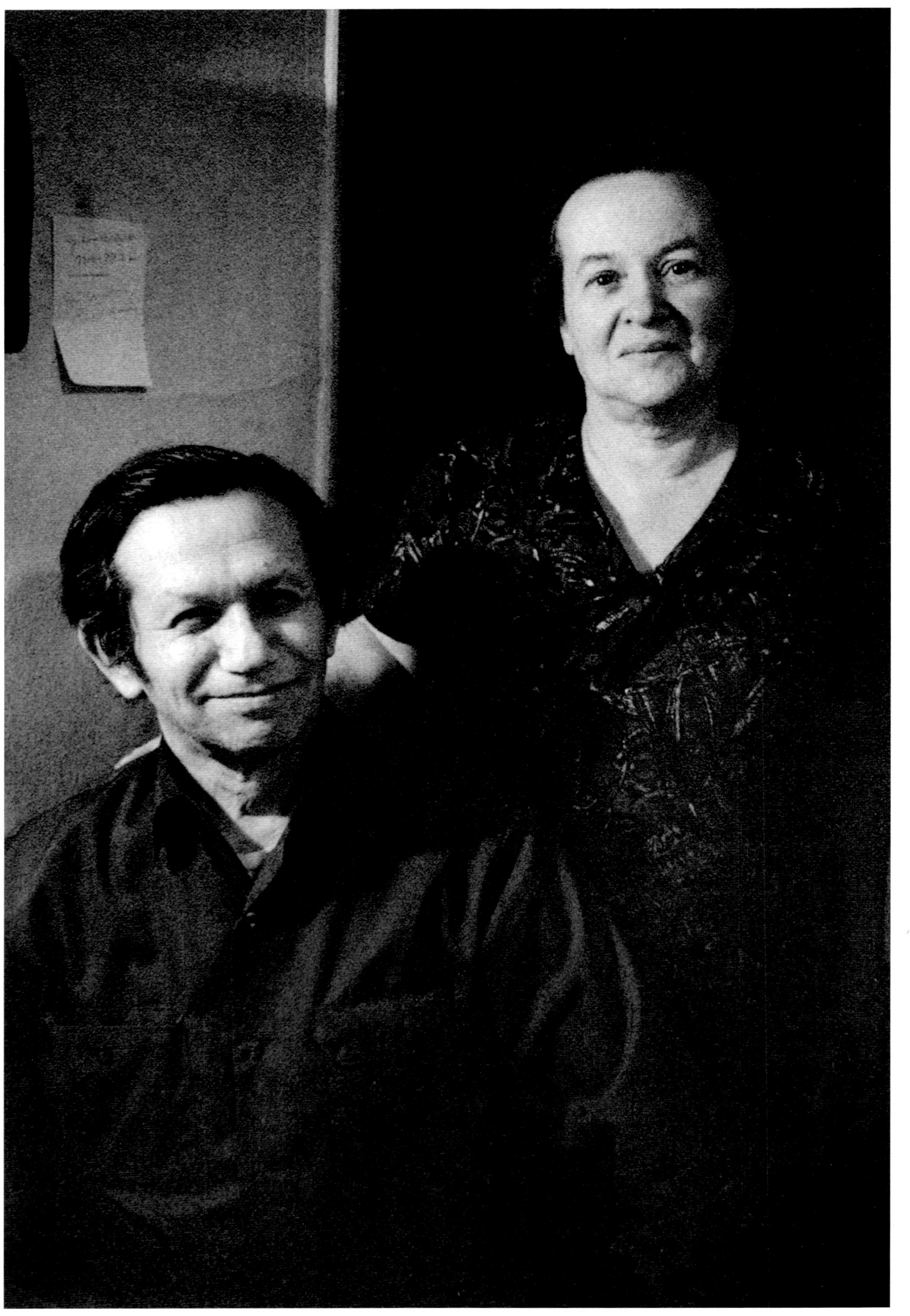

Mommie and Daddy, Brooklyn
New York, 1972

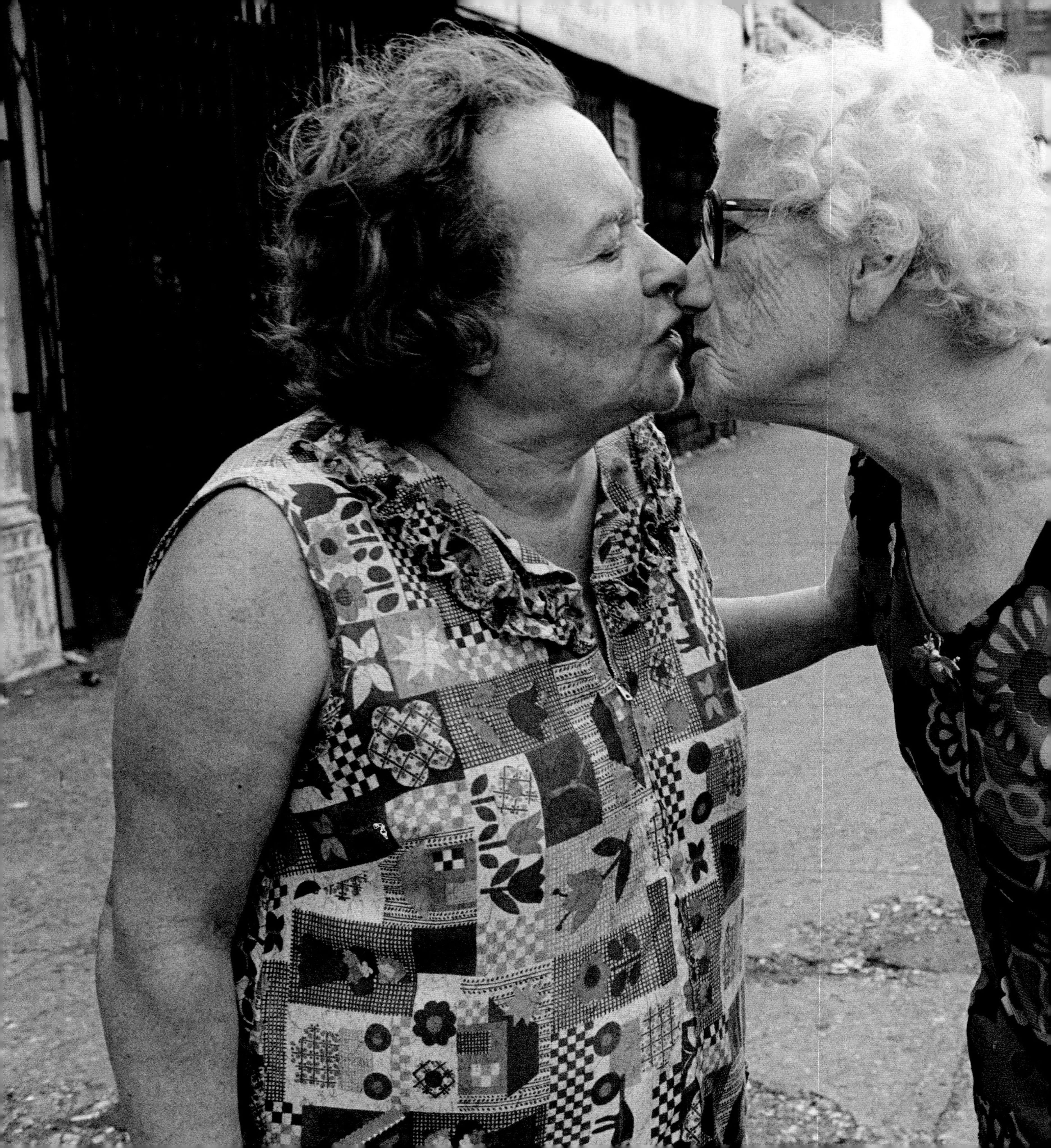

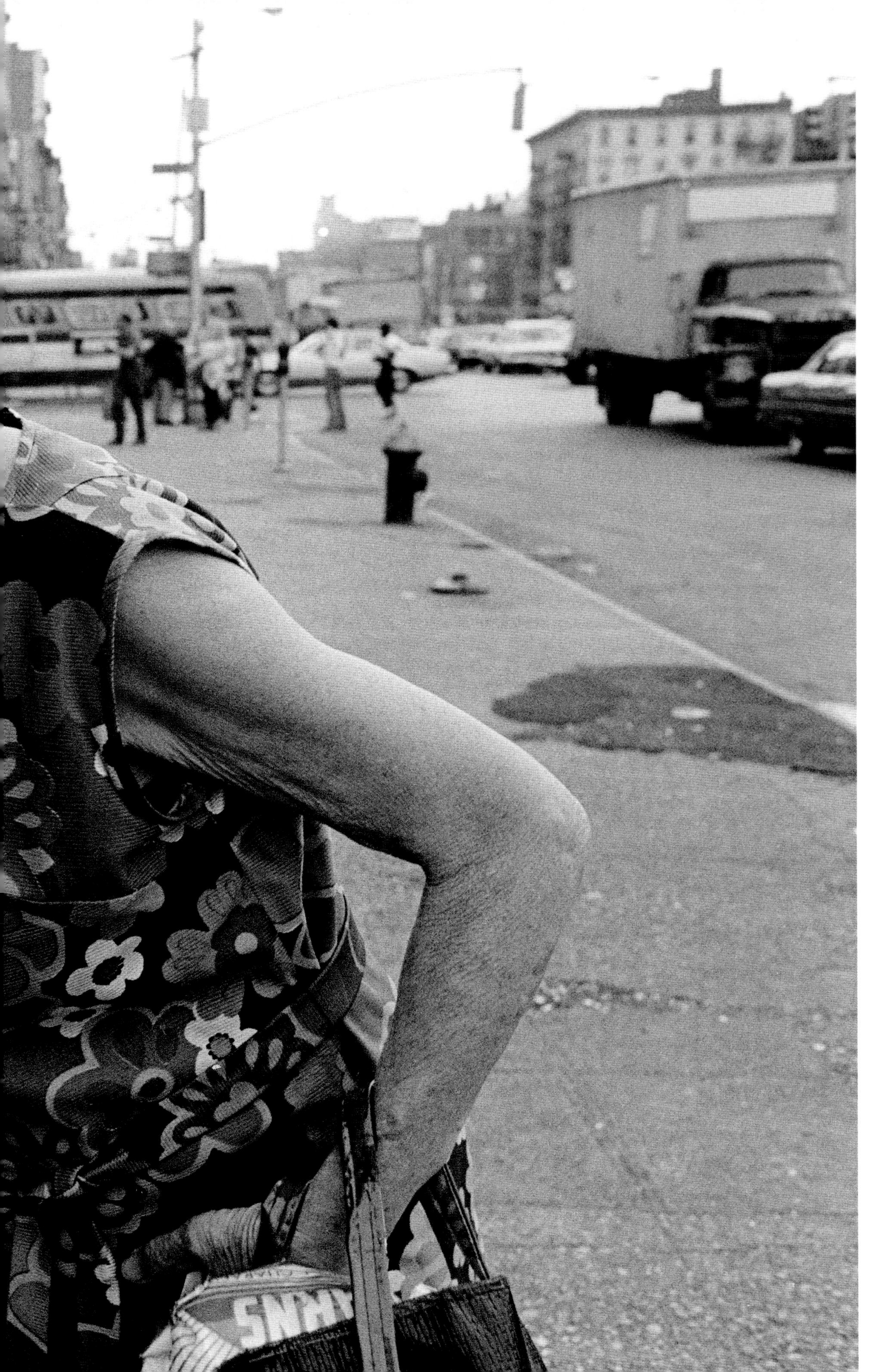

Mommie Kissing Bubbie on Delancey Street New York, 1979

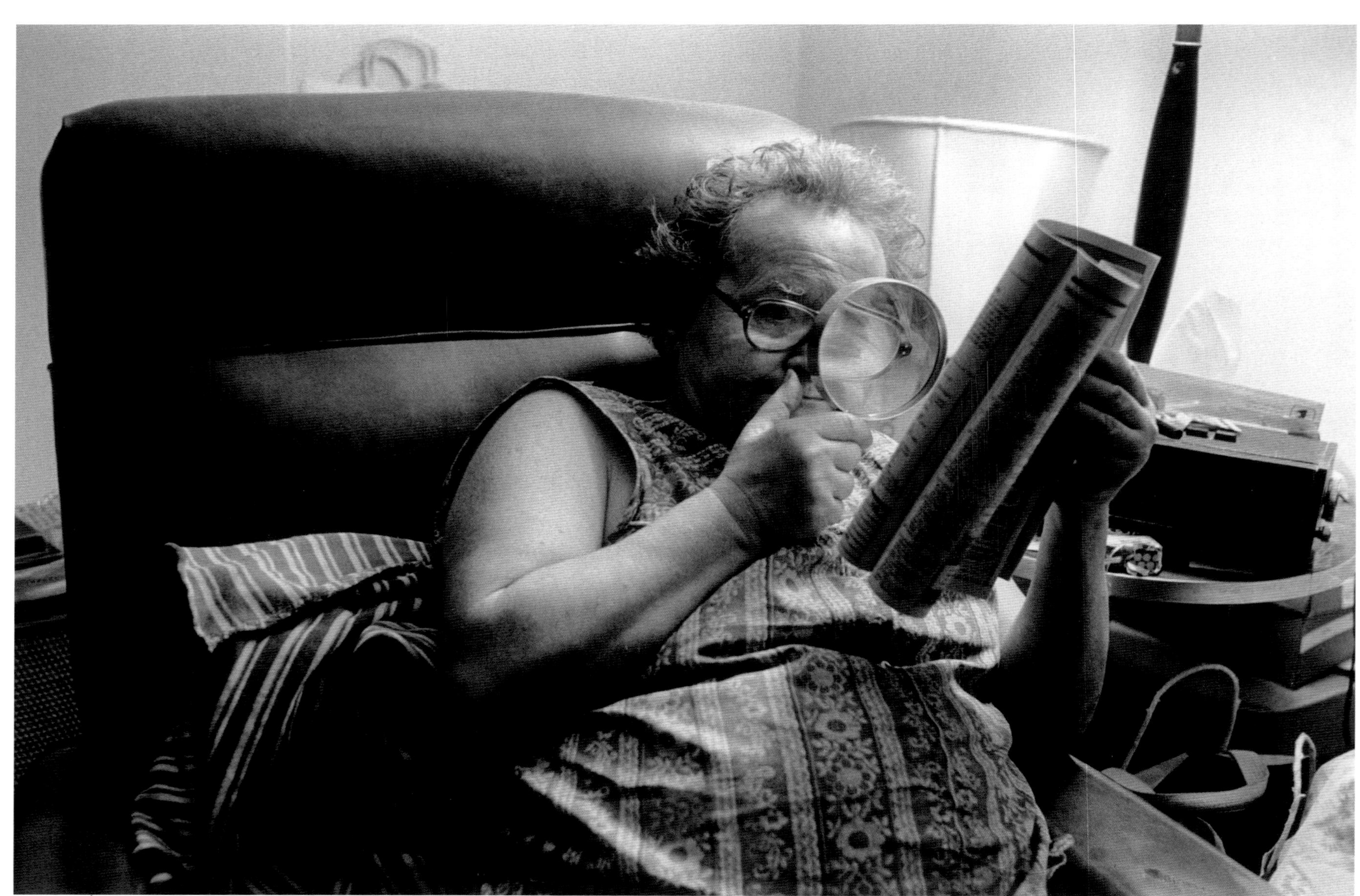

Mommie Reading
with Magnifying Glass
New York, 1983

Mommie Drinking Coffee on Apartment Balcony
New York, 1984

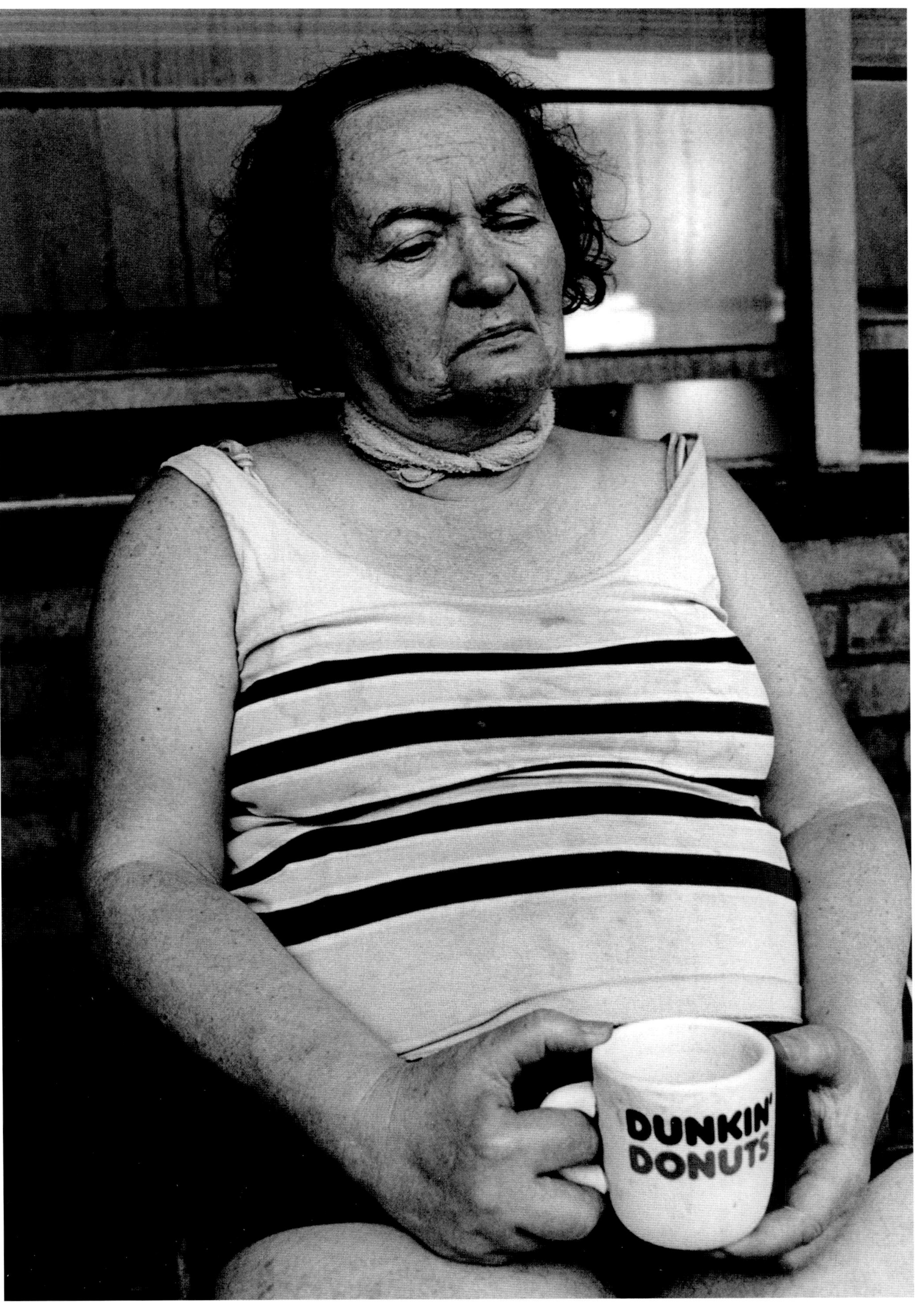
DUNKIN'
DONUTS

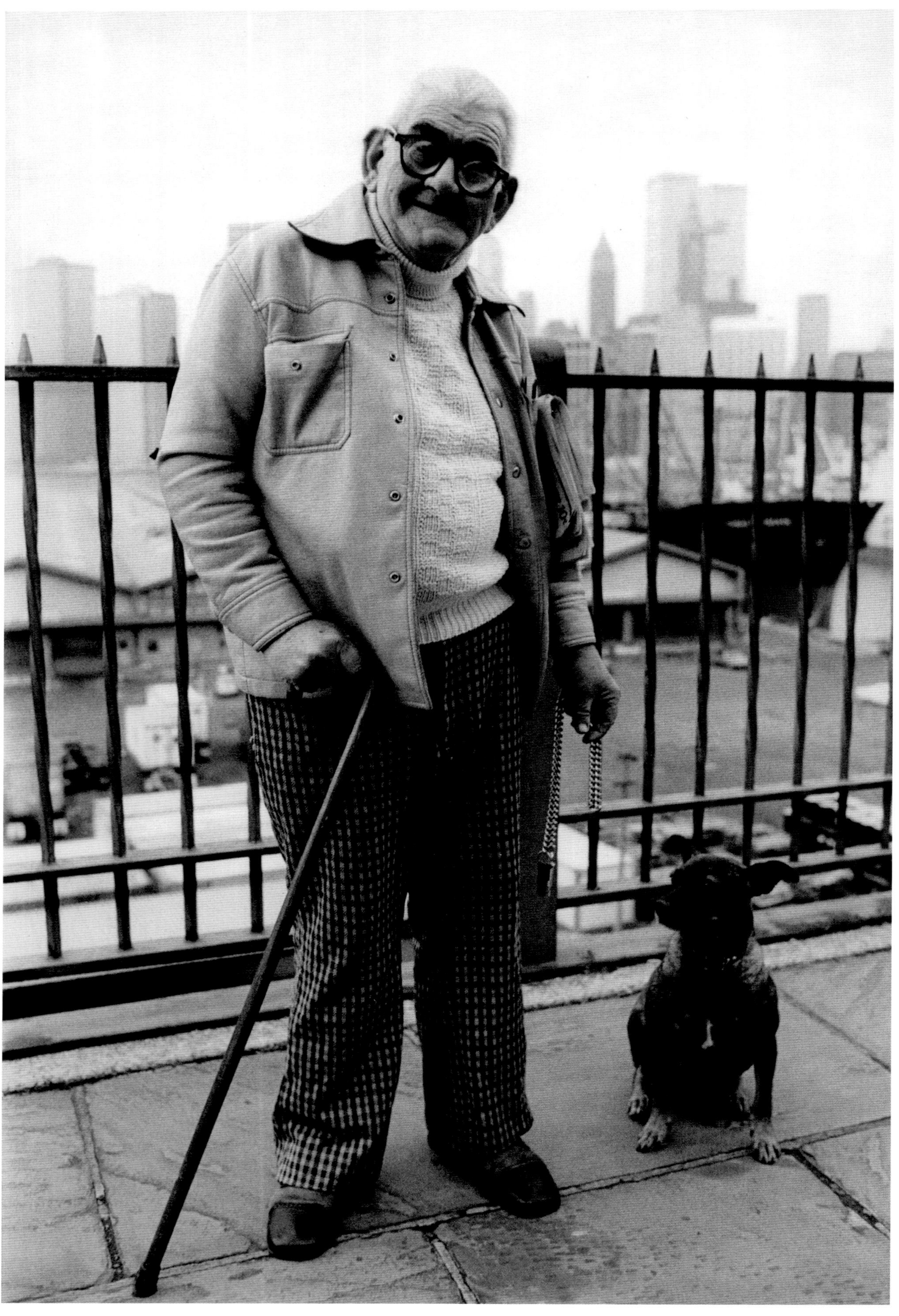

Man with Dog on Brooklyn Heights Promenade New York, 1982

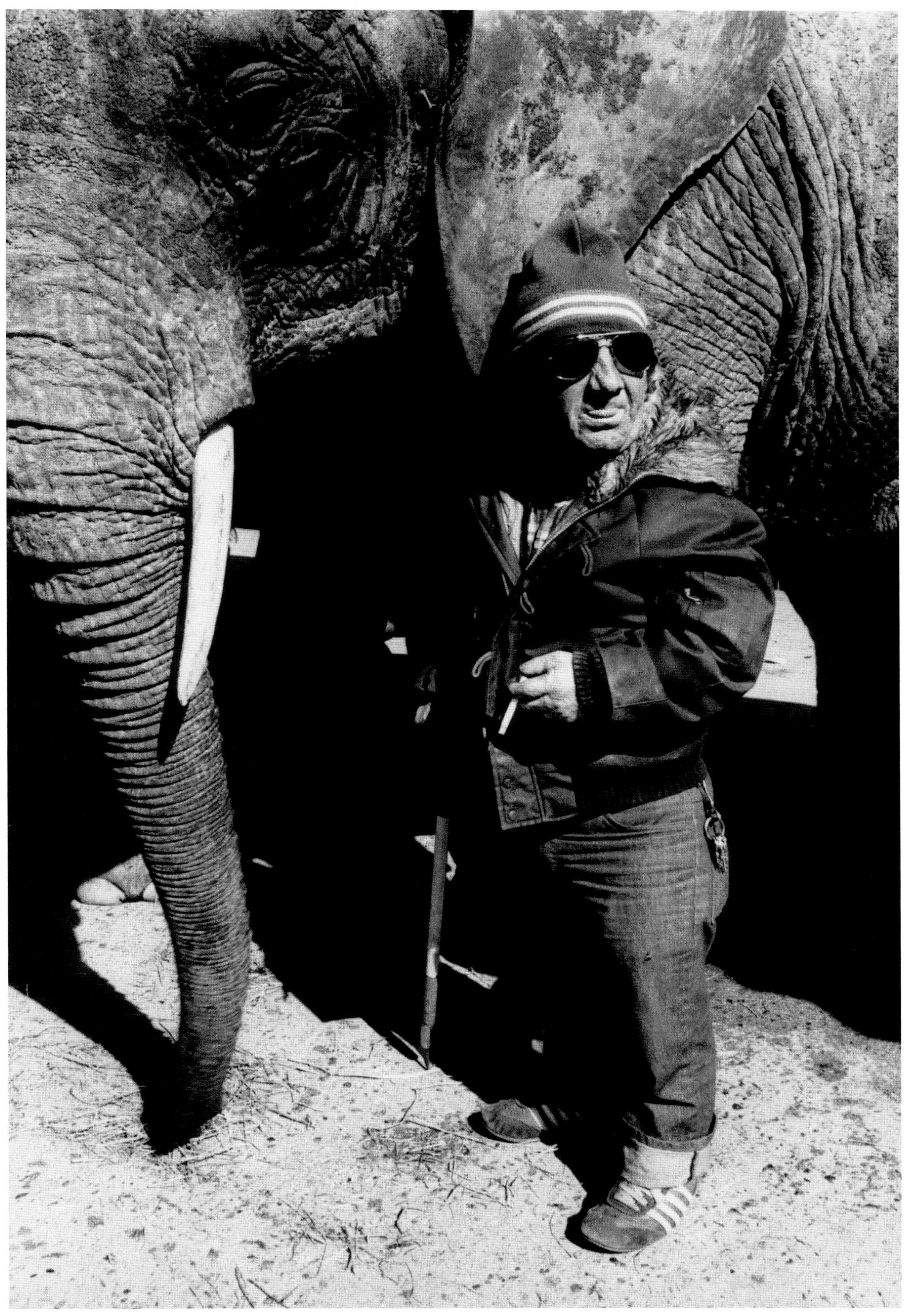

Circus Parade to Madison
Square Garden
New York, 1979

Avenue C Bodega,
Lower East Side
New York, 1980

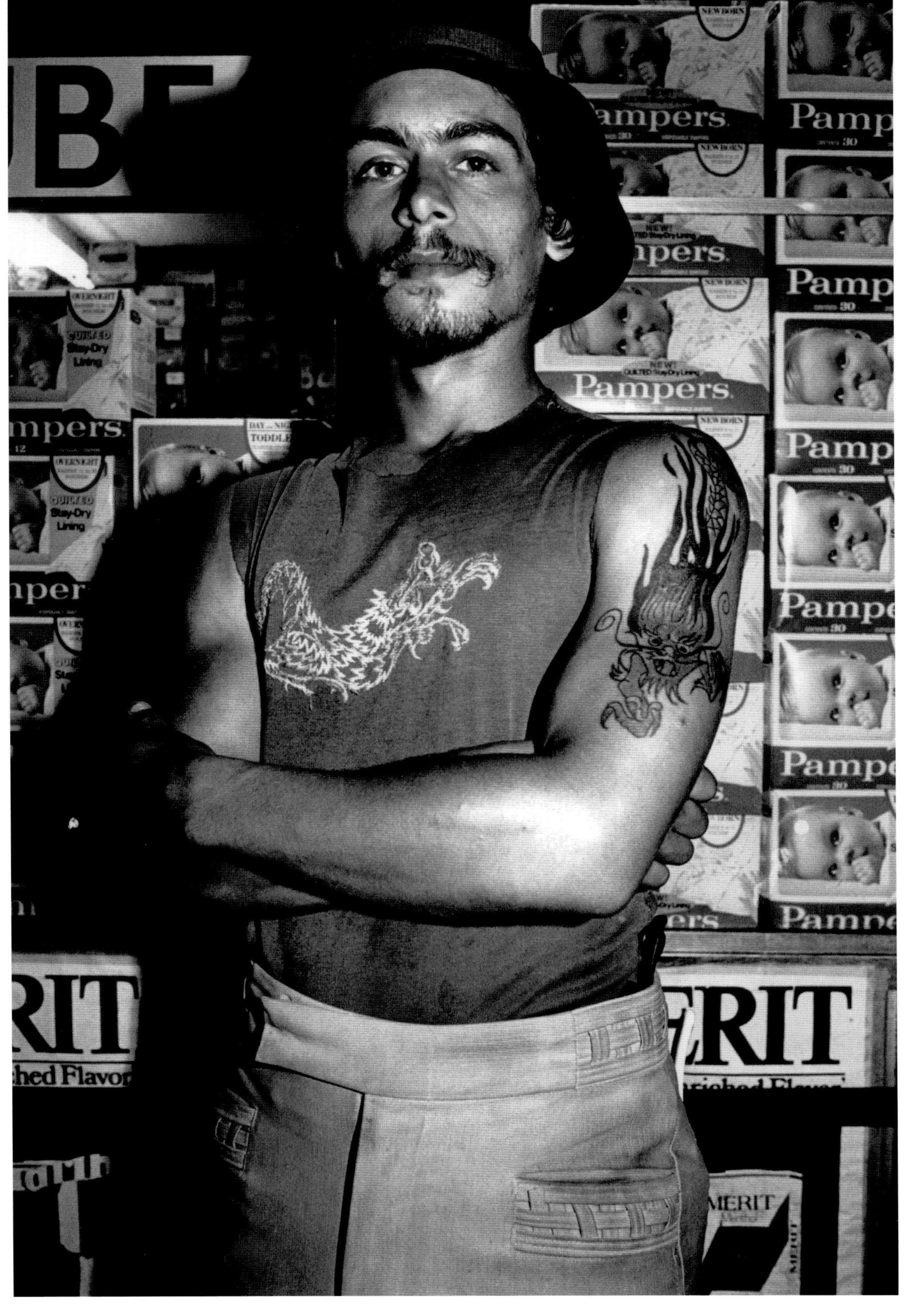
Pampers.
NEWBORN
OVERNIGHT
QUILTED
Stay-Dry
Lining
MERIT

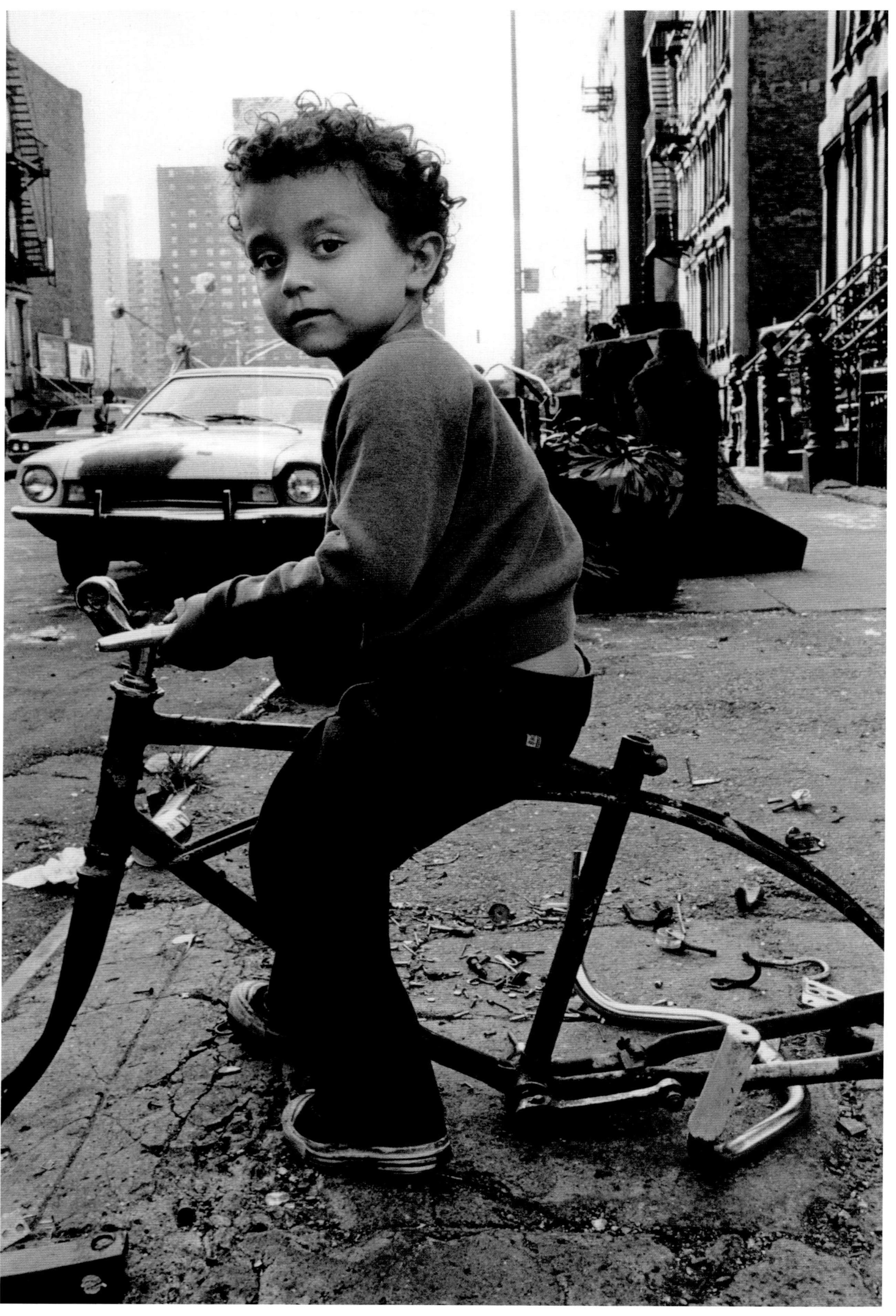

No Wheels, El Barrio
New York, 1978

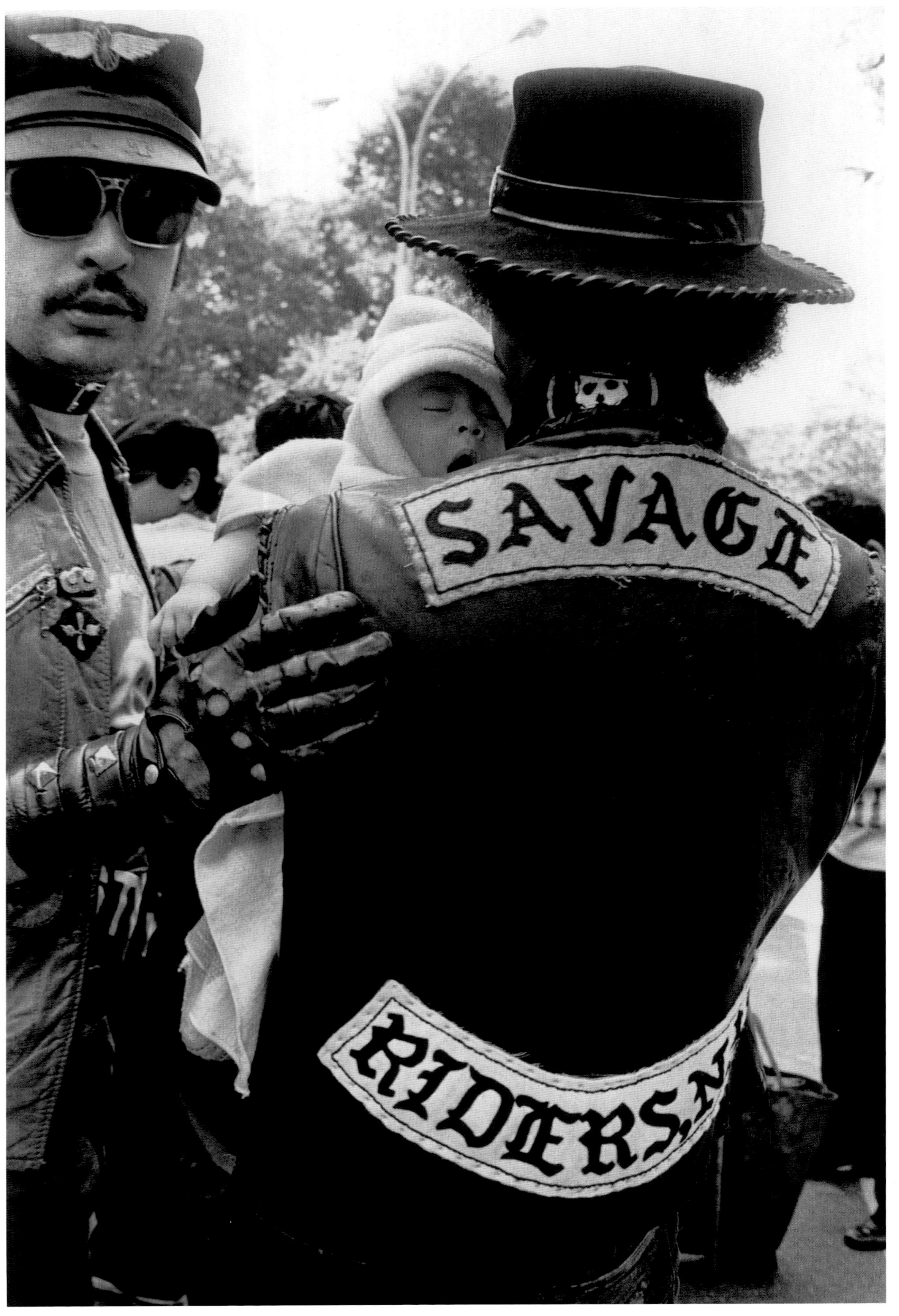

Savage Riders at the Puerto Rican Day Parade New York, 1980

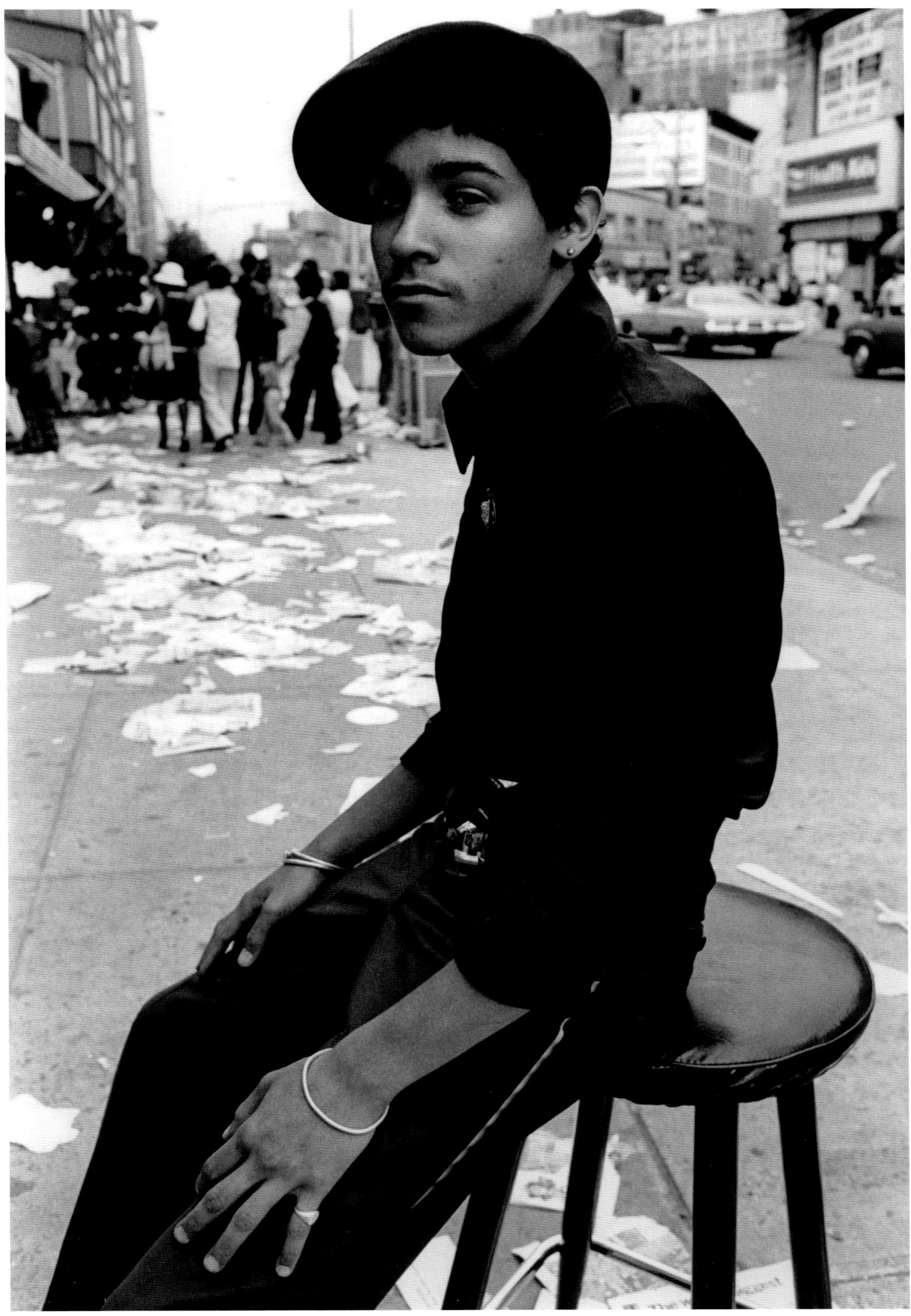

Third Avenue Shopping, El Barrio
New York, 1978

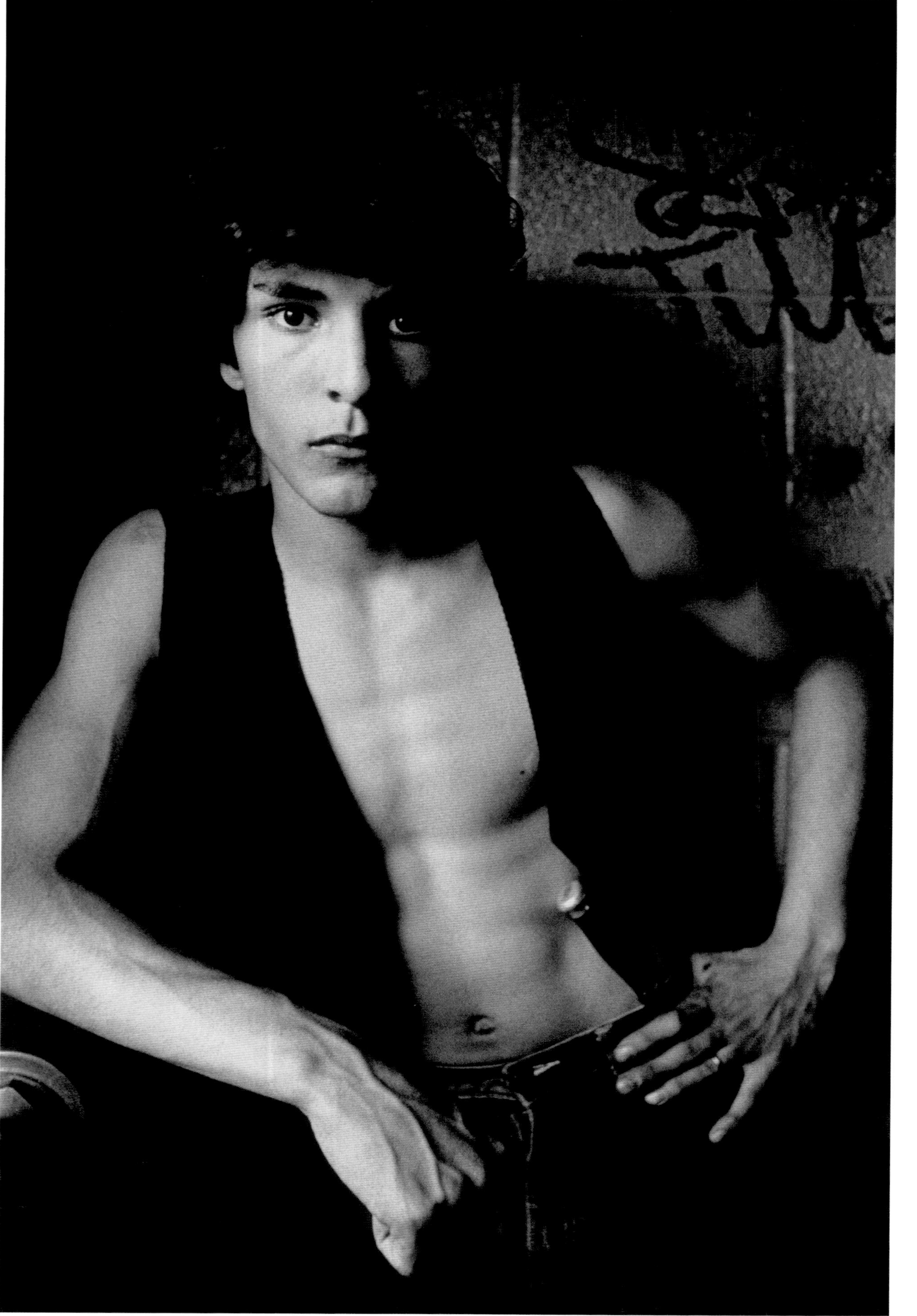

Johnny Cintron, Lower East Side
New York, 1980

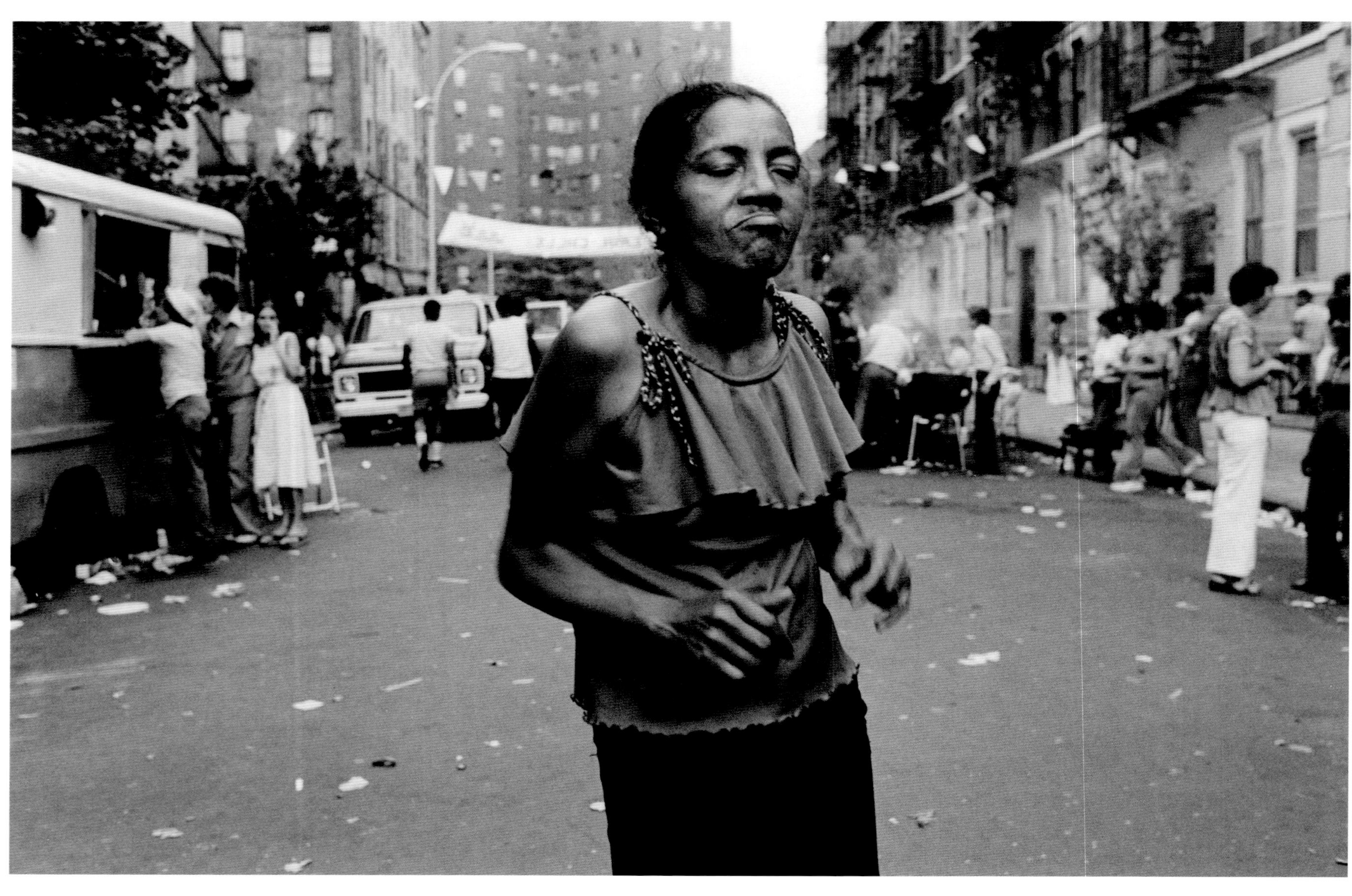

Block Party on East 7th Street
New York, 1977

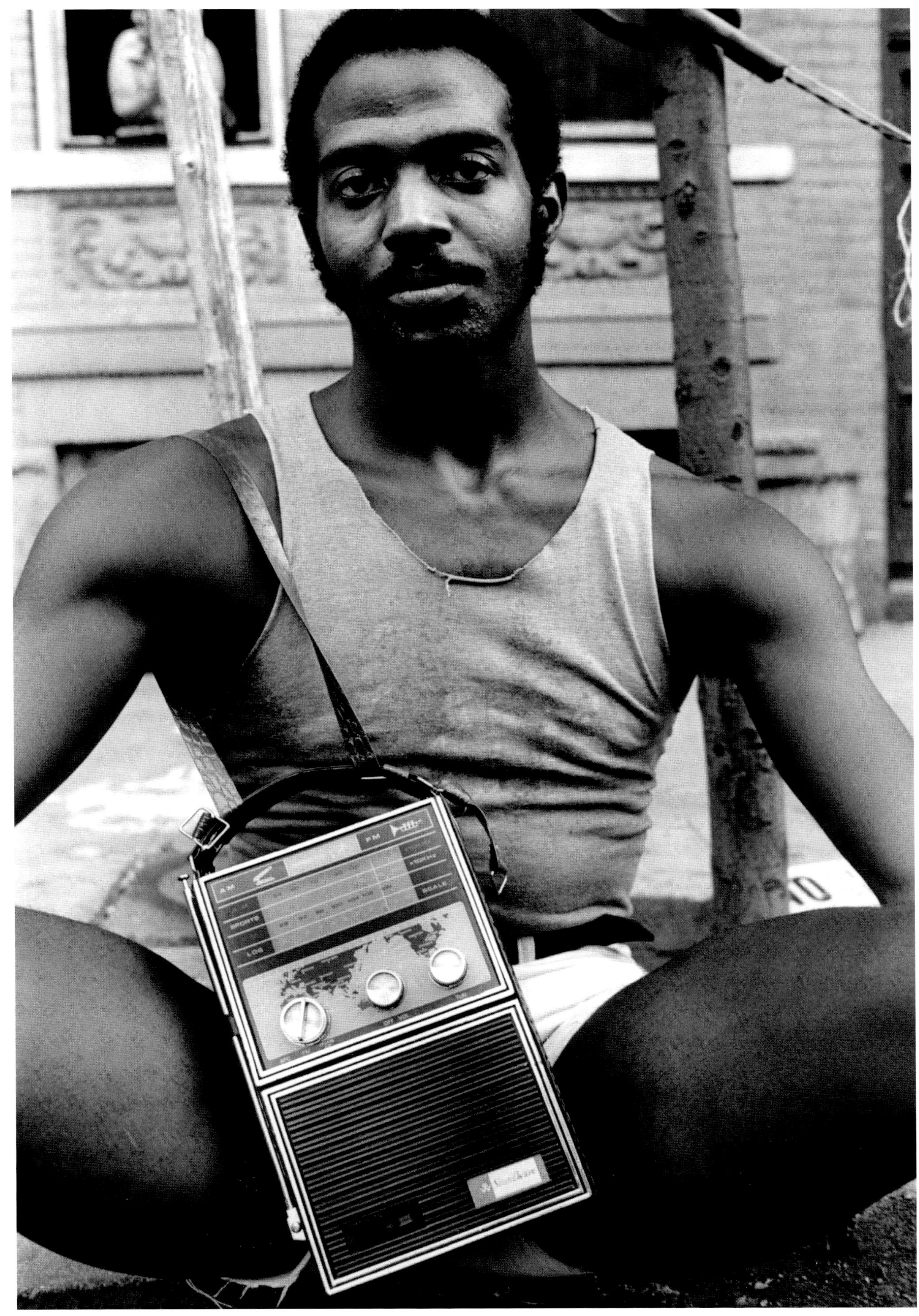

Guy with Radio, East 7th Street
New York, 1977

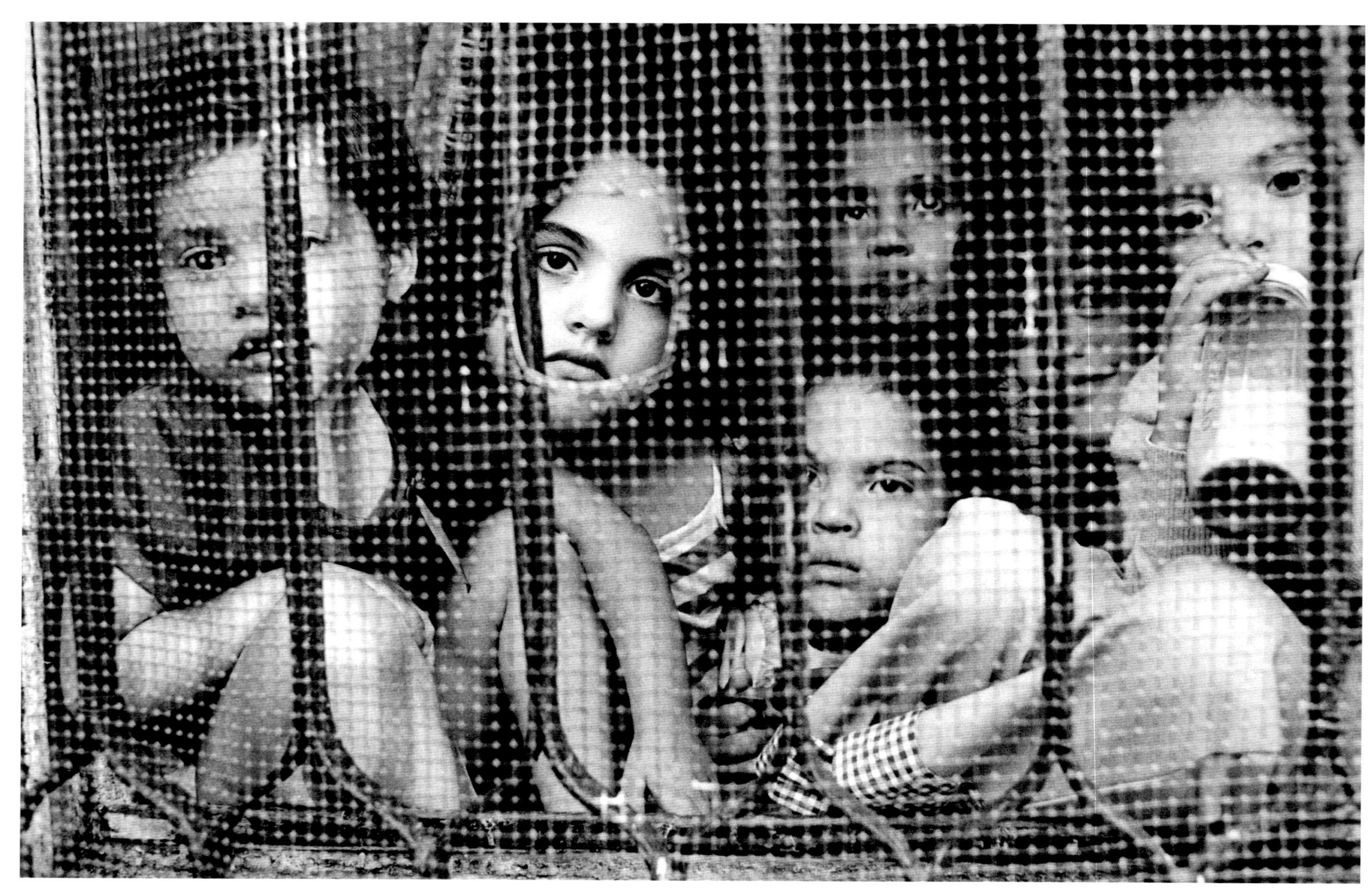

La Familia Rivera en El Barrio
Nueva York, 1978

West 42nd Street, 1982

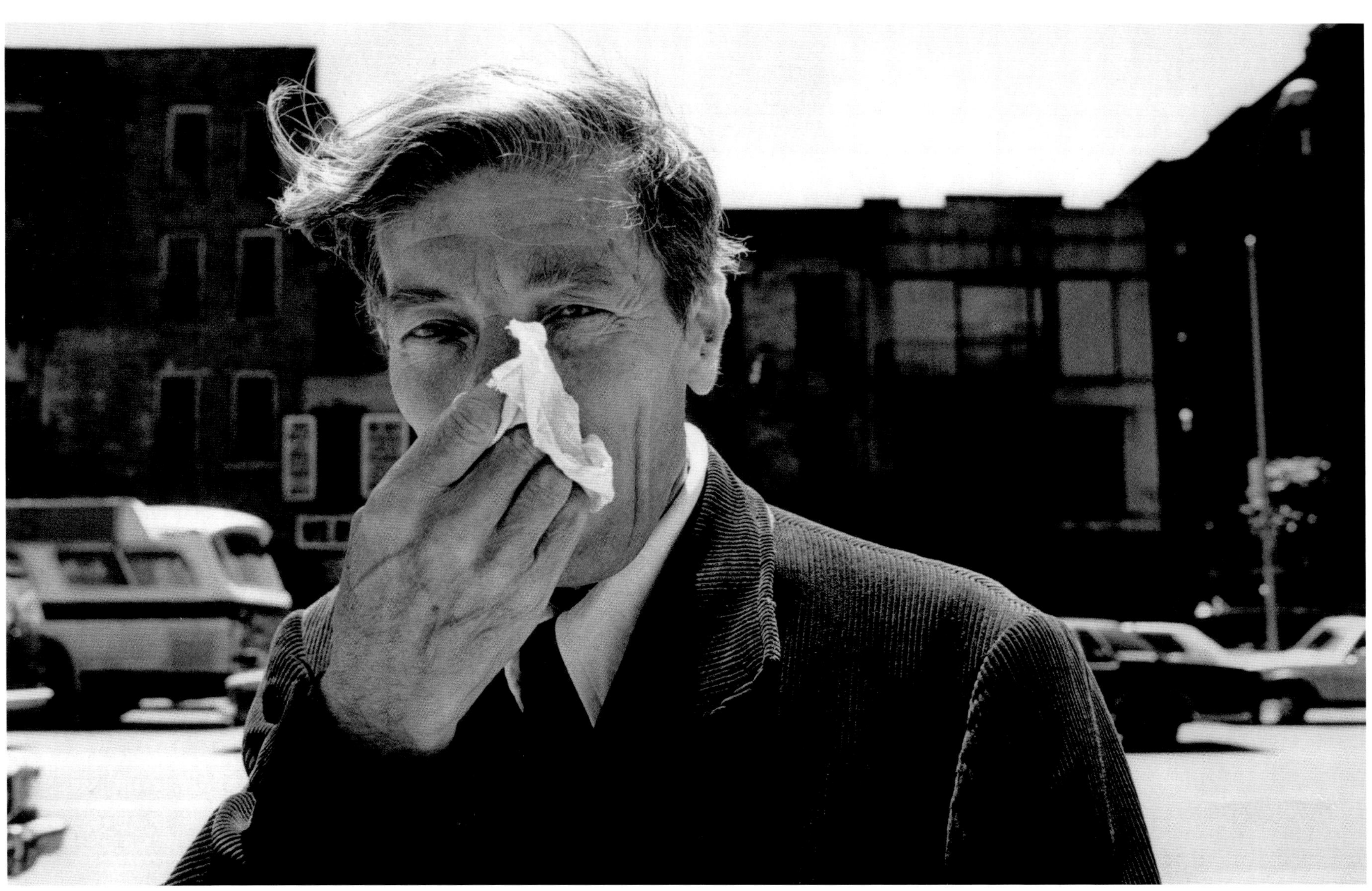

Bar in Coney Island
New York, 1976

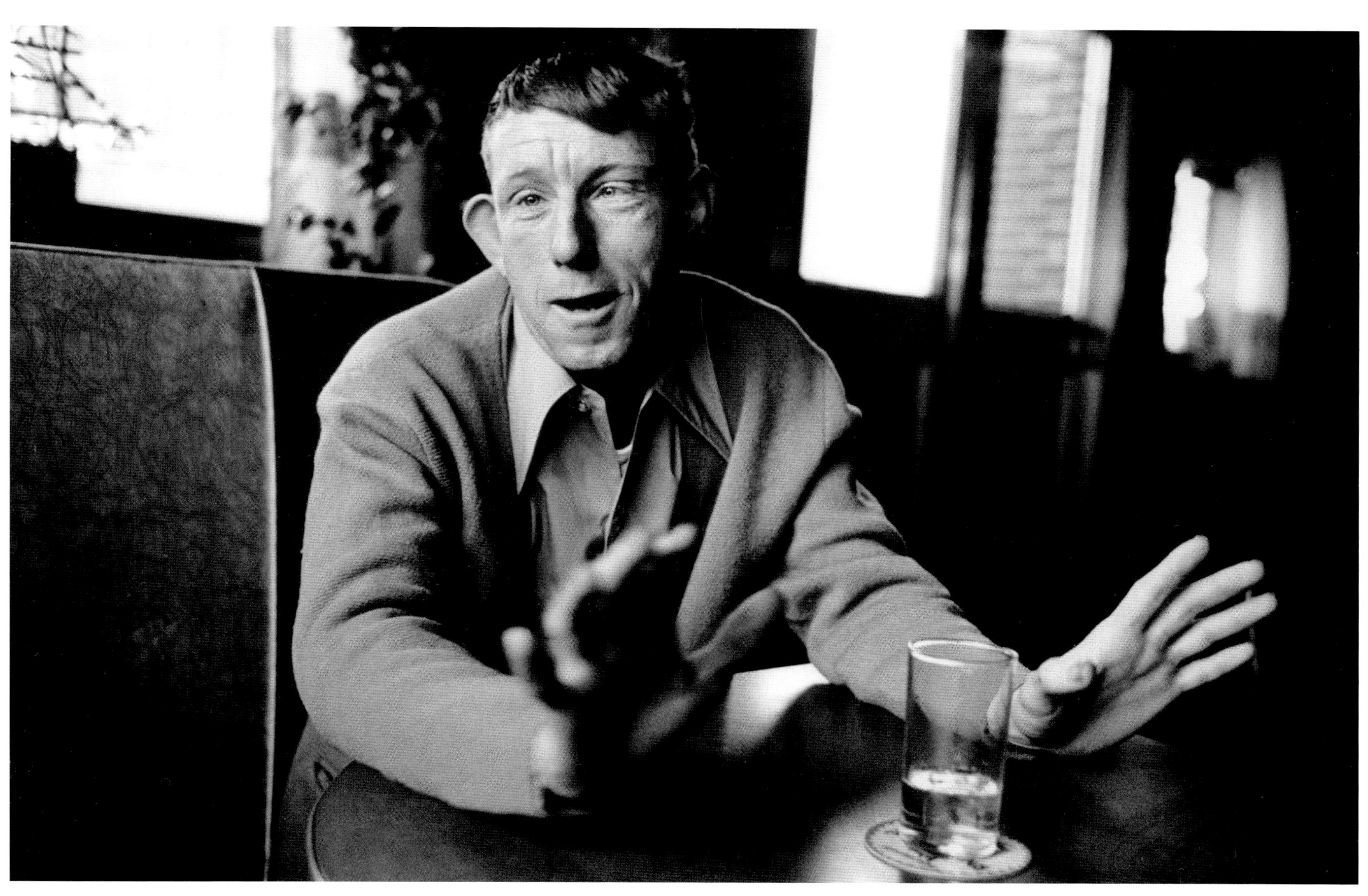

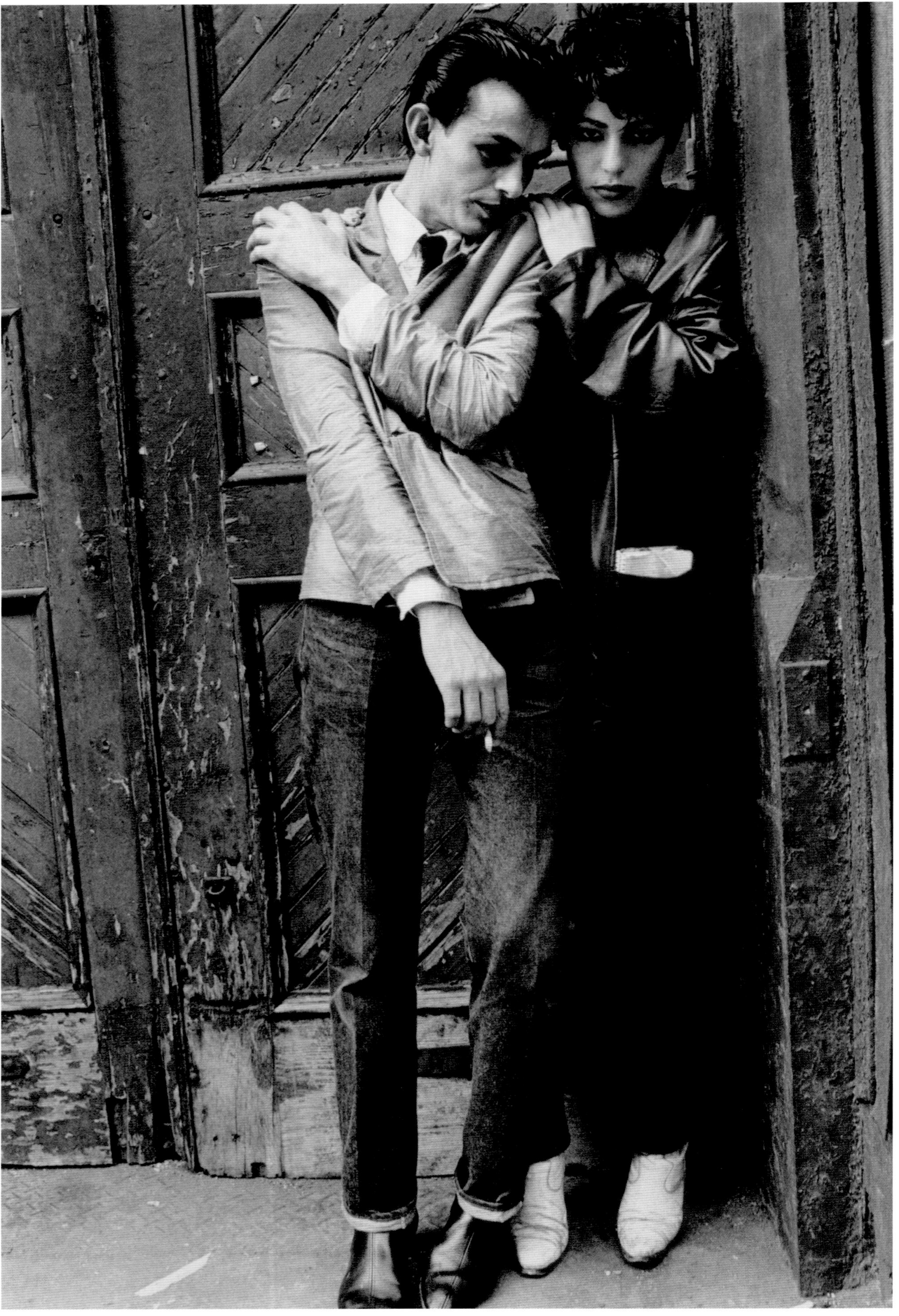

Doorway in SoHo
New York, 1980

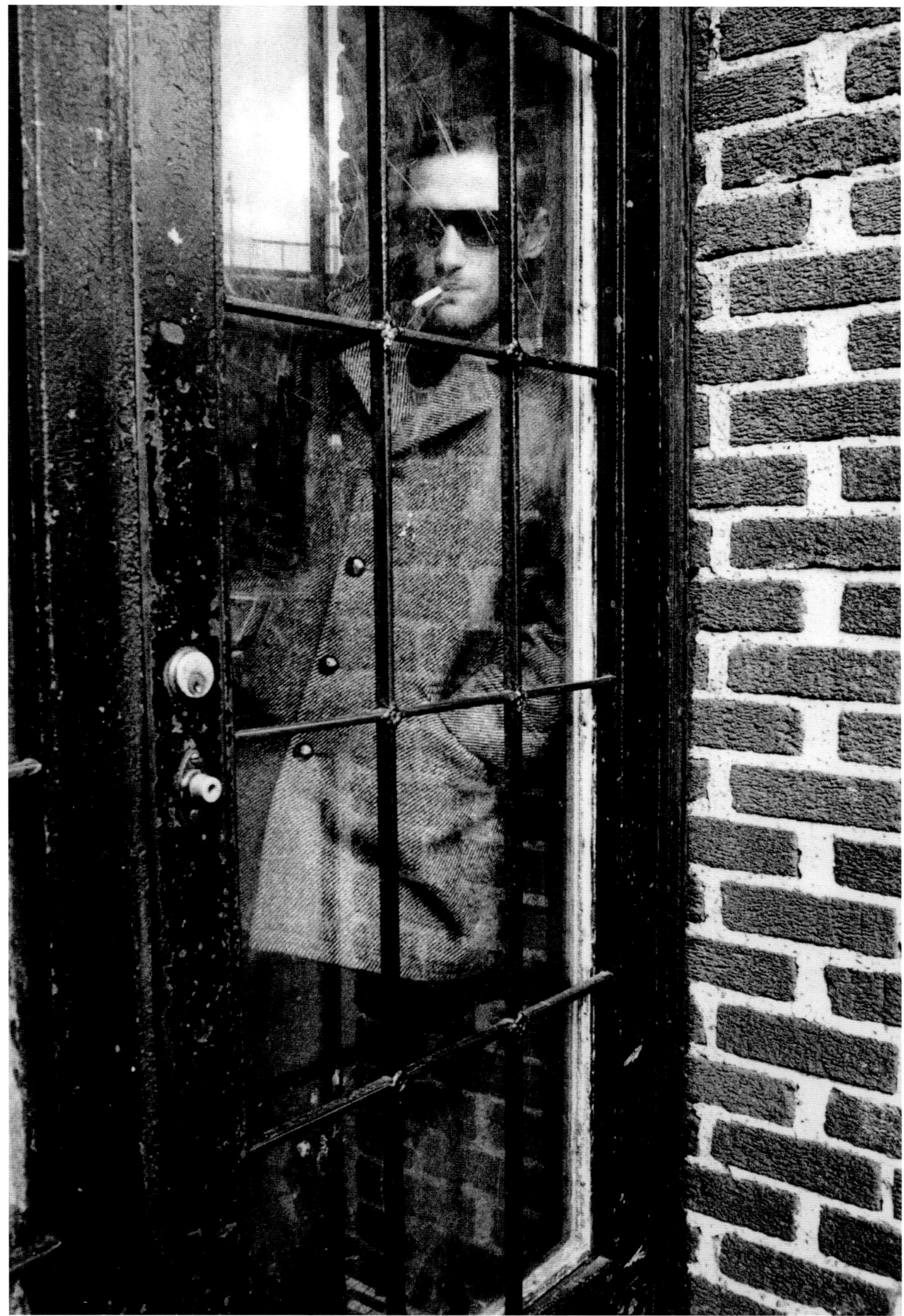

Doorway in Brooklyn
New York, 1980

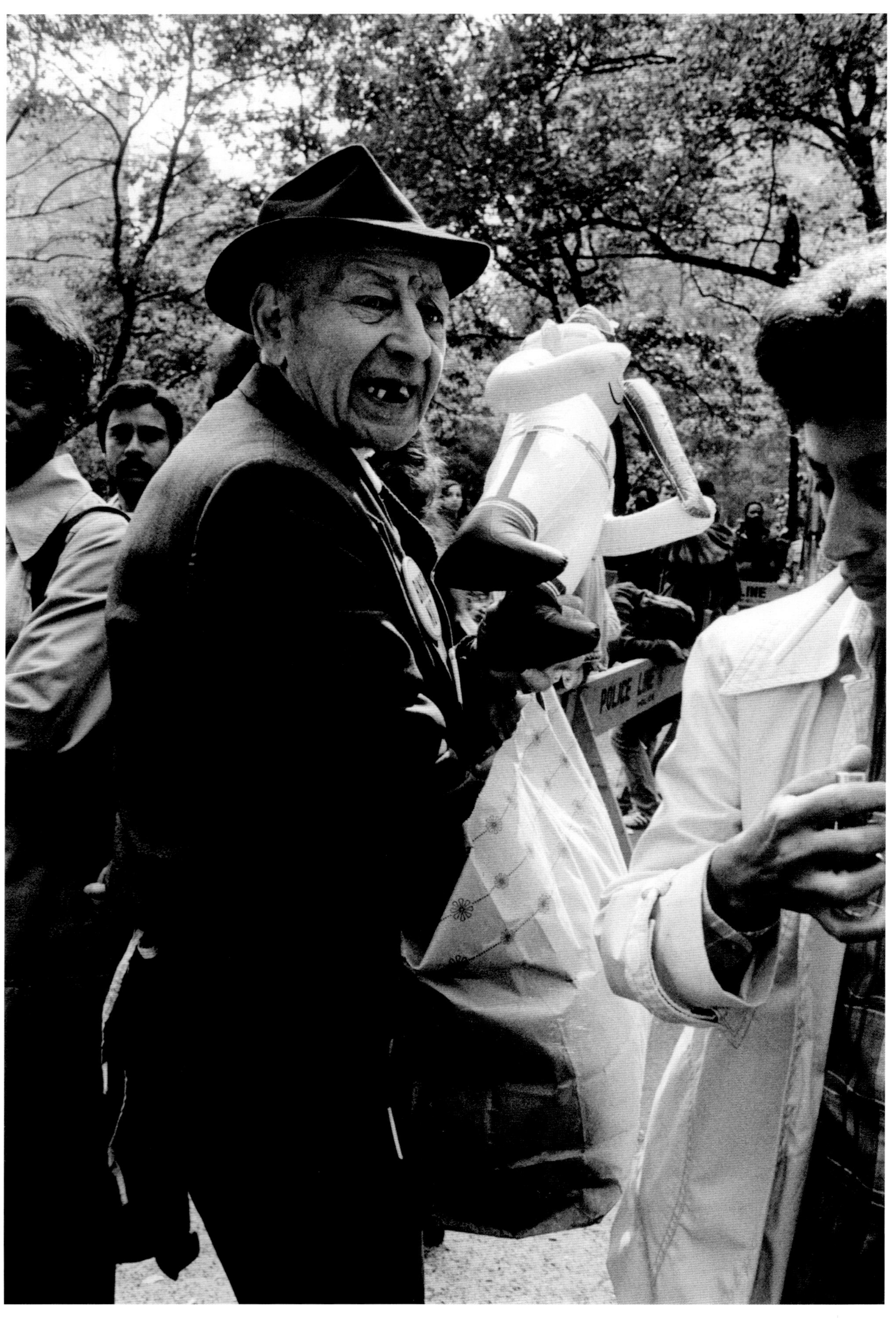

Selling Souvenirs at Yankee Victory Parade, City Hall Park New York, 1978

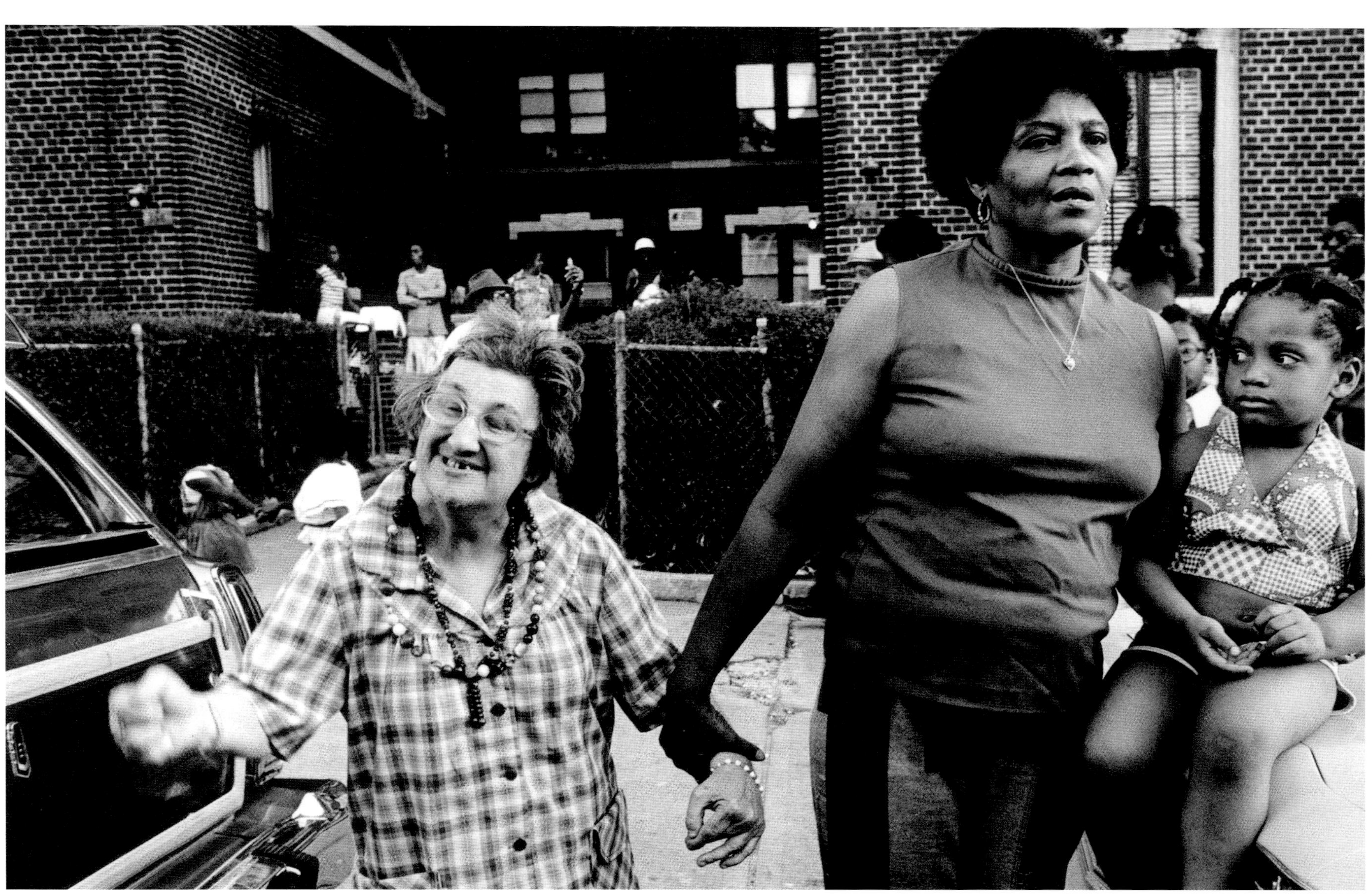

**West Indian Day Parade,
Brooklyn
New York, 1978**

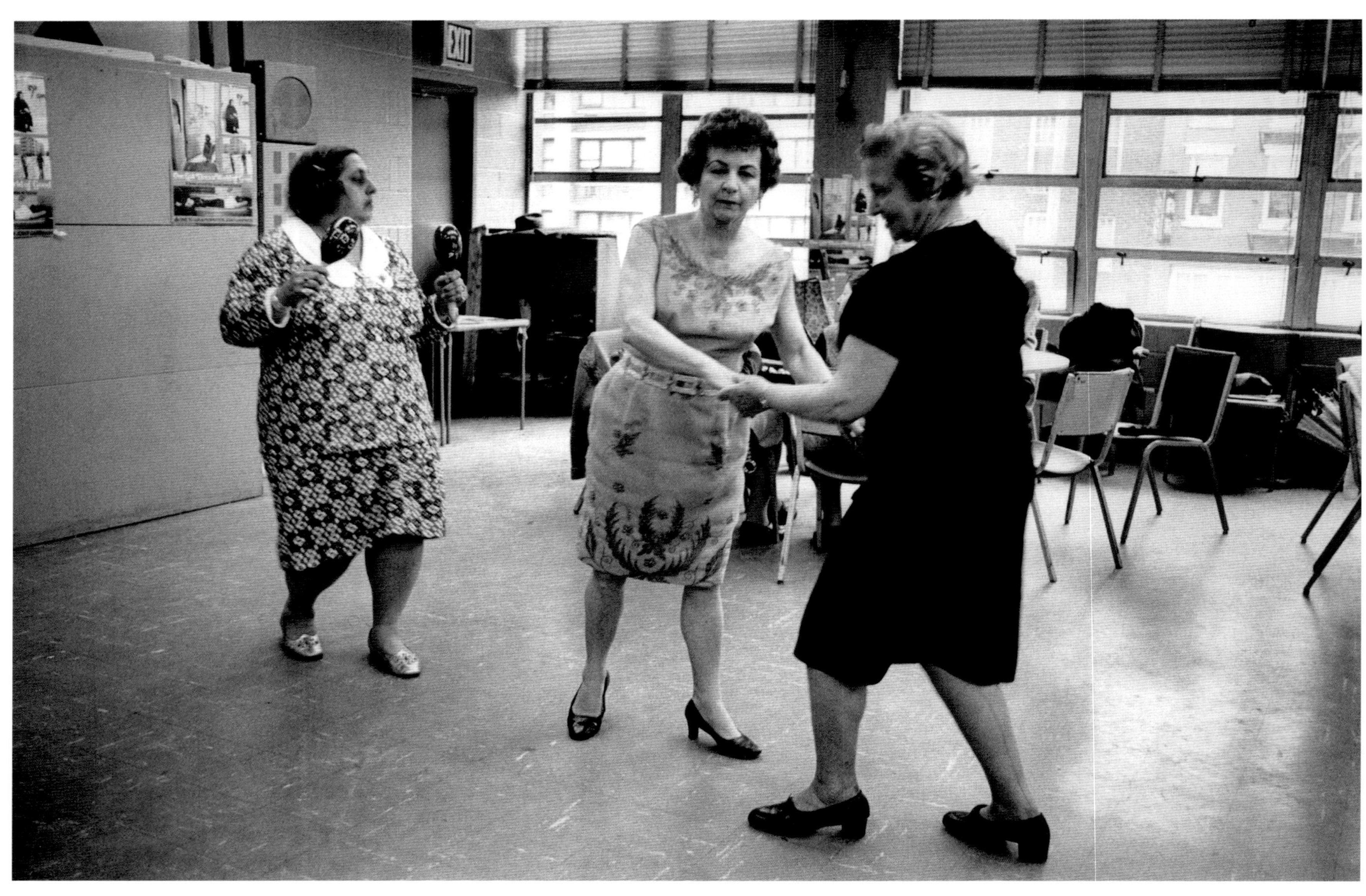

Midtown Y on East 14th Street
New York, 1975

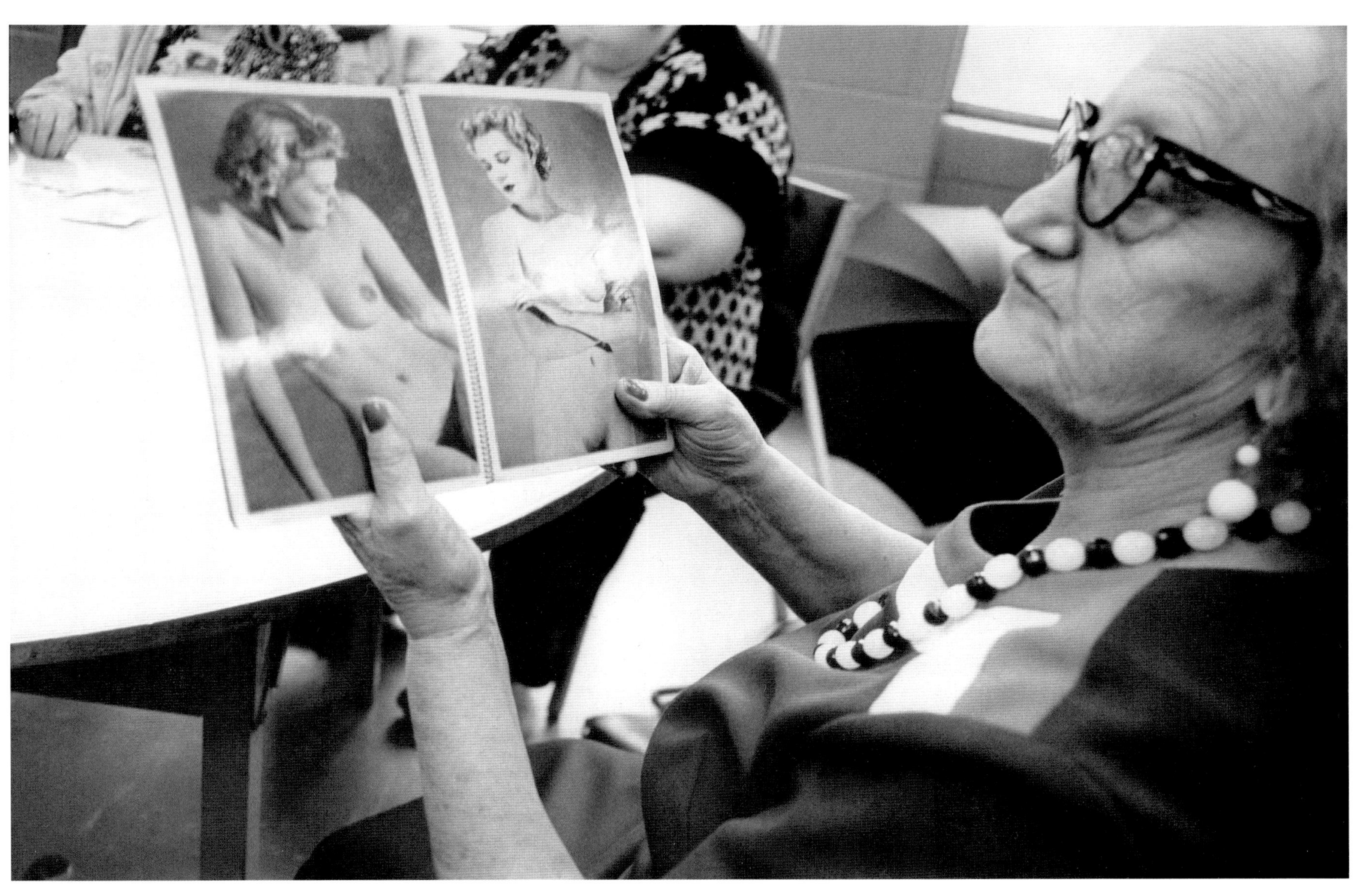

Midtown Y on East 14th Street
New York, 1975

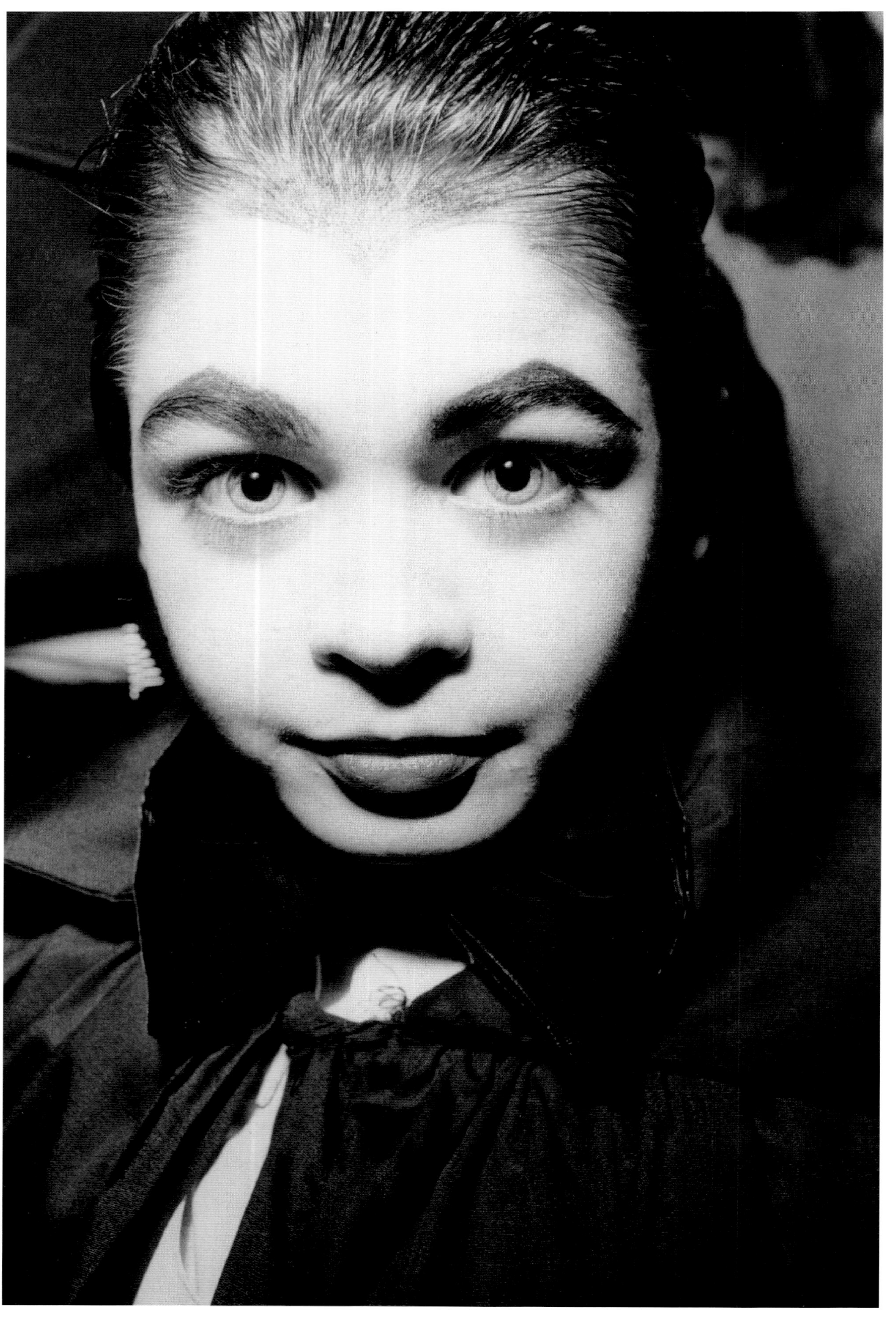

Dracula, Halloween Parade in
the West Village
New York, 1978

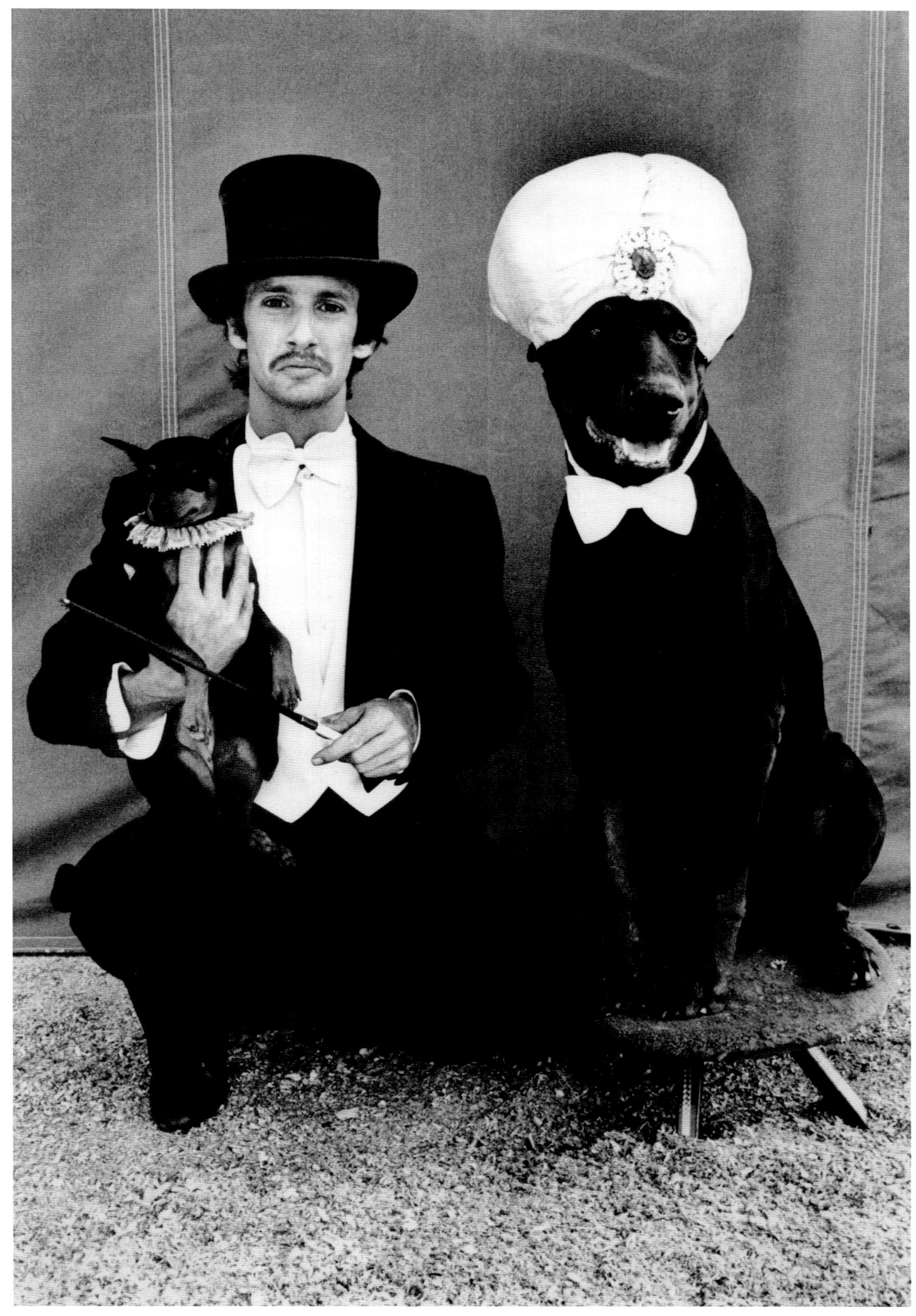

Lloyd Steir and Dogs at the Big Apple Circus New York, 1976

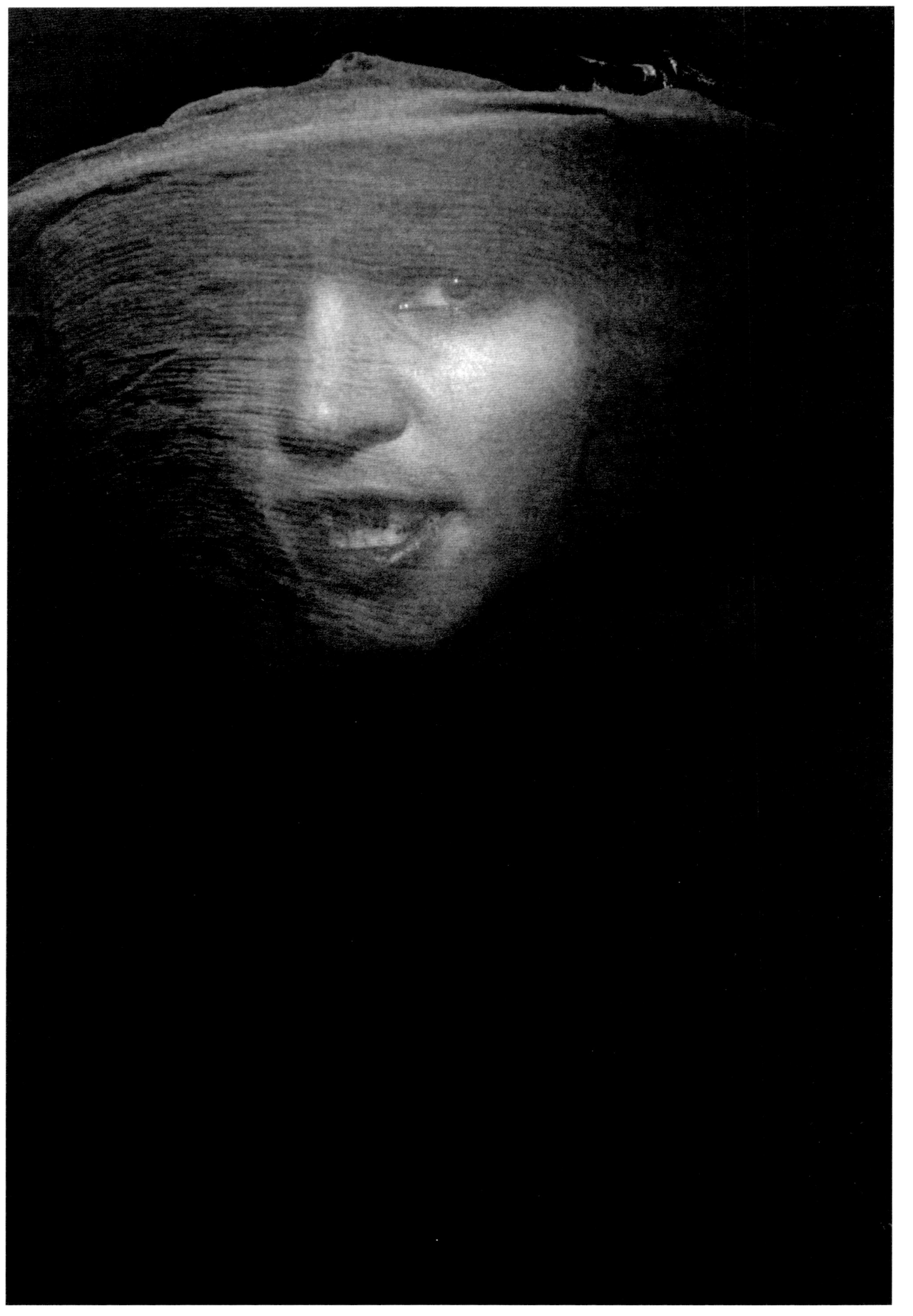

Woman Vampire
in Halloween Parade,
West Village
New York, 1979

George Rossovich Walks Out
New York, 1978

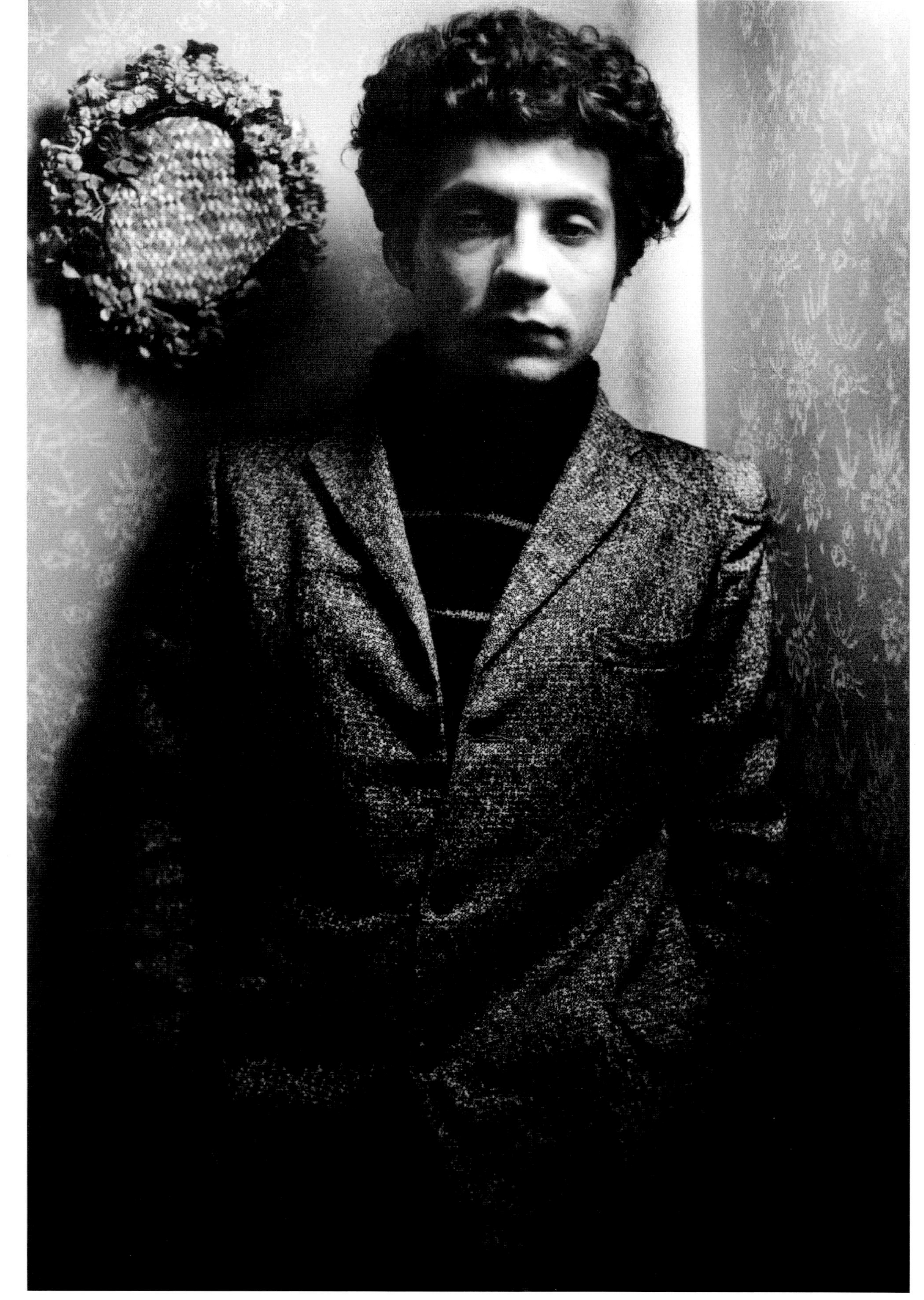

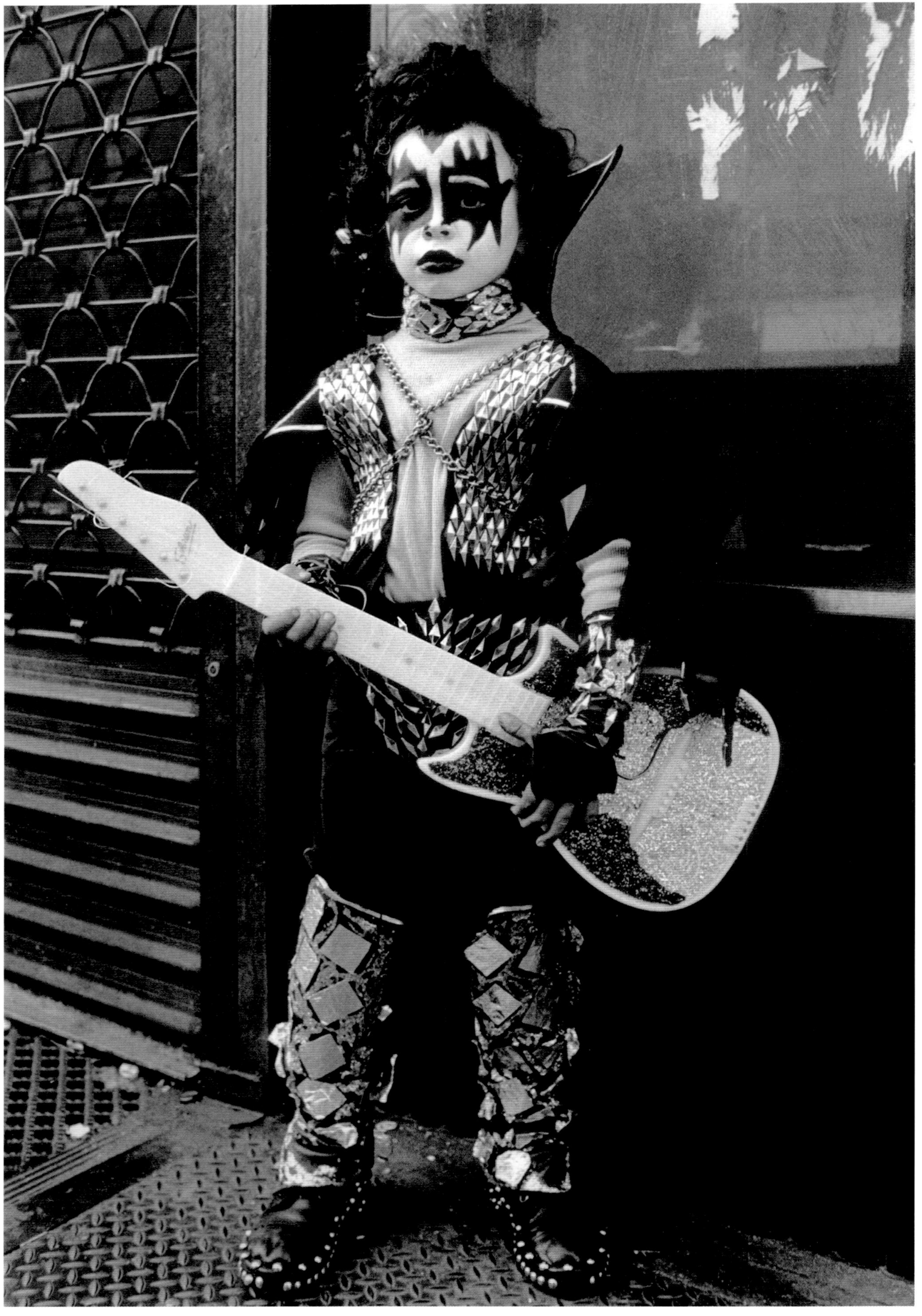

KISS, Halloween Parade,
West Village
New York, 1978

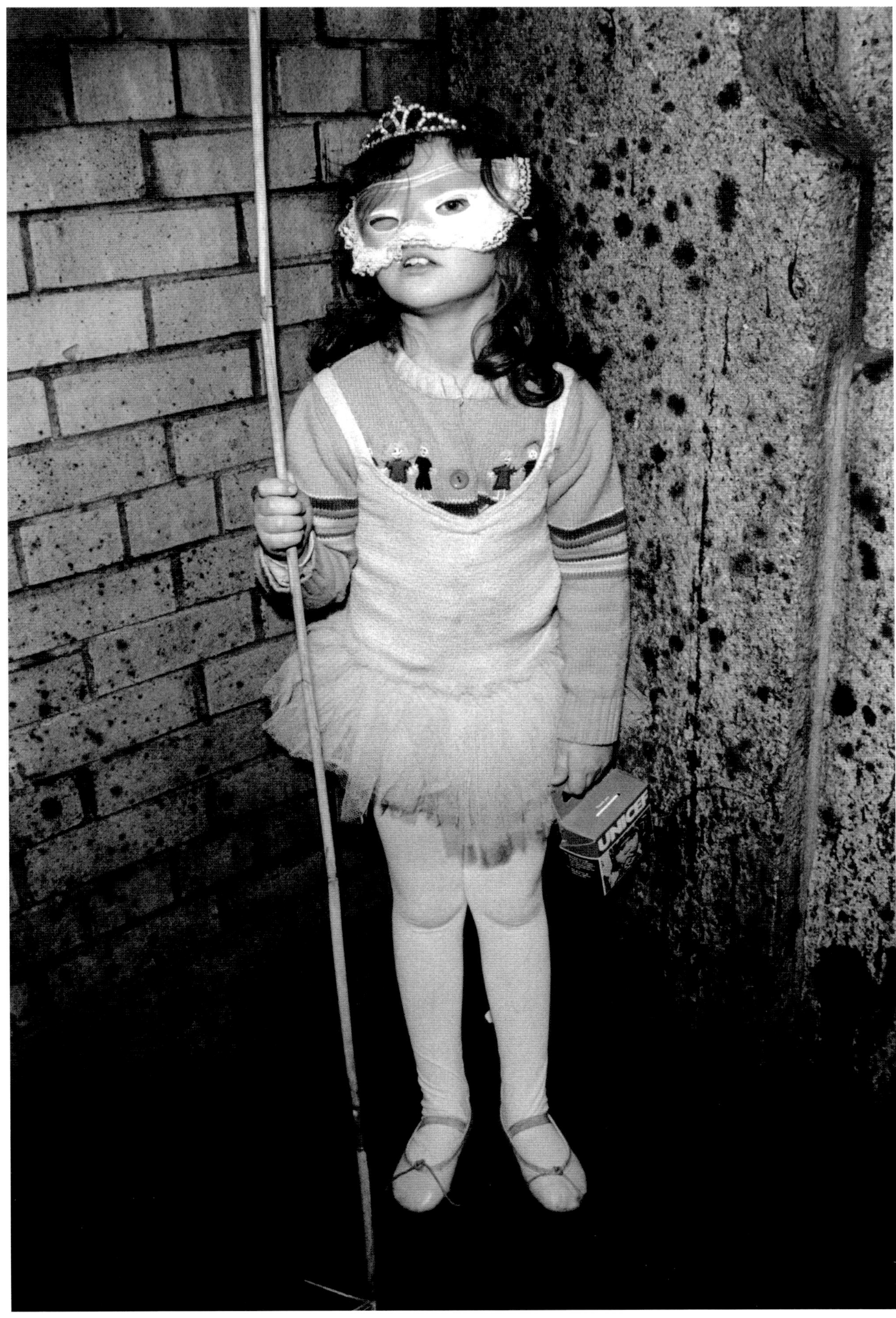

Ballerina, Halloween Parade,
Westbeth
New York, 1978

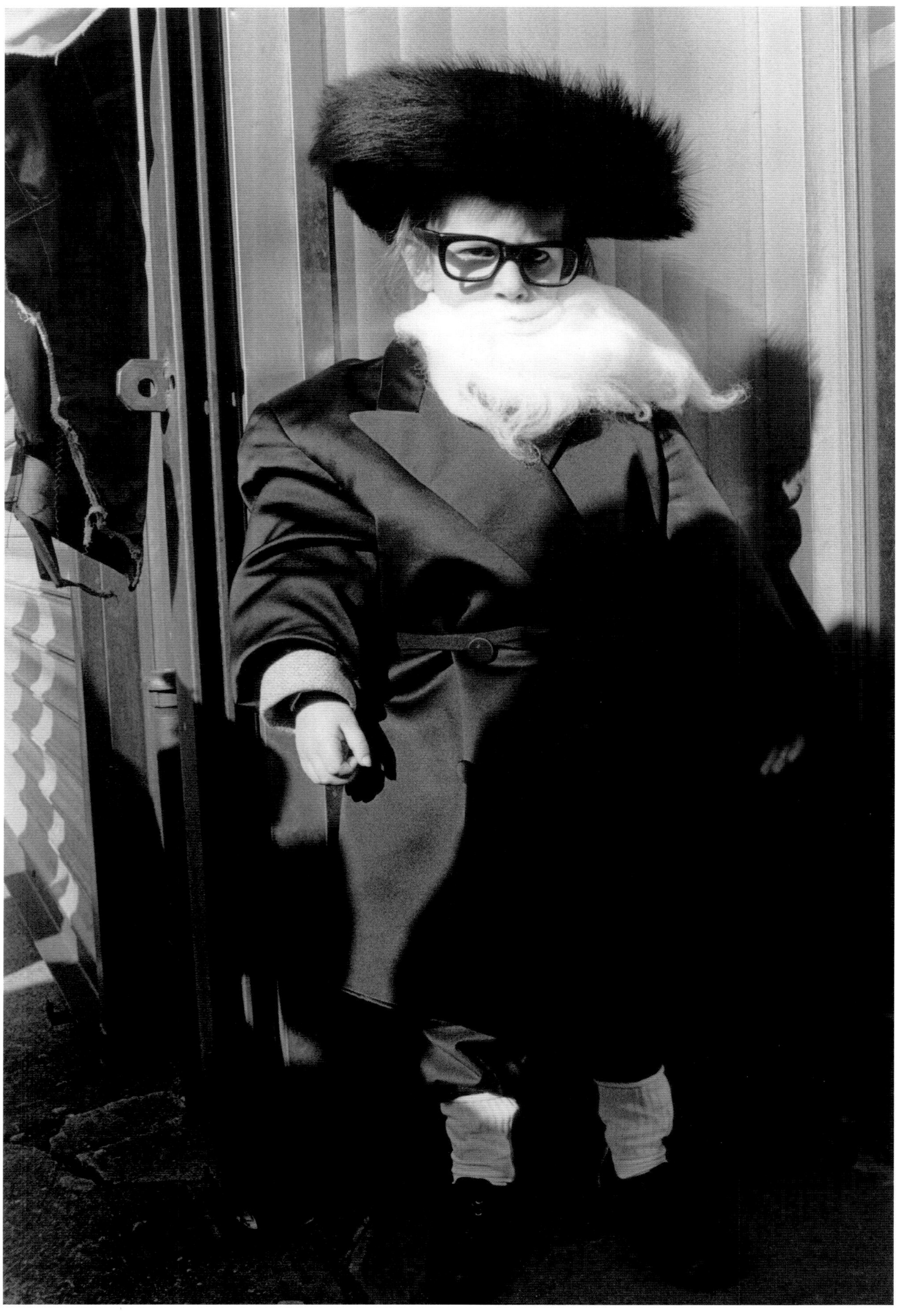

Little Rabbi, Purim,
Brooklyn
New York, 1988

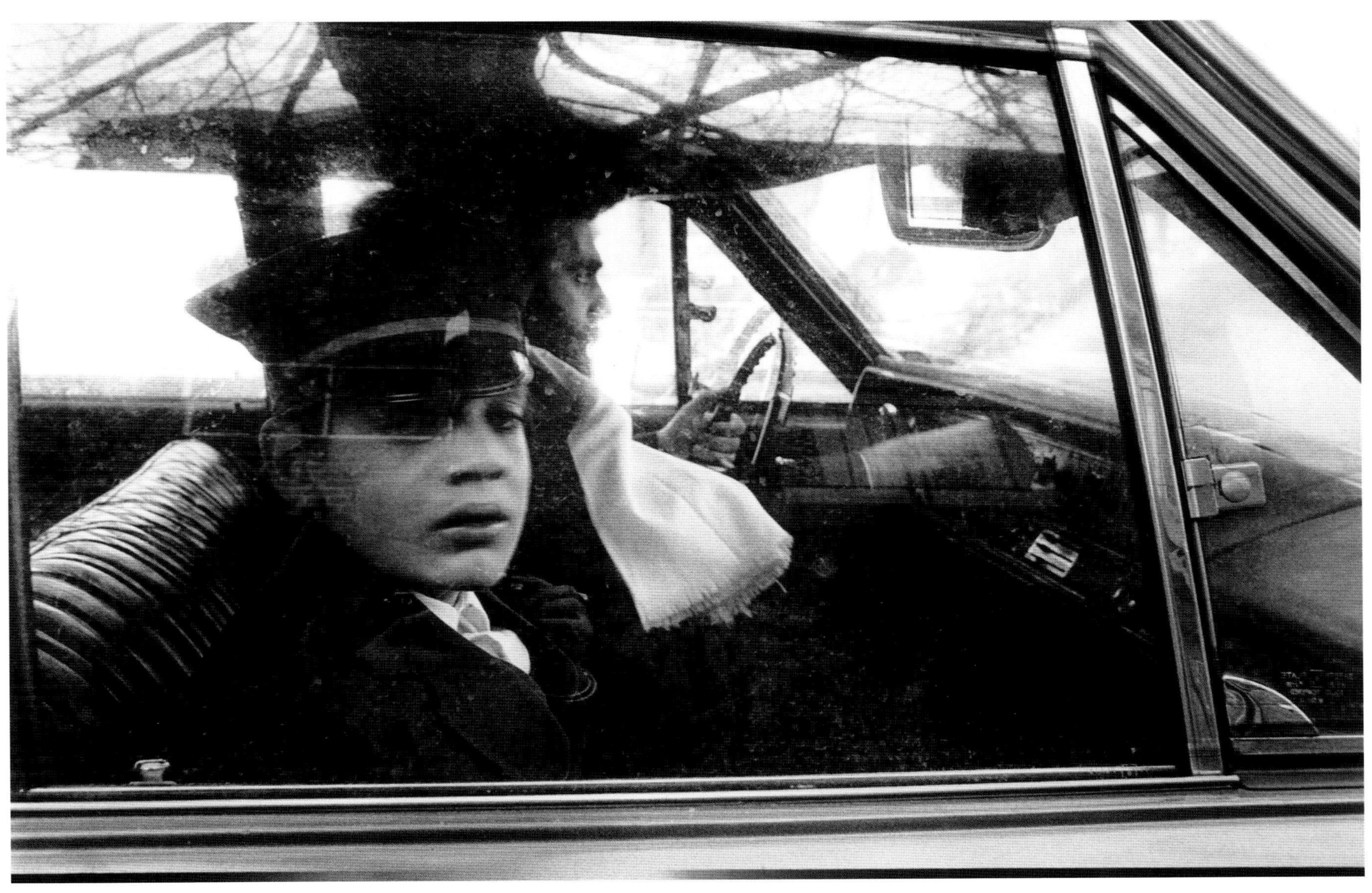

**Boy in Car on Purim,
Brooklyn
New York, 1988**

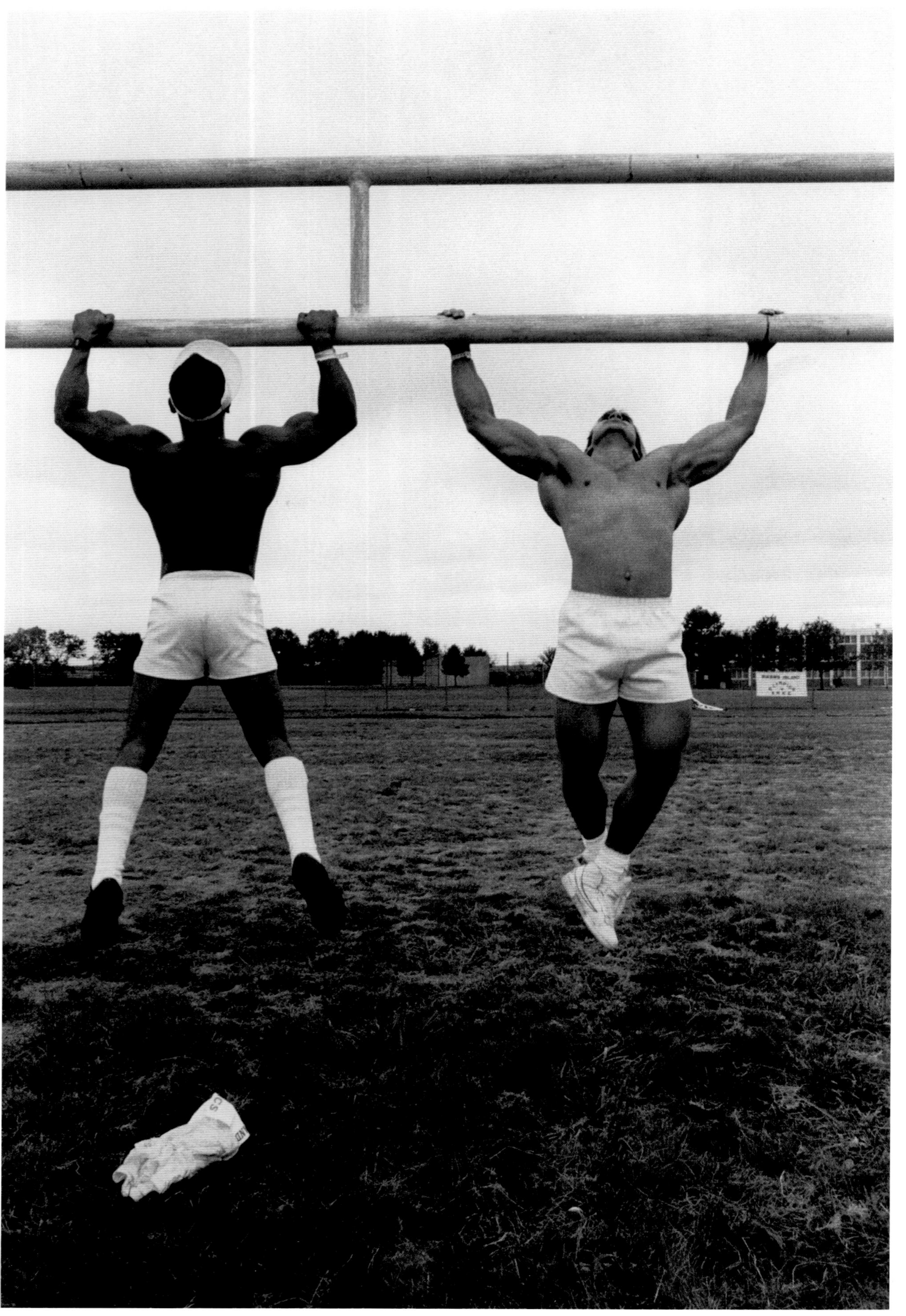

Rikers Island Olympics
New York, 1987

Riis Nude Bay,
Queens
New York, 1980

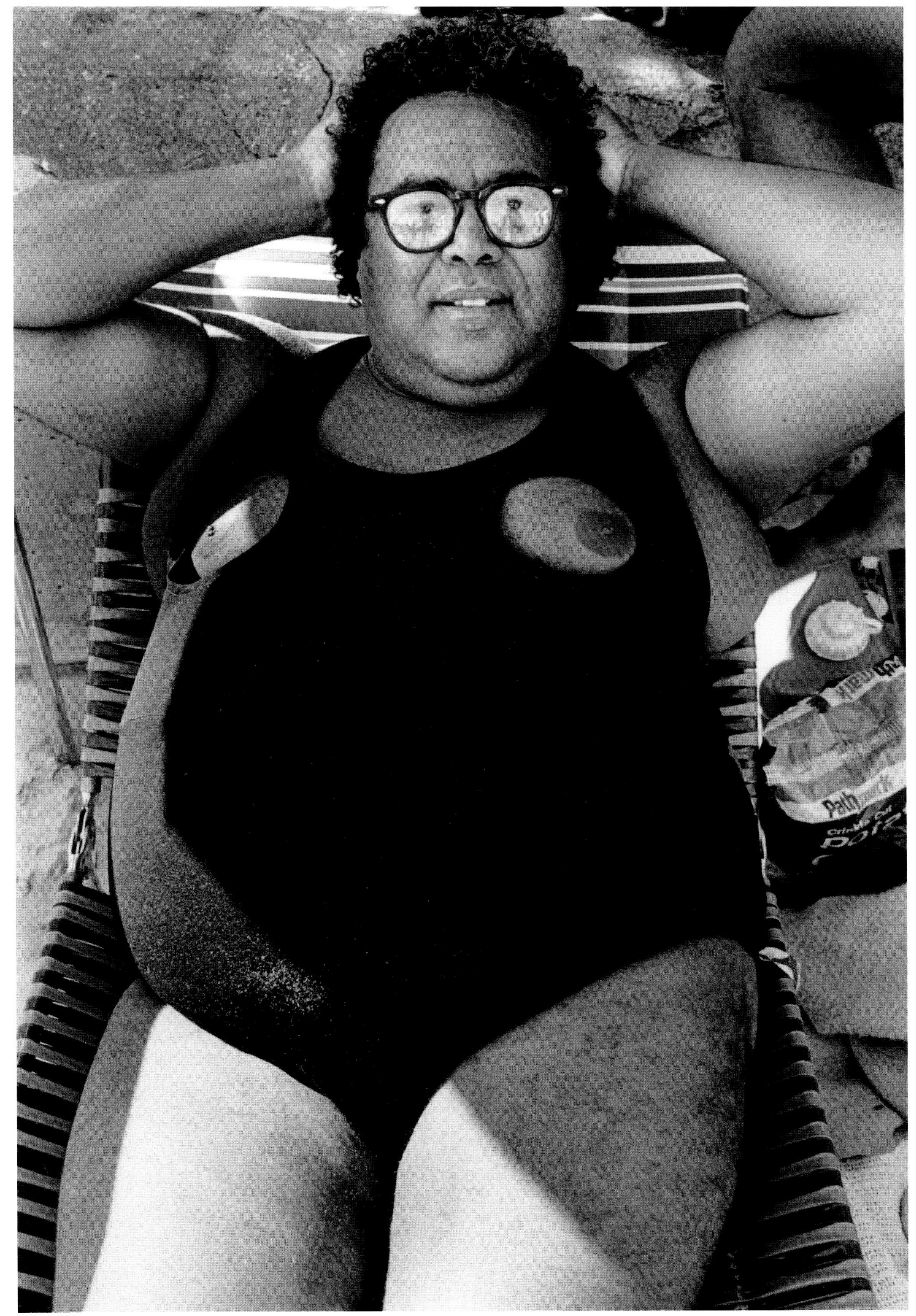

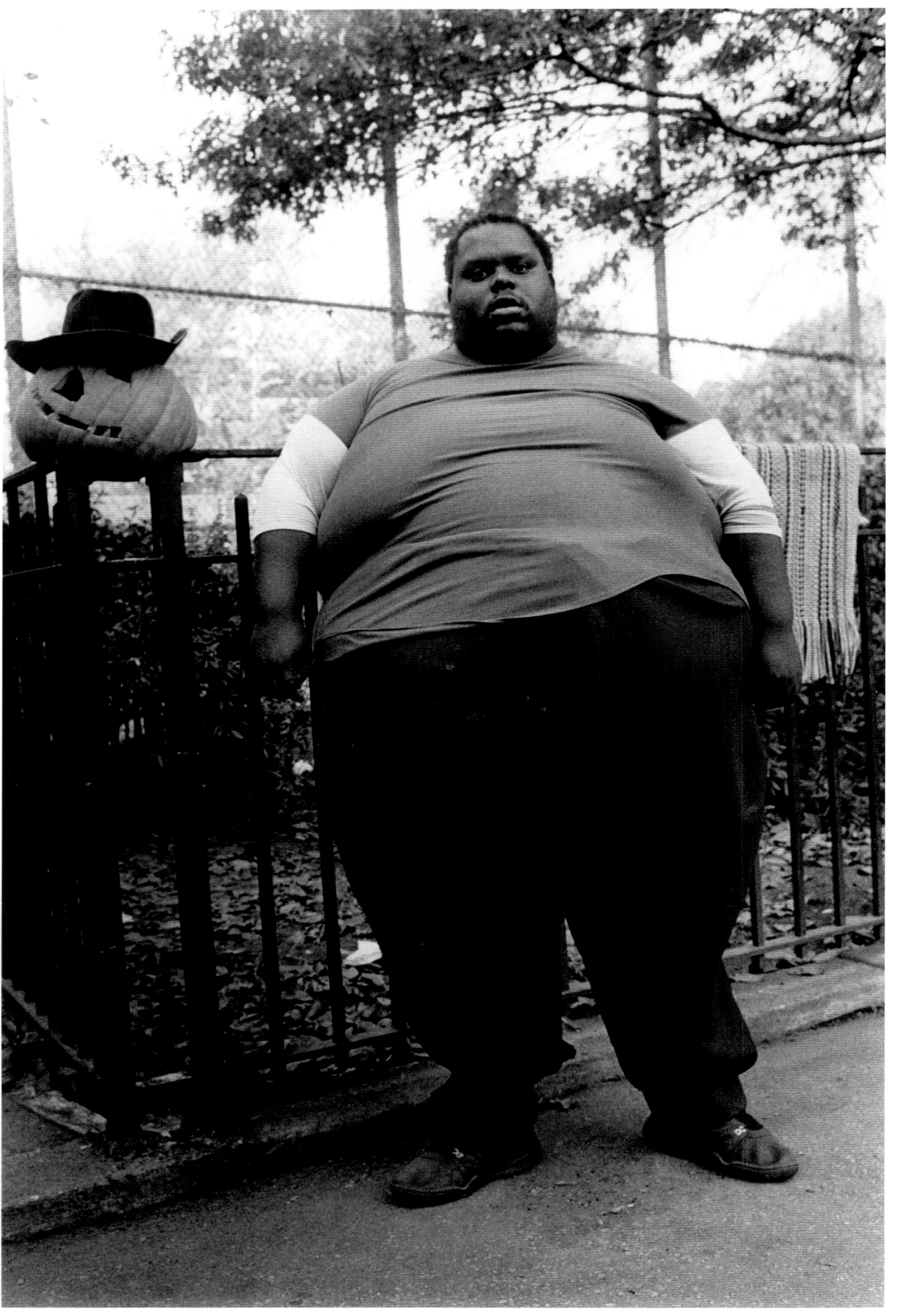

Halloween,
Tompkins Square Park
New York, 1989

Sid's Basketball Game,
Coney Island
New York, 1976

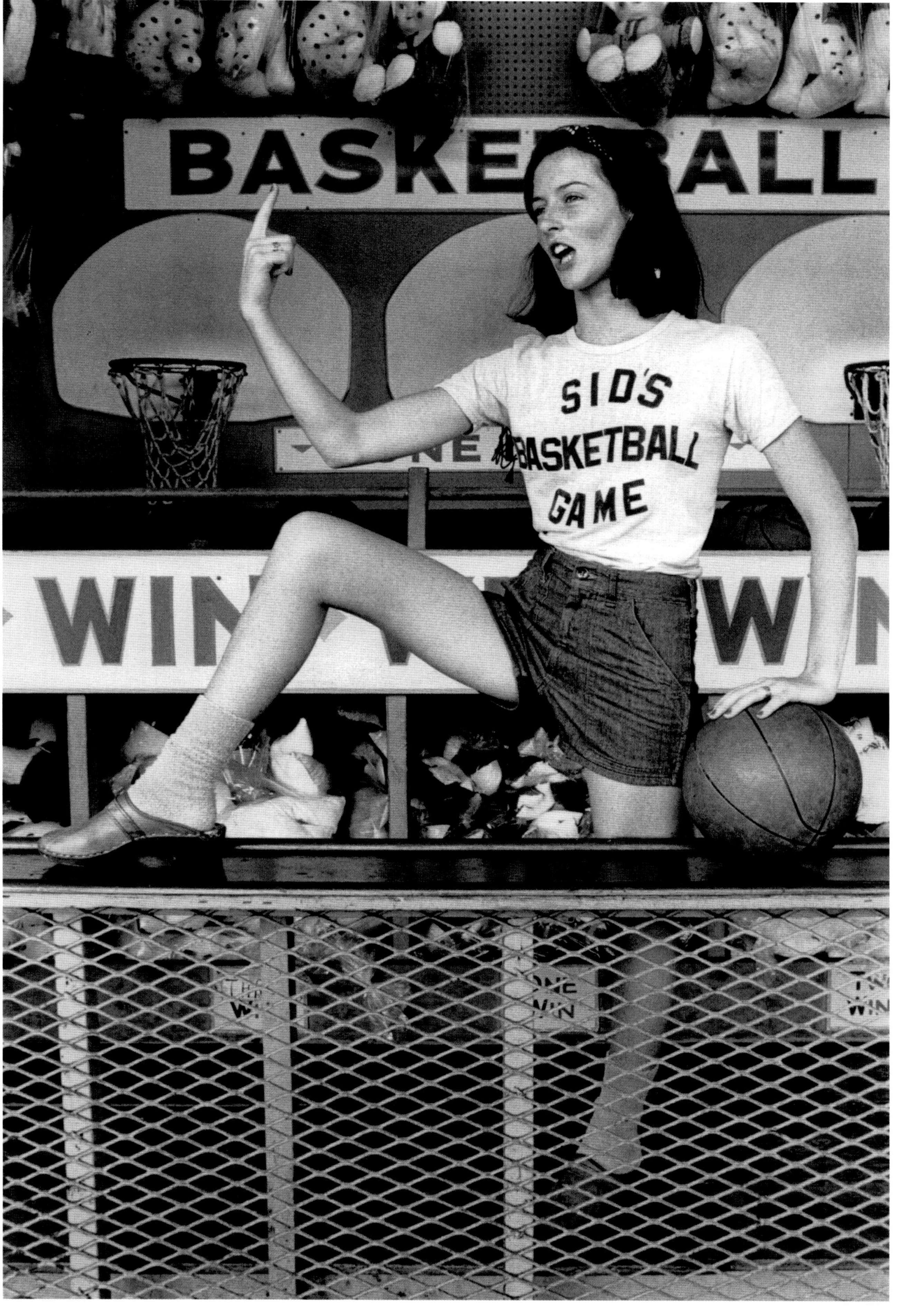
SID'S
BASKETBALL
GAME
WIN

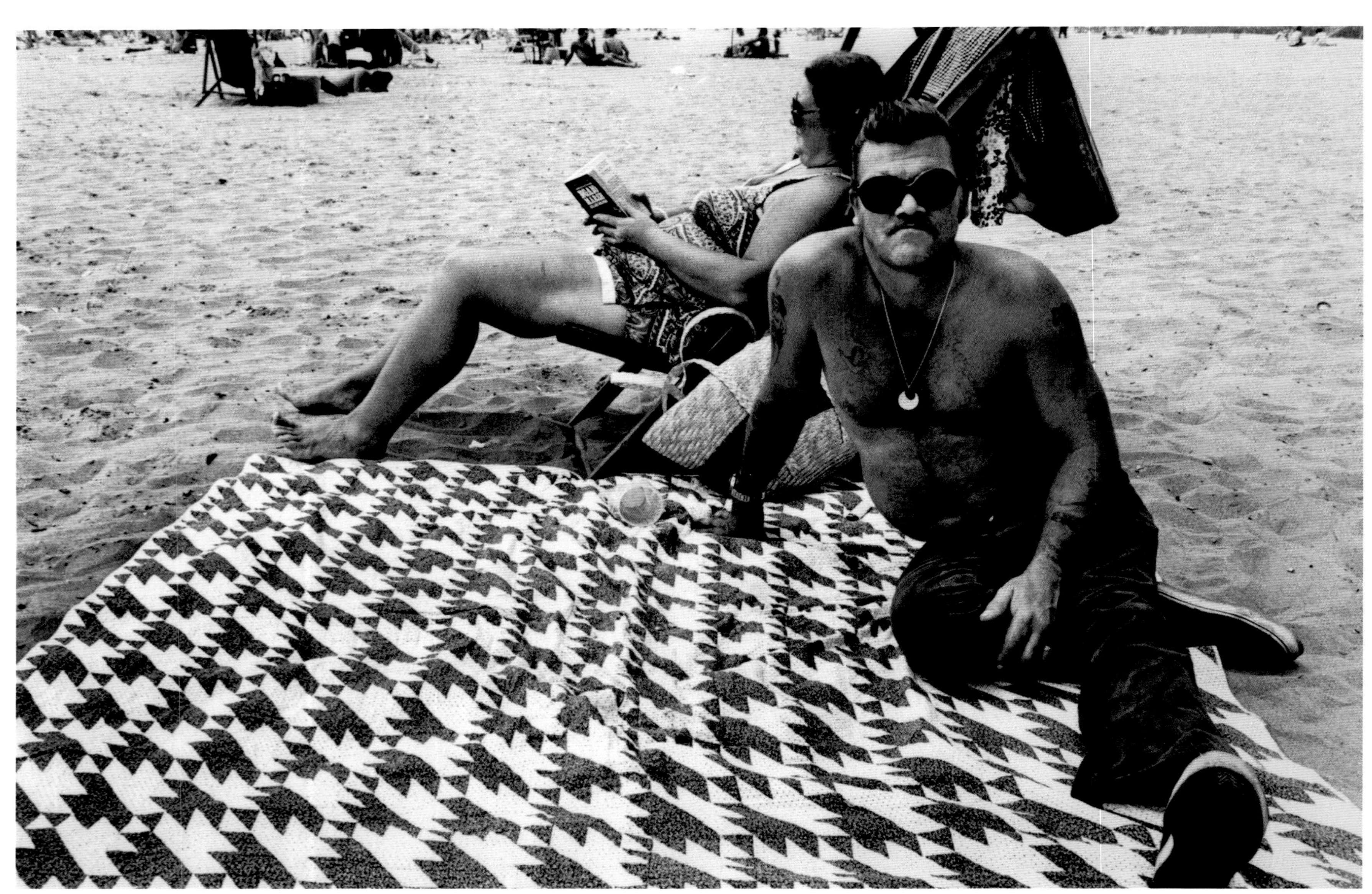

Houndstooth Blanket
on Coney Island Beach
New York, 1976

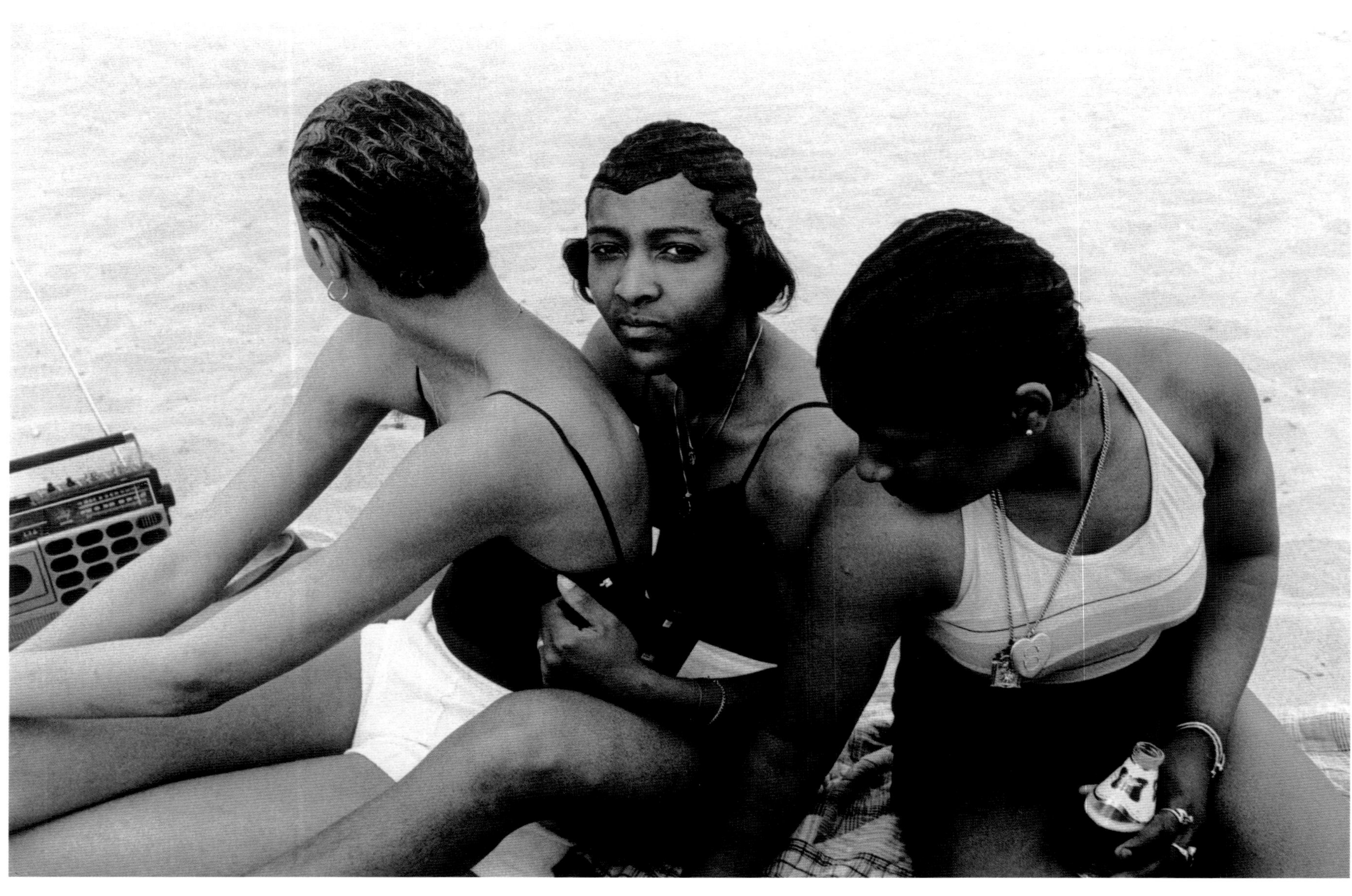

Women on Riis Beach
New York, 1980

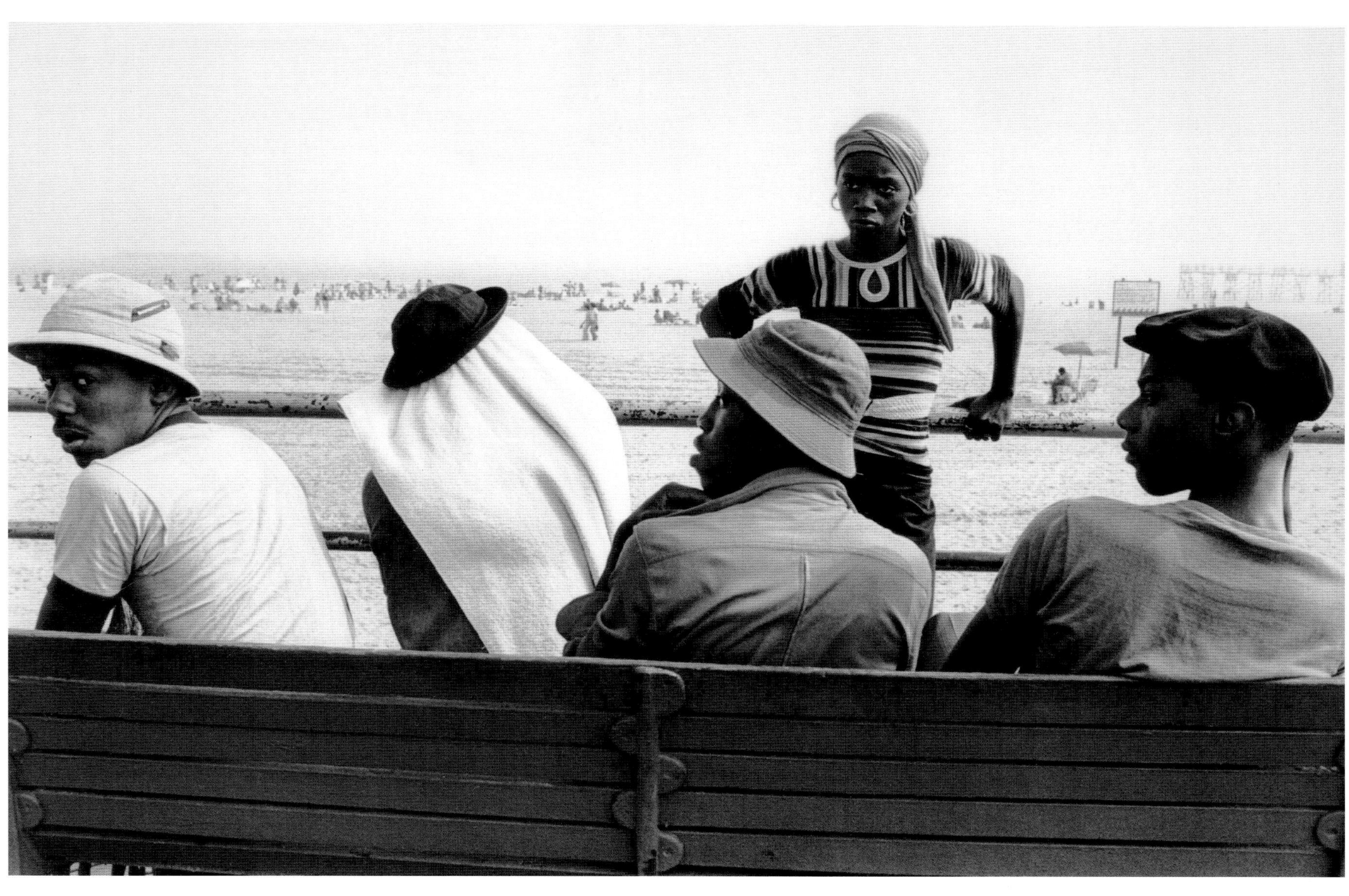

Boardwalk, Coney Island
New York, 1976

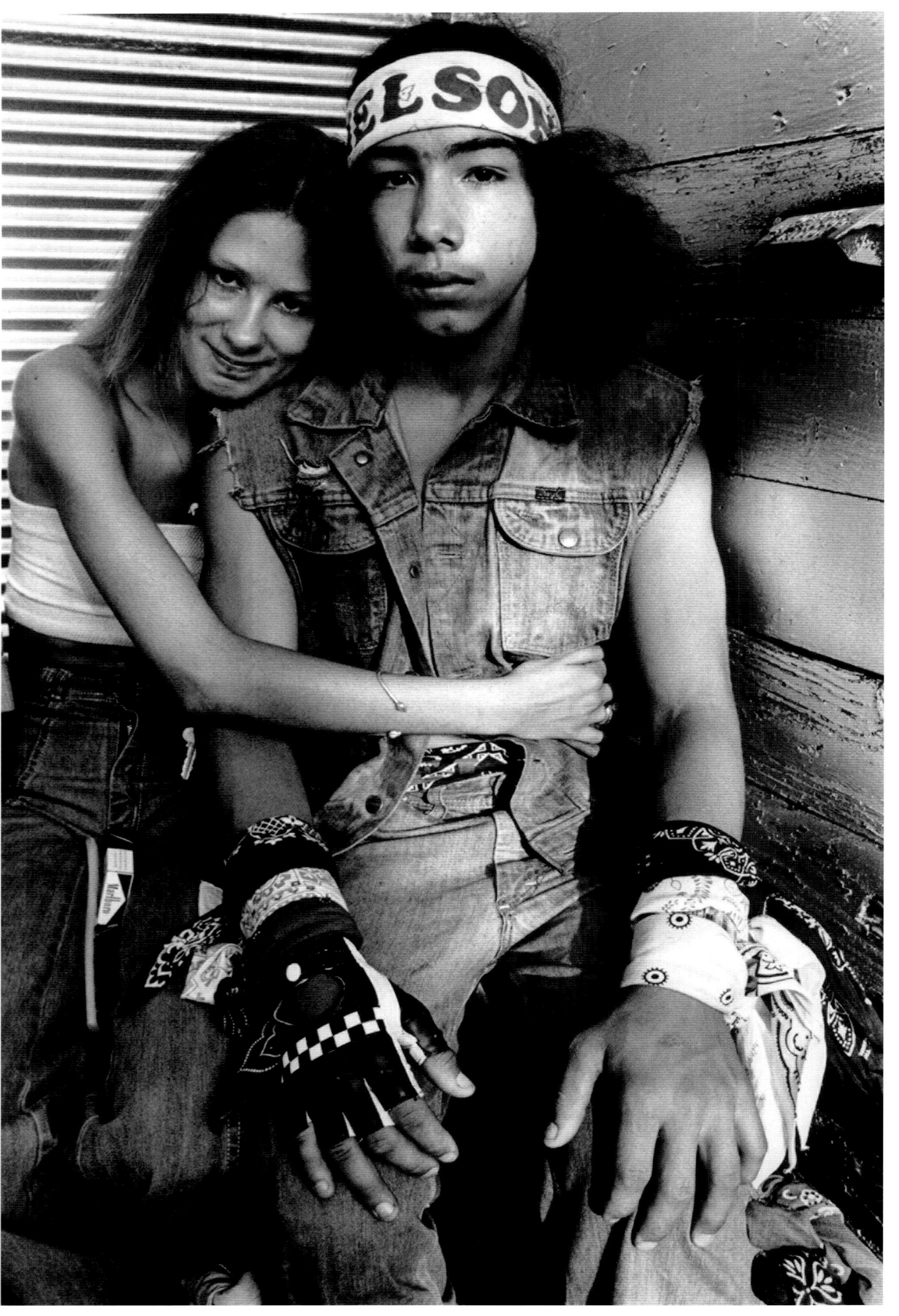

Nelson Rivera,
Tornado Roller Coaster,
Coney Island
New York, 1976

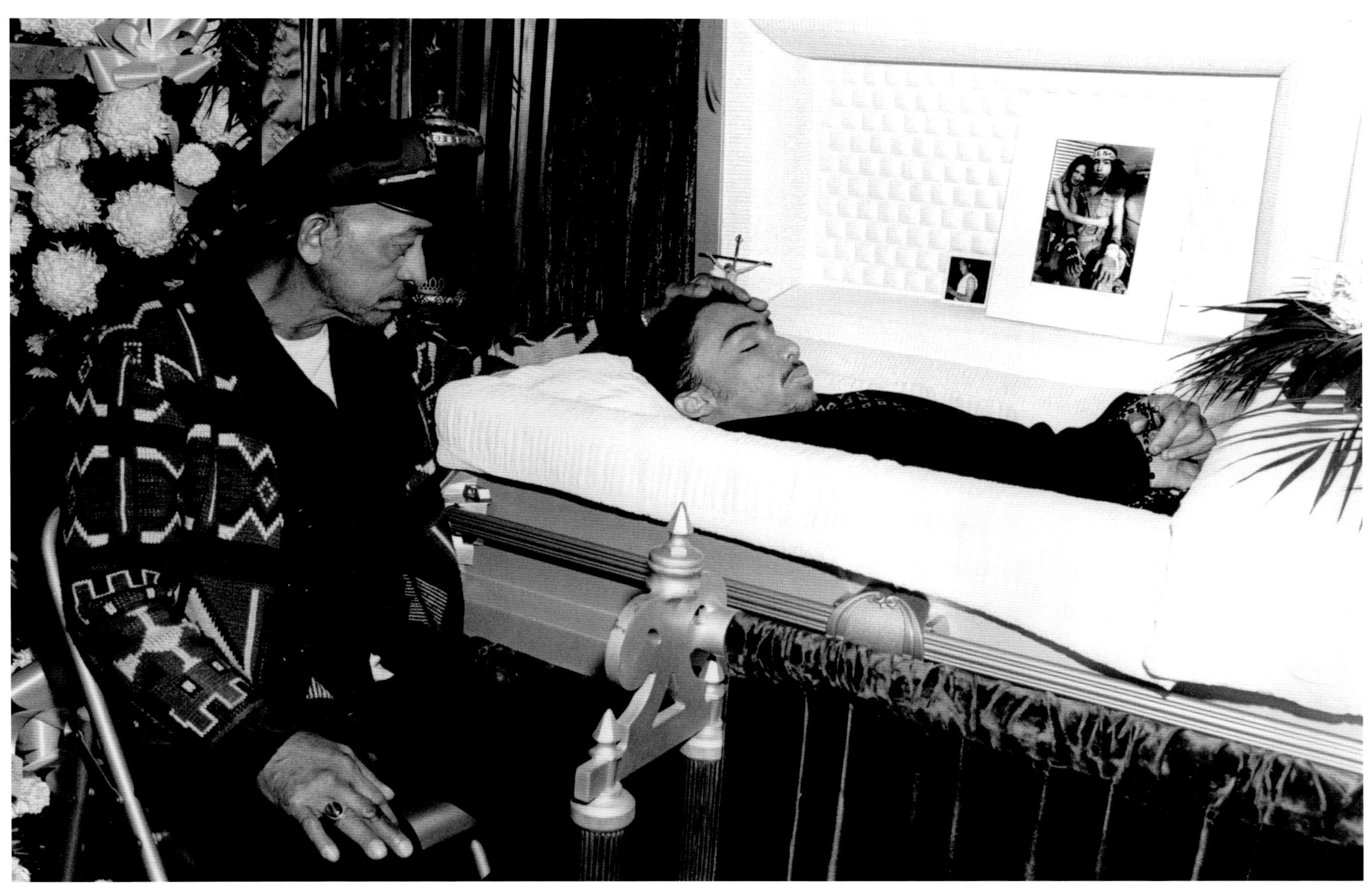

Nelson Rivera at Home,
Coney Island
New York, 1976

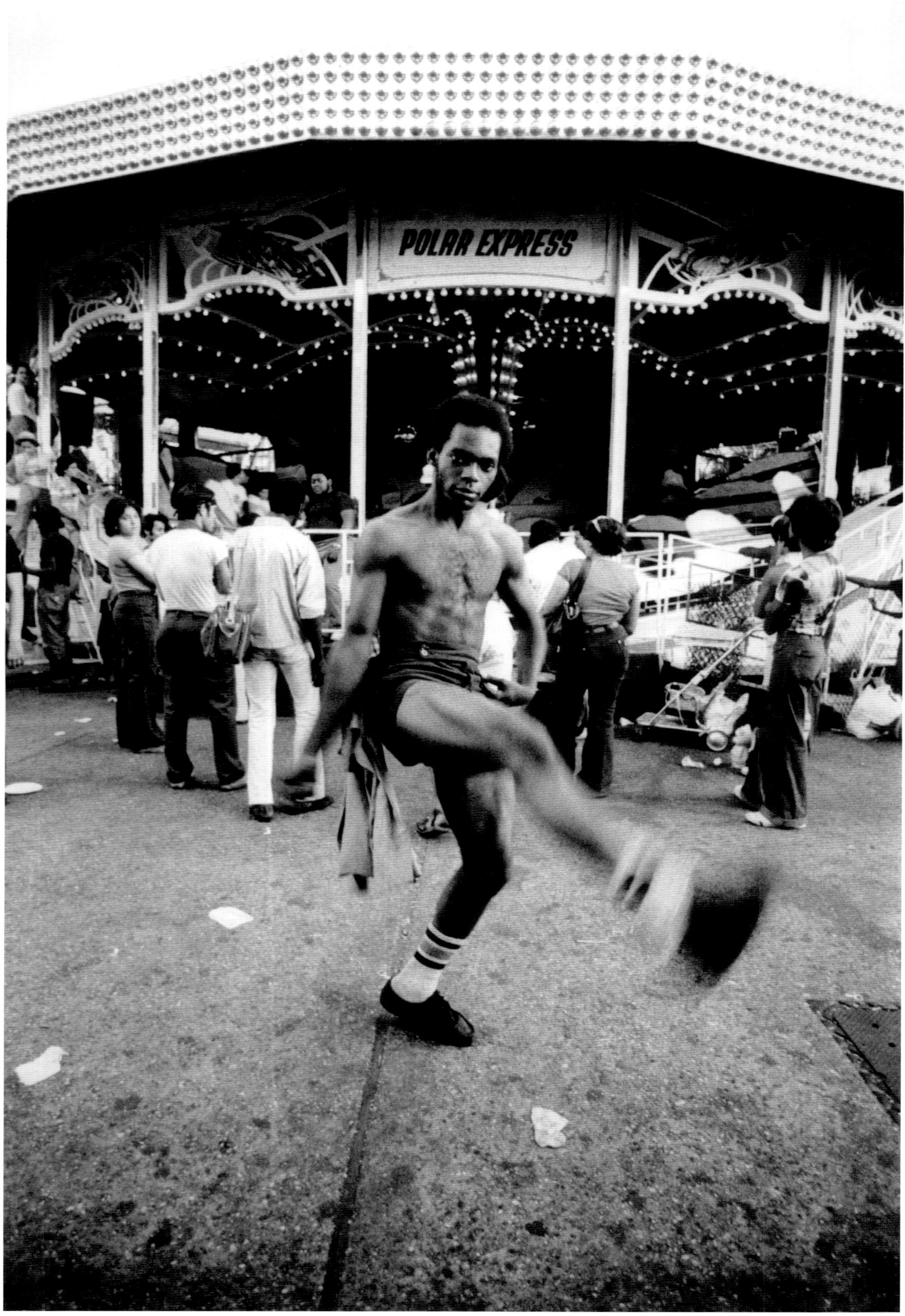

Polar Express, Coney Island
New York, 1976

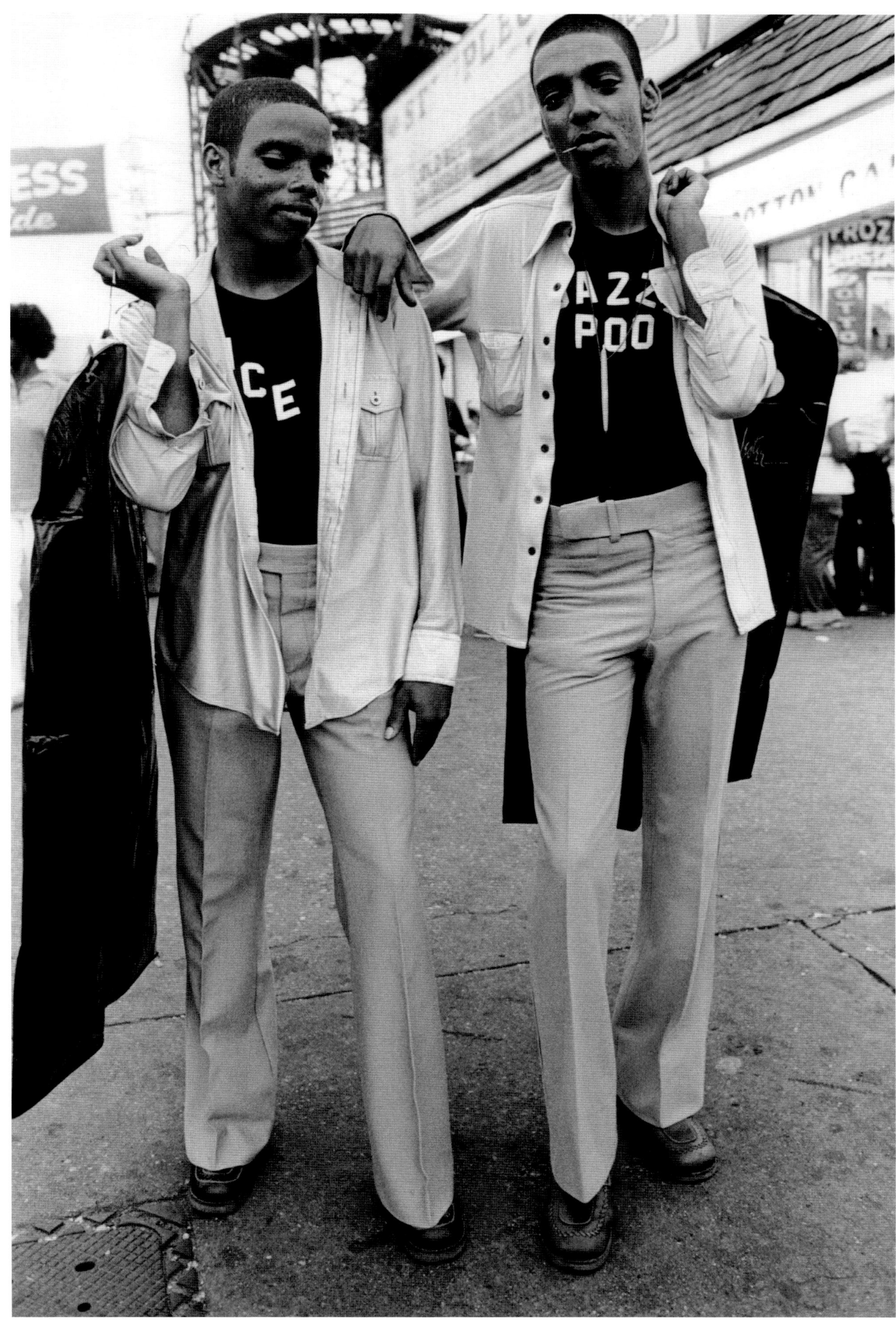

Brothers with Their Vines,
Coney Island
New York, 1976

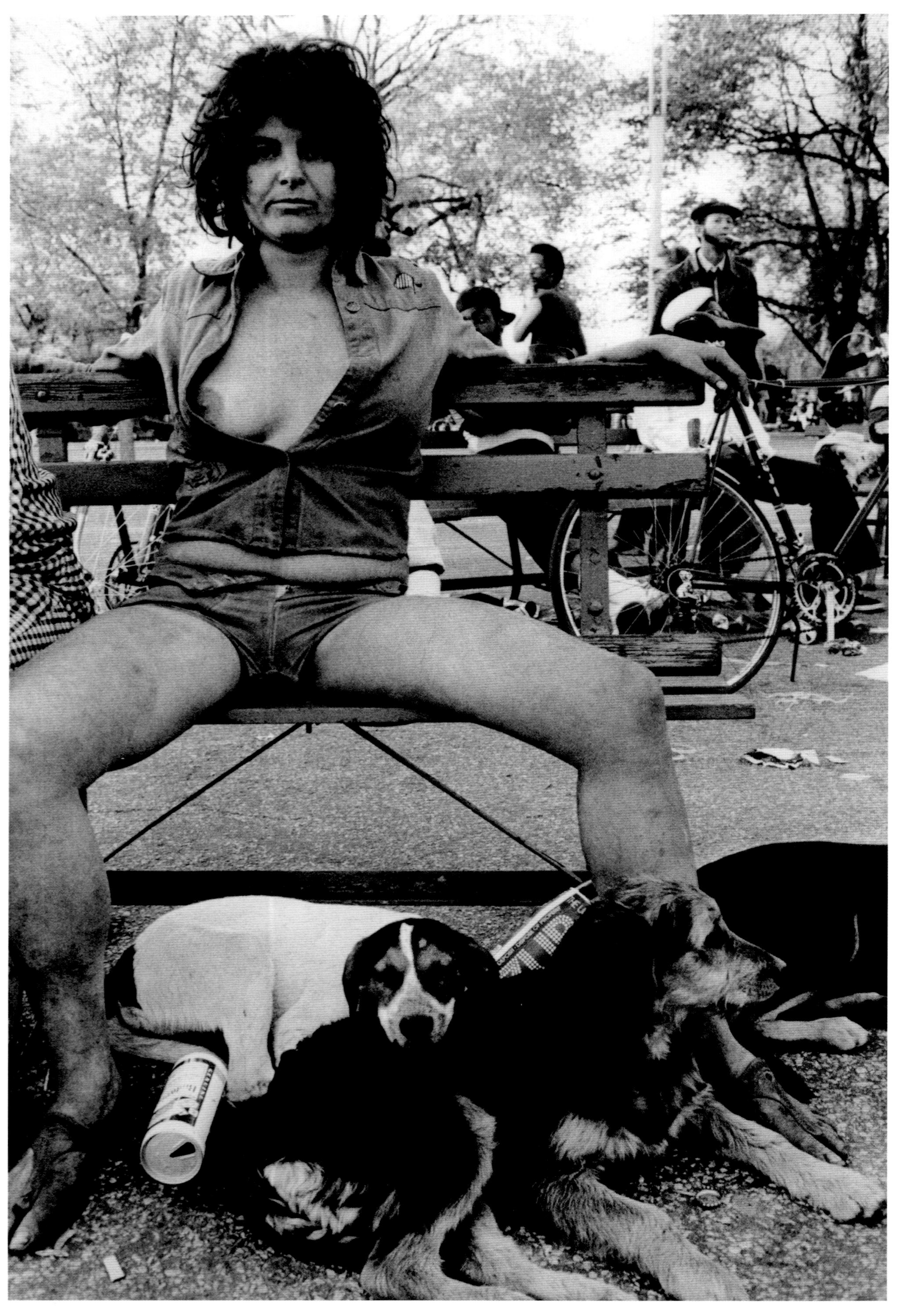

Woman with Dogs
in Central Park
New York, 1980

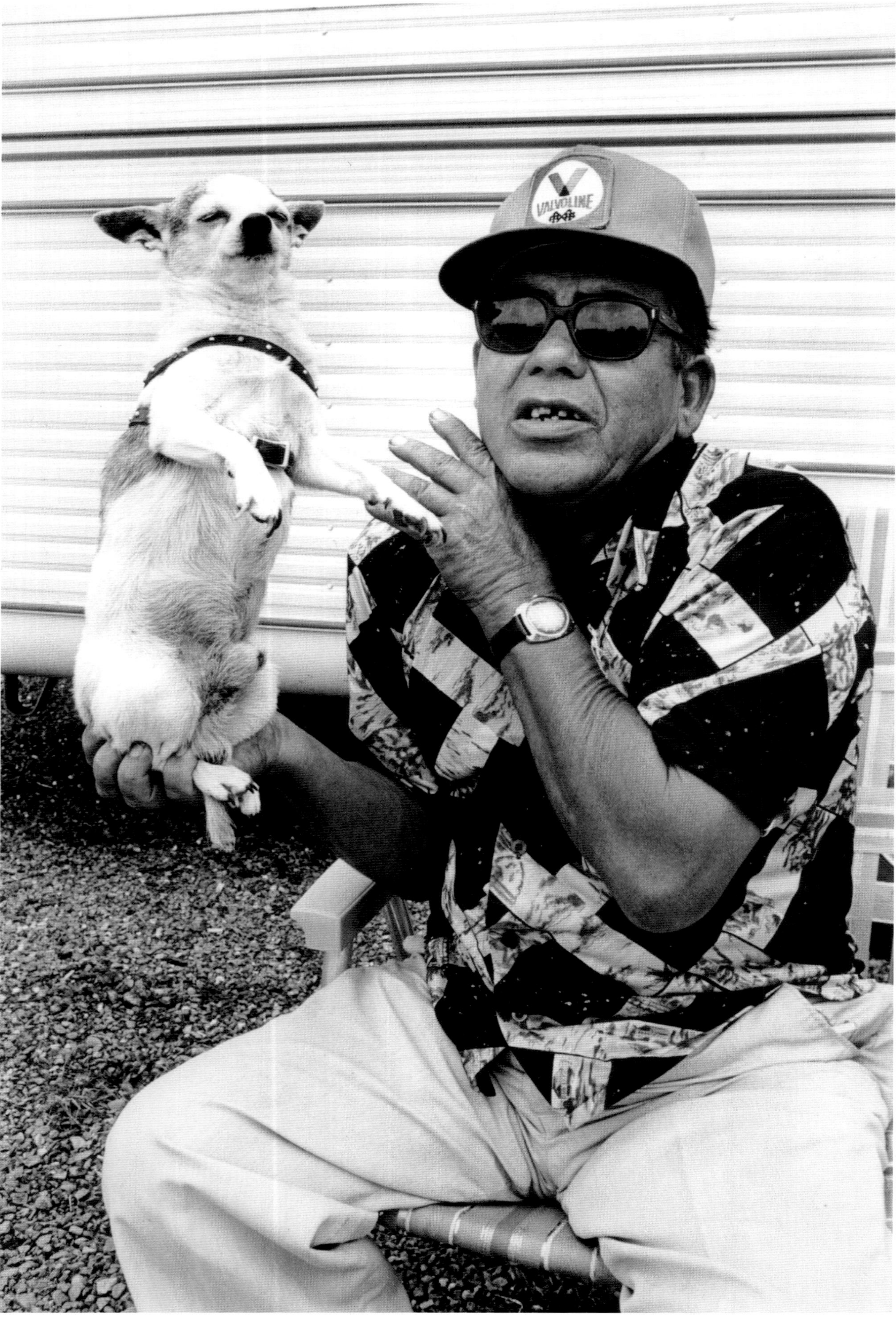

Husband with Chihuahua, 1980

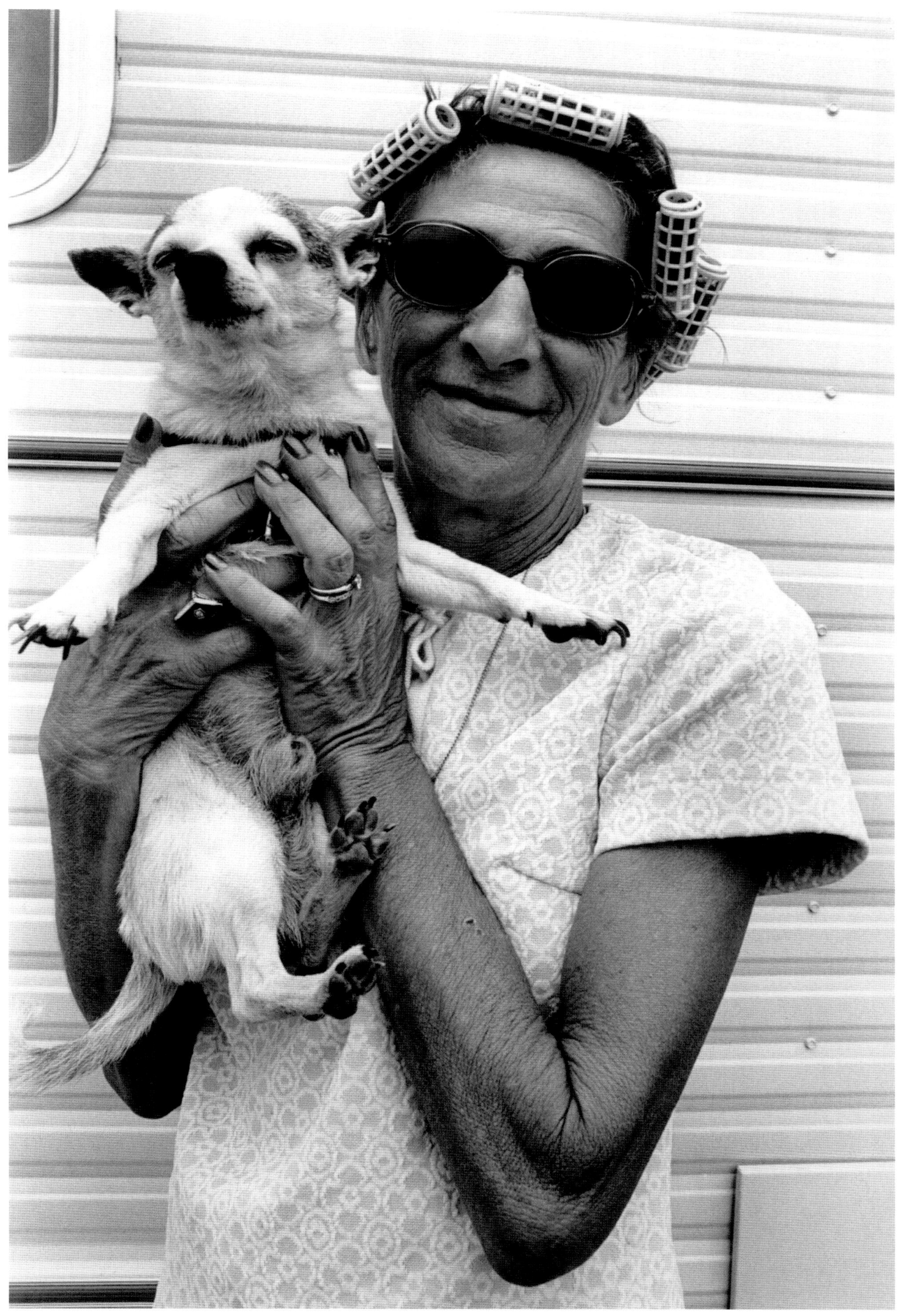

Wife with Chihuahua, 1980

Dog, Coney Island
New York, 1976

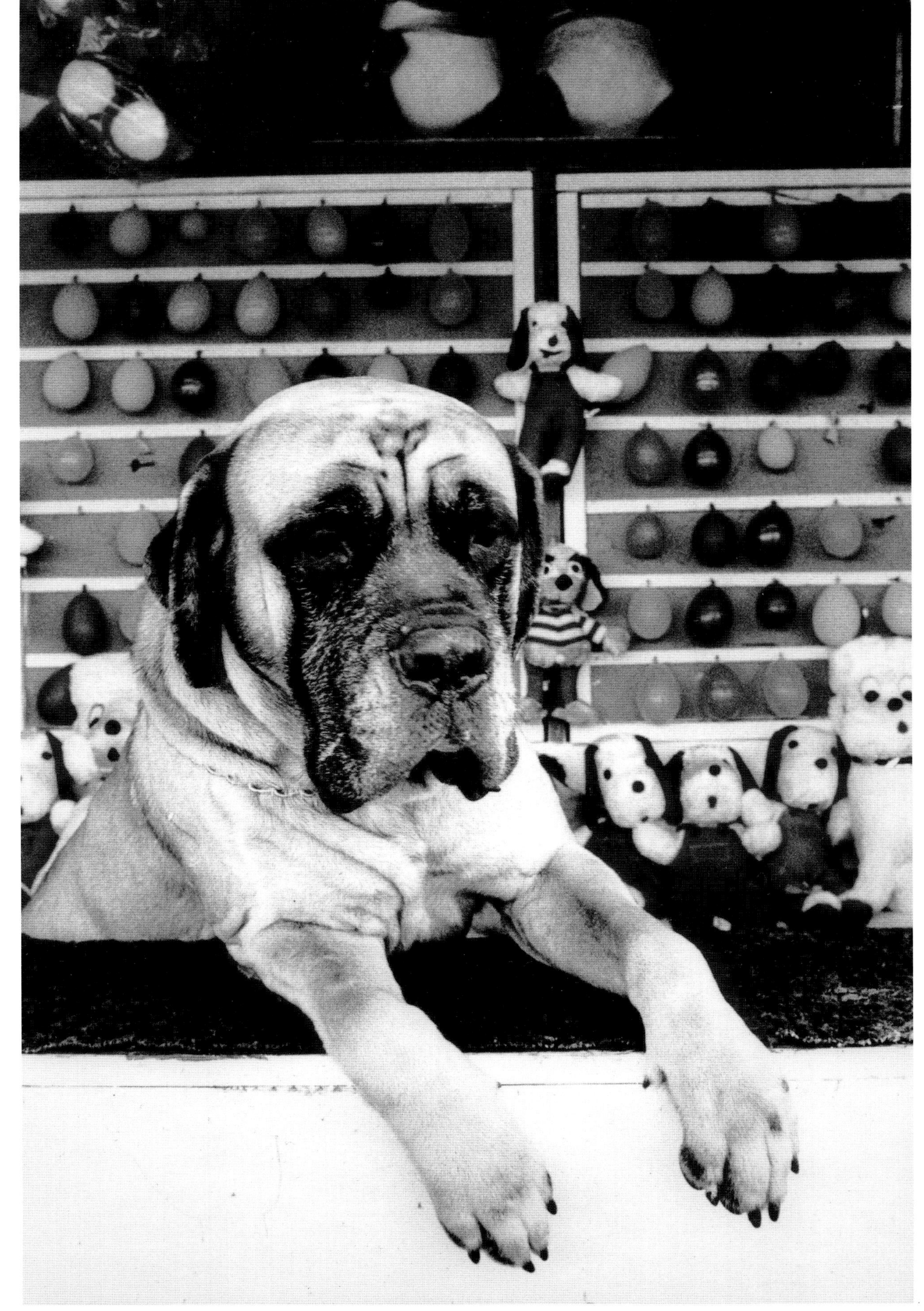

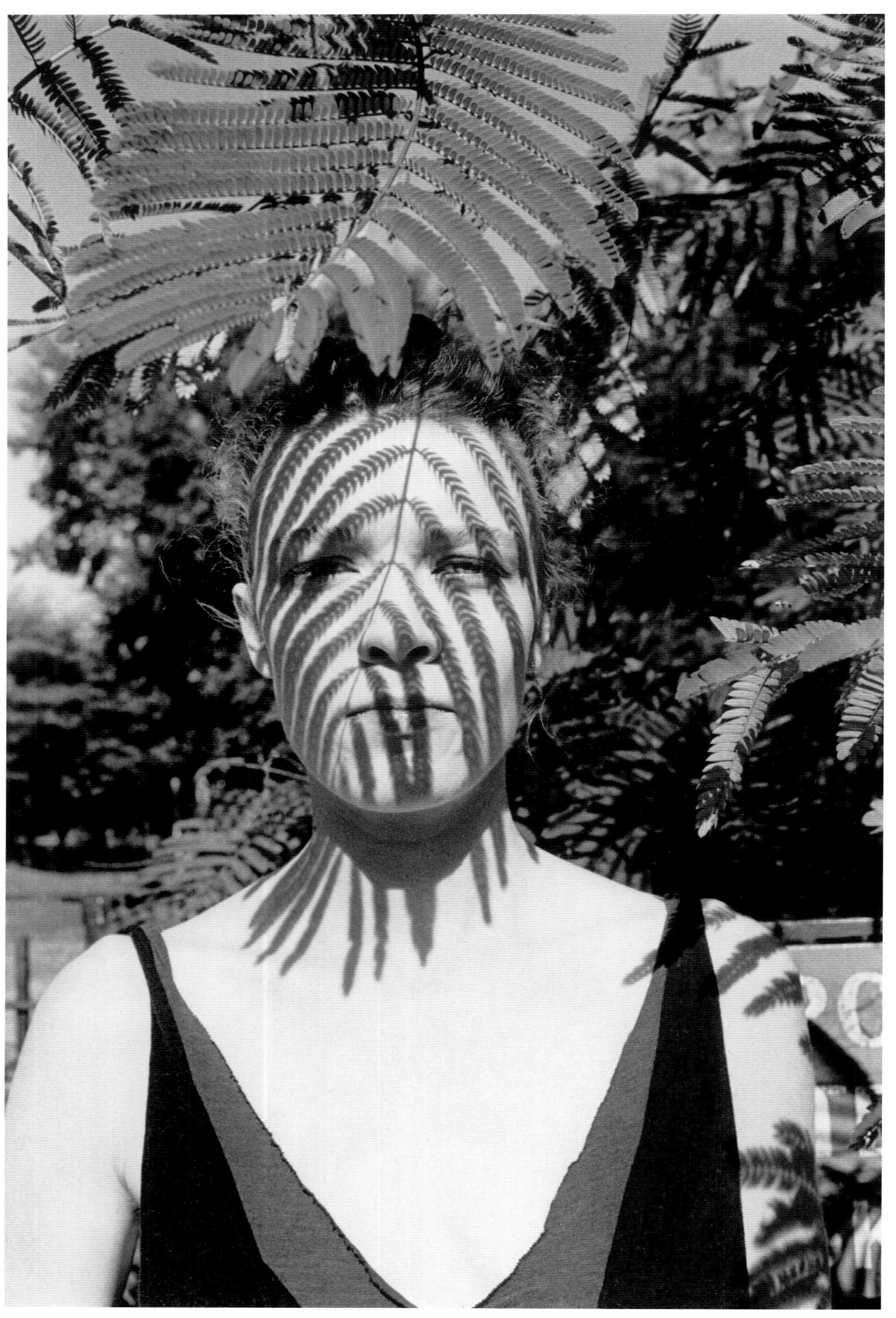

Woman under a Leaf,
Tompkins Square Park
New York, 1983

Elvira Madigan Dress
New York, 1974

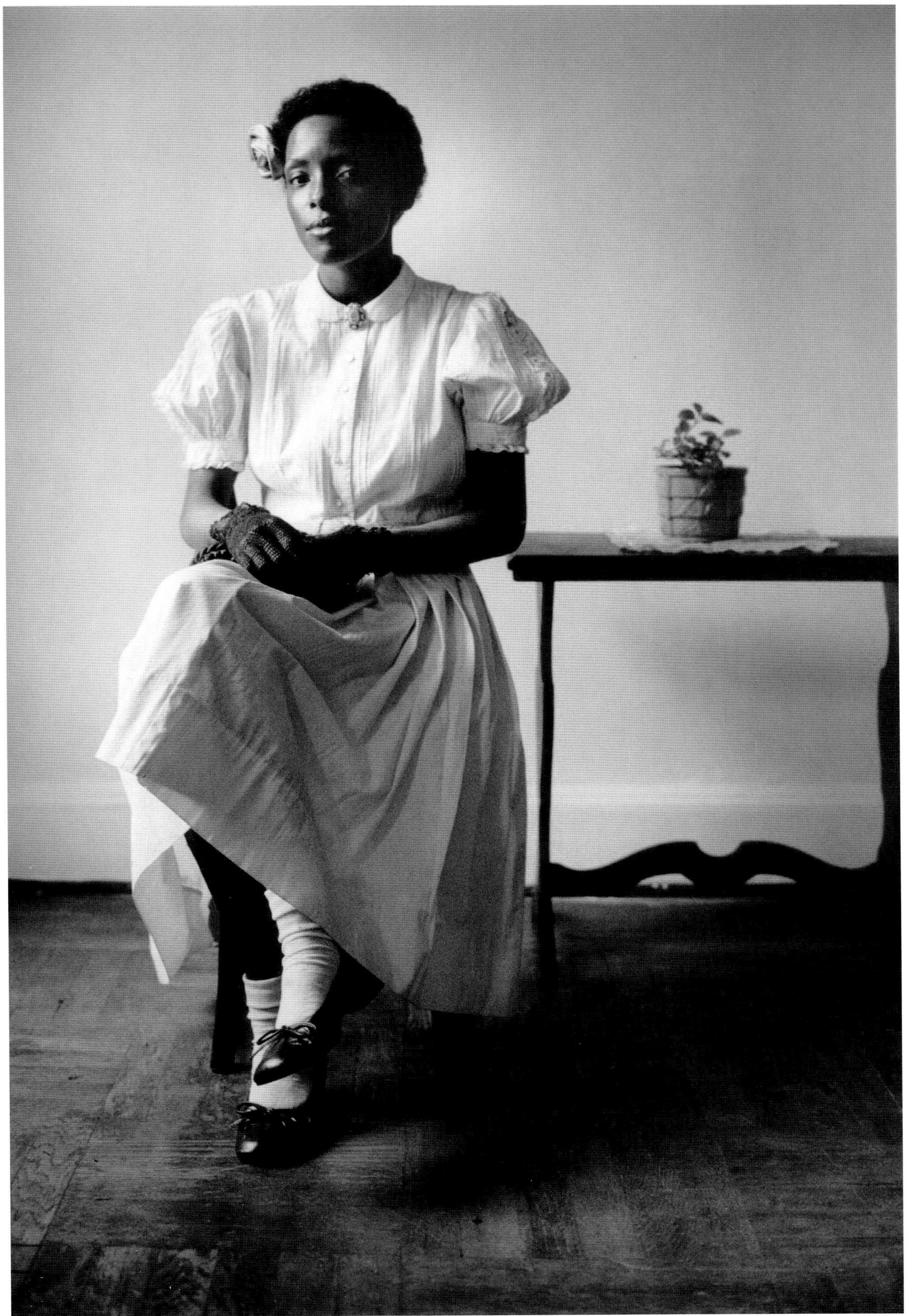

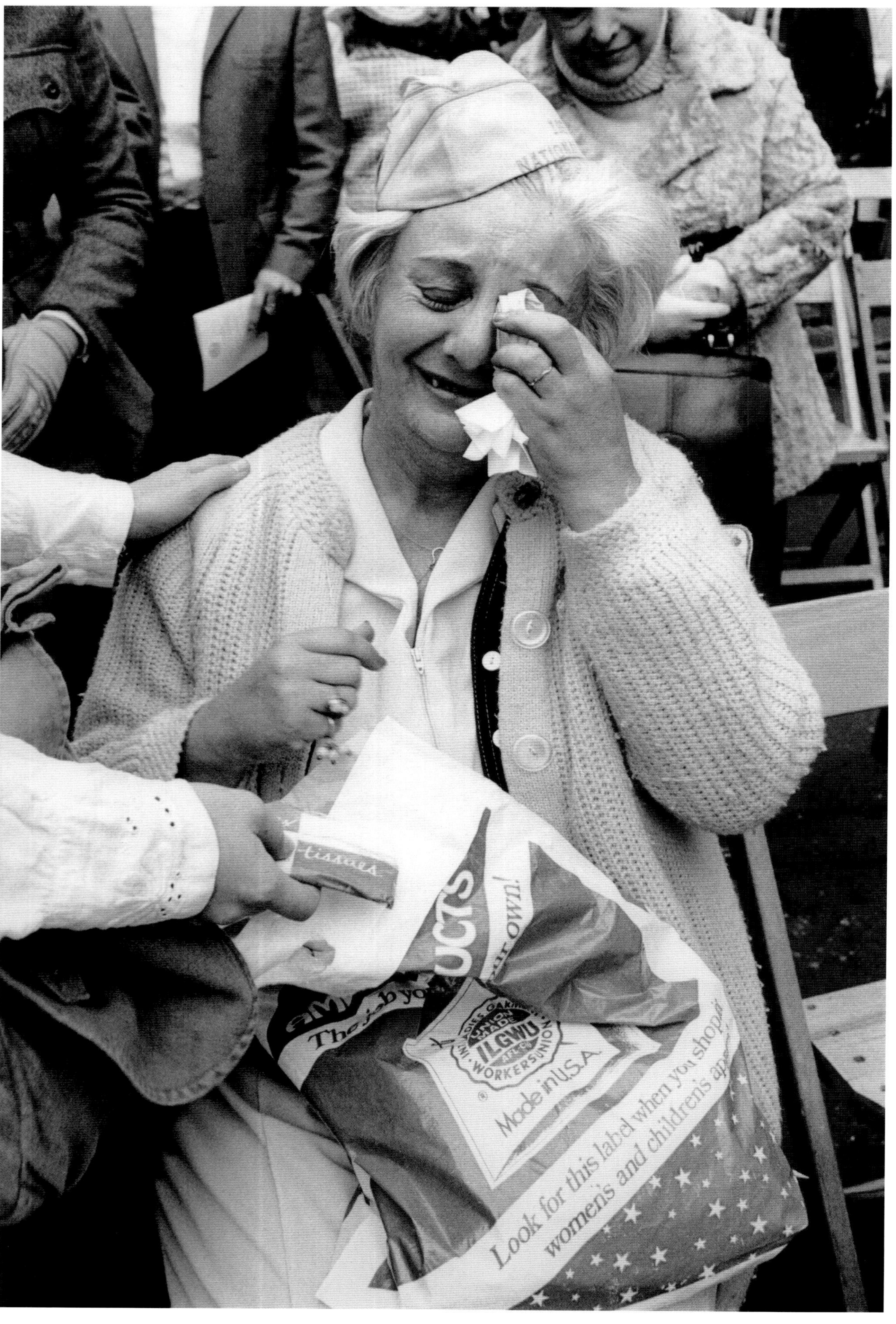

Woman Crying,
Veterans Day Parade
New York, 1983

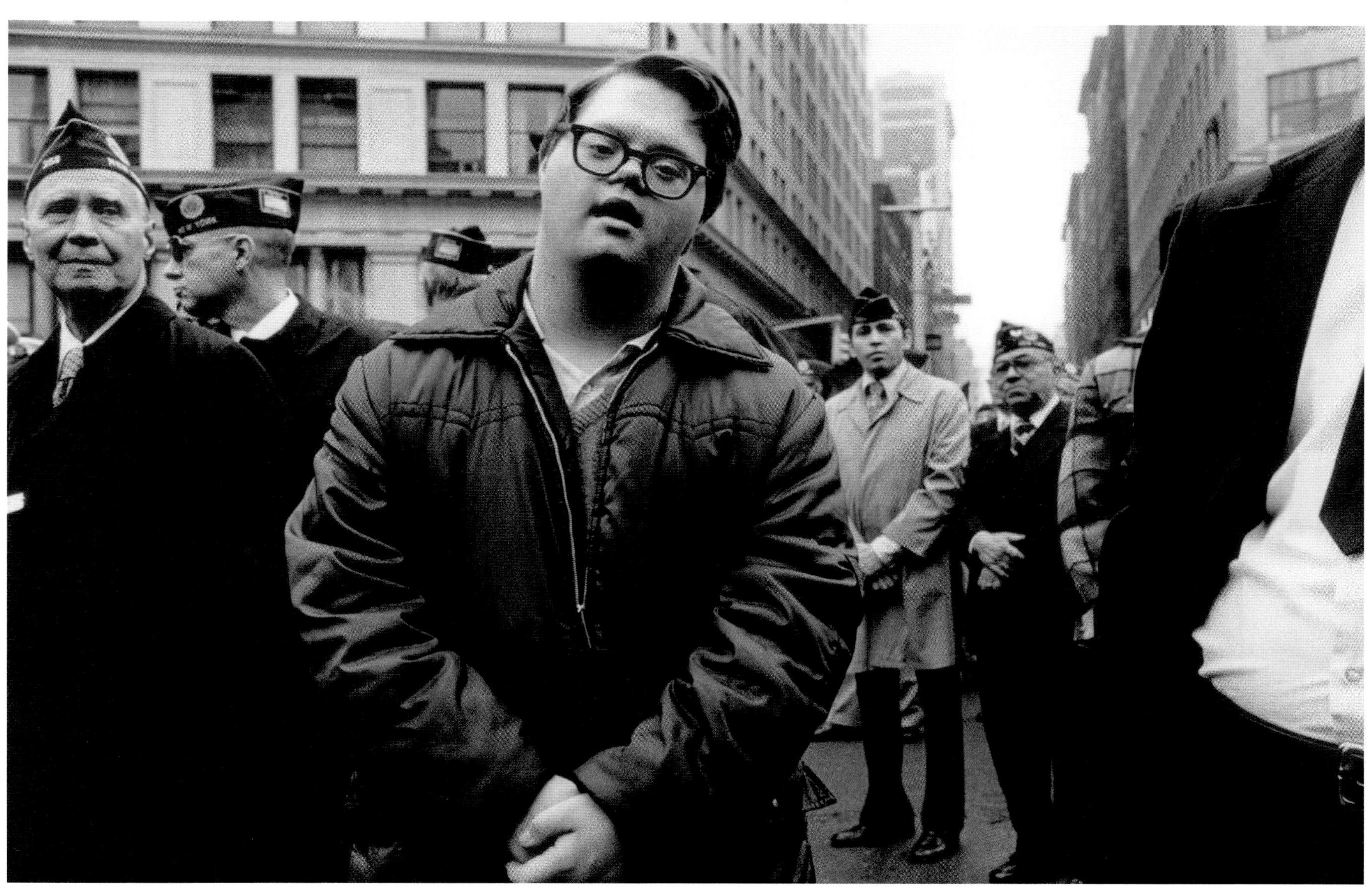

Young Man,
Veterans Day Parade
New York, 1979

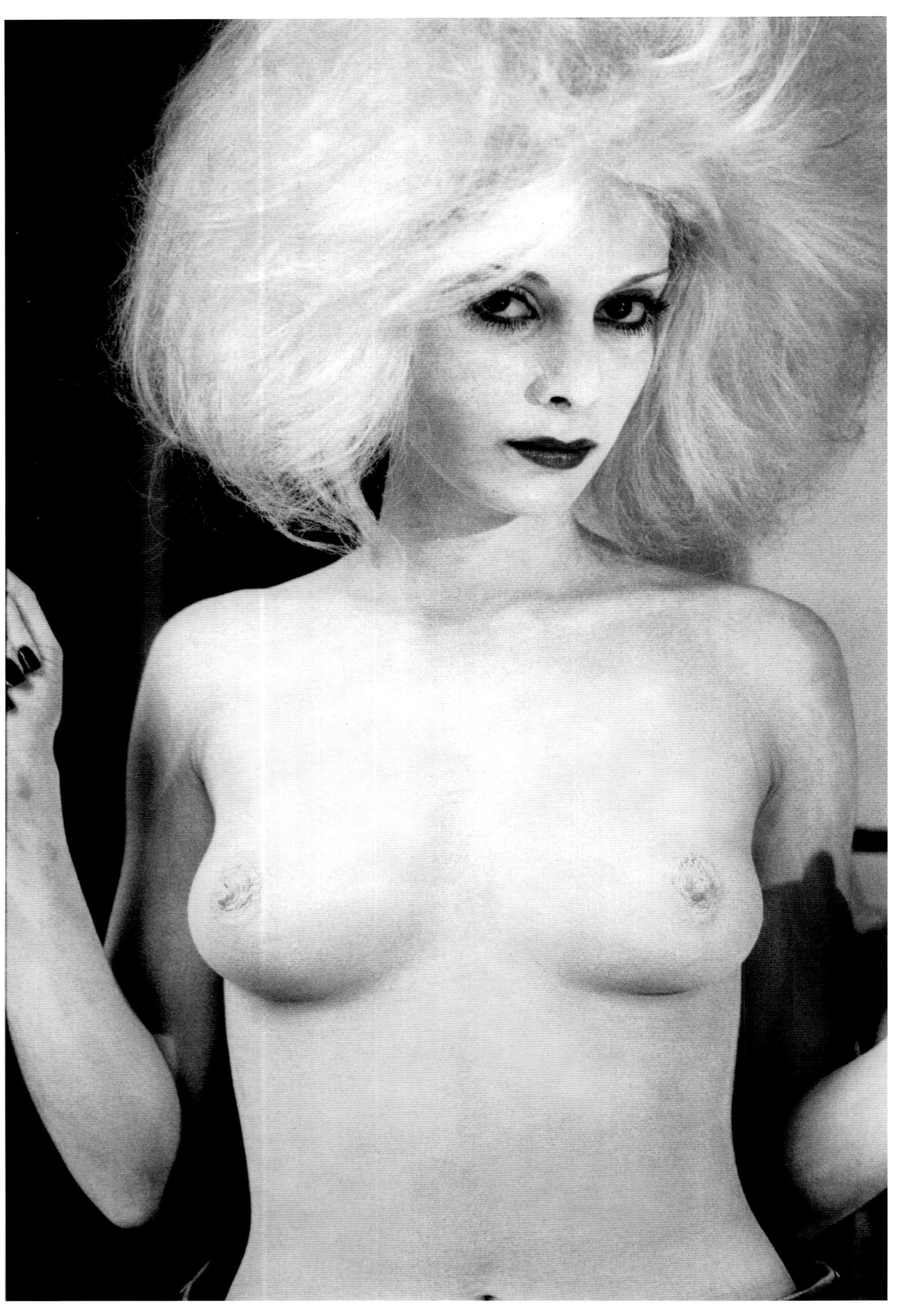

**Kish Manasse's
Photography Studio,
Fifth Avenue
New York, 1972**

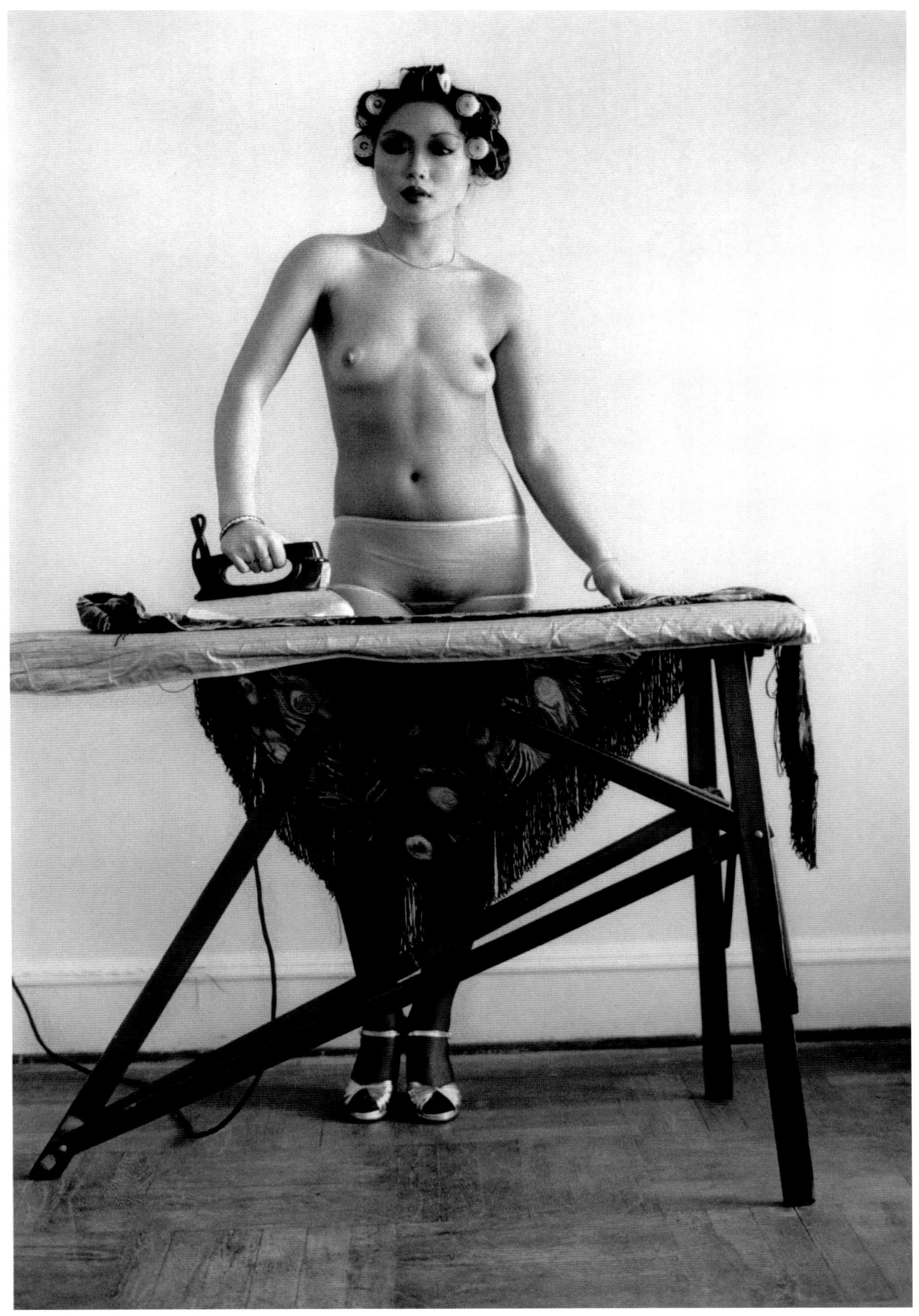

Eddie Sun's Friend Ironing
New York, 1972

Michael Spano in His Darkroom
New York, 1984

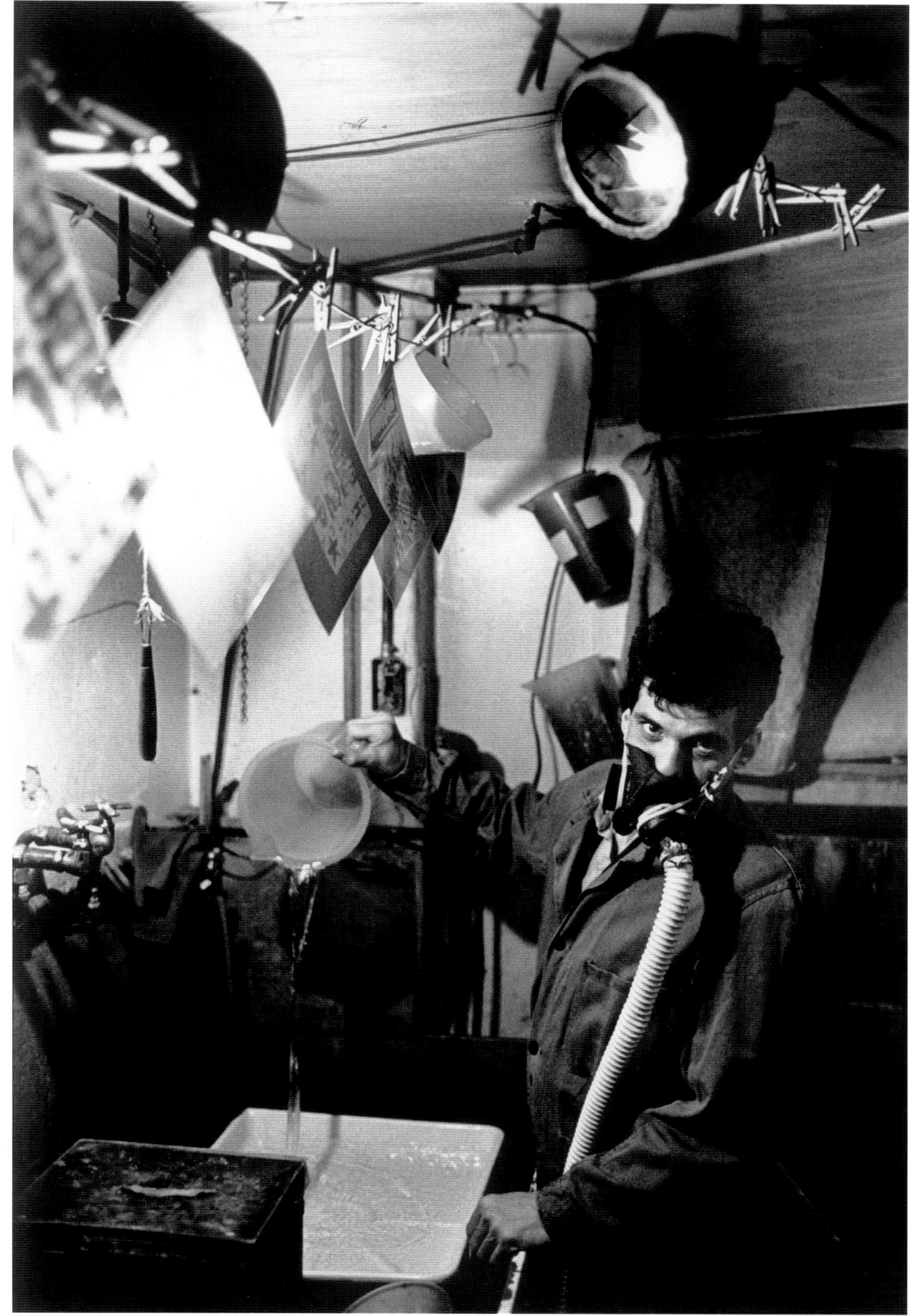

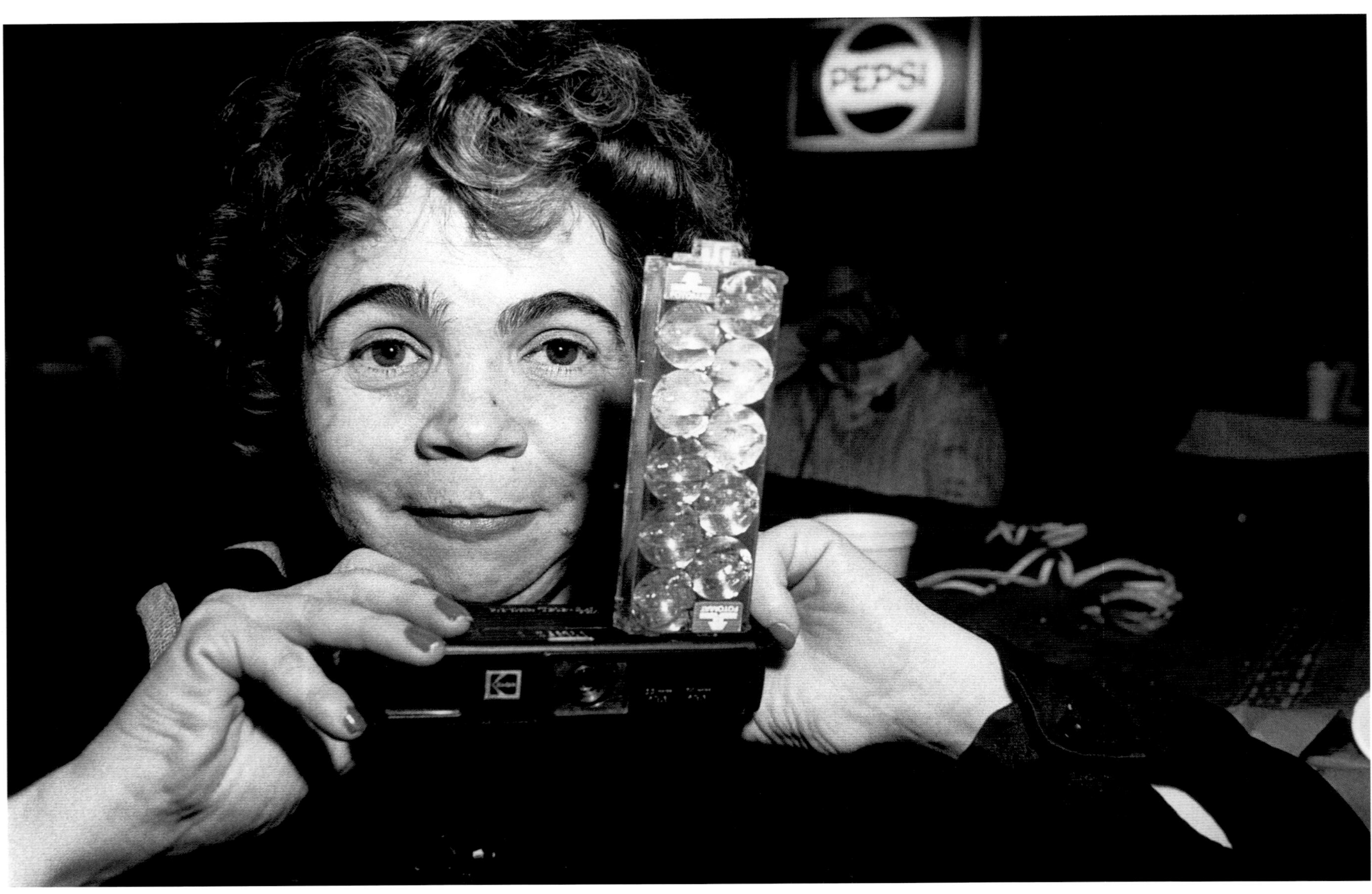
PEPSI

Instamatic Camera
New York, 1983

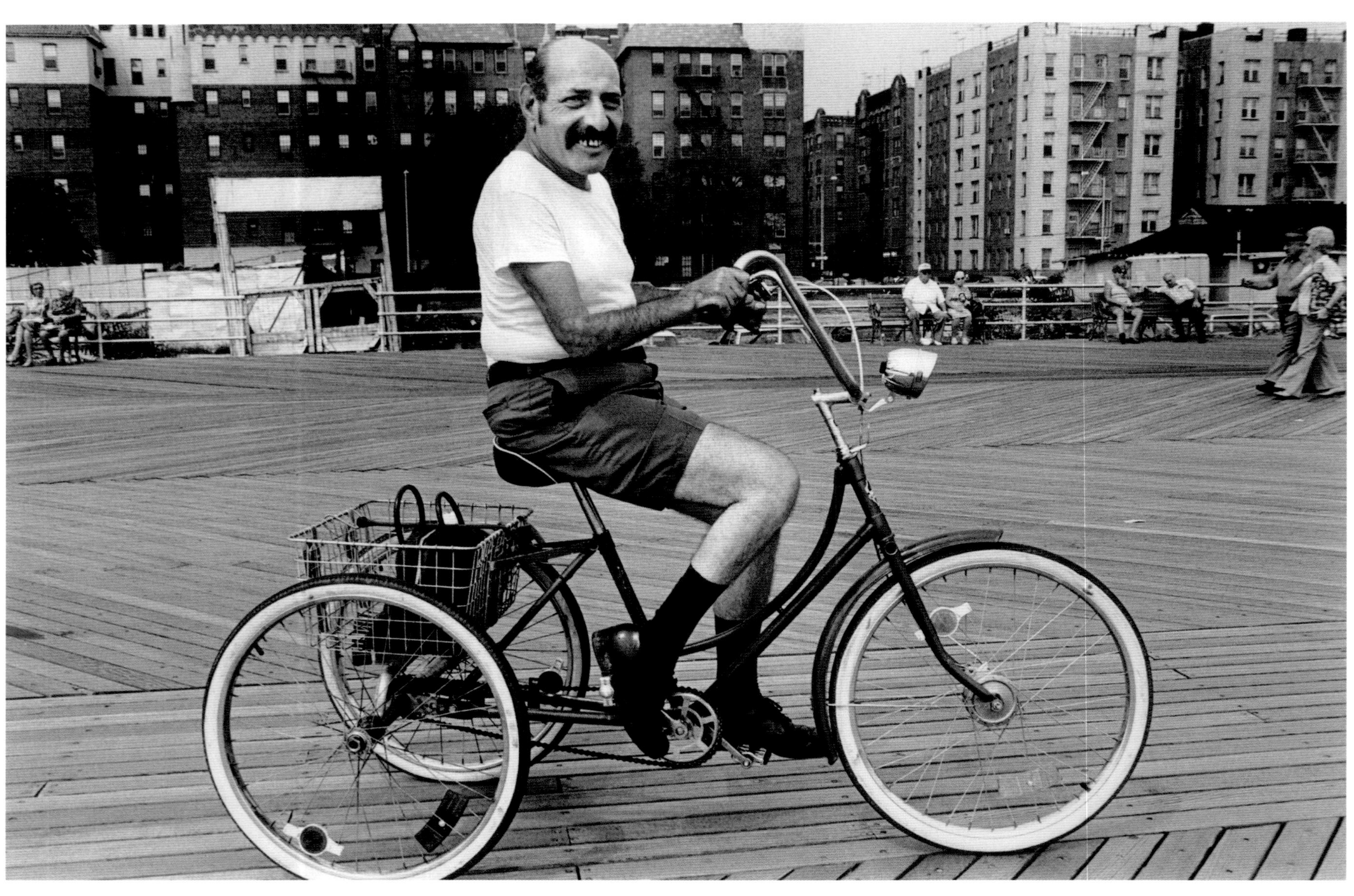

Tricycle on the Boardwalk,
Brighton Beach
New York, 1976

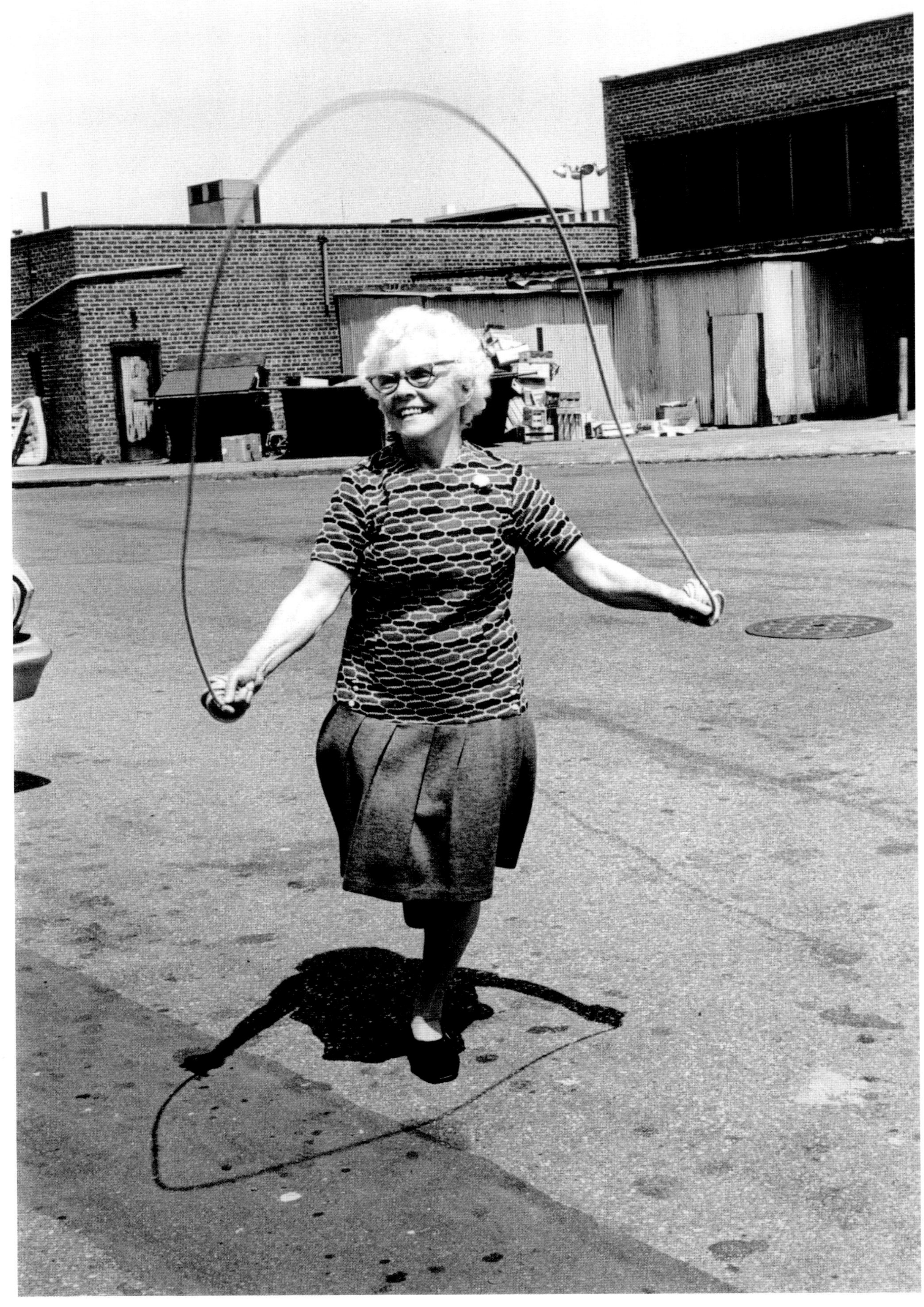

Isabel Croft Jumping Rope,
Brooklyn
New York, 1972

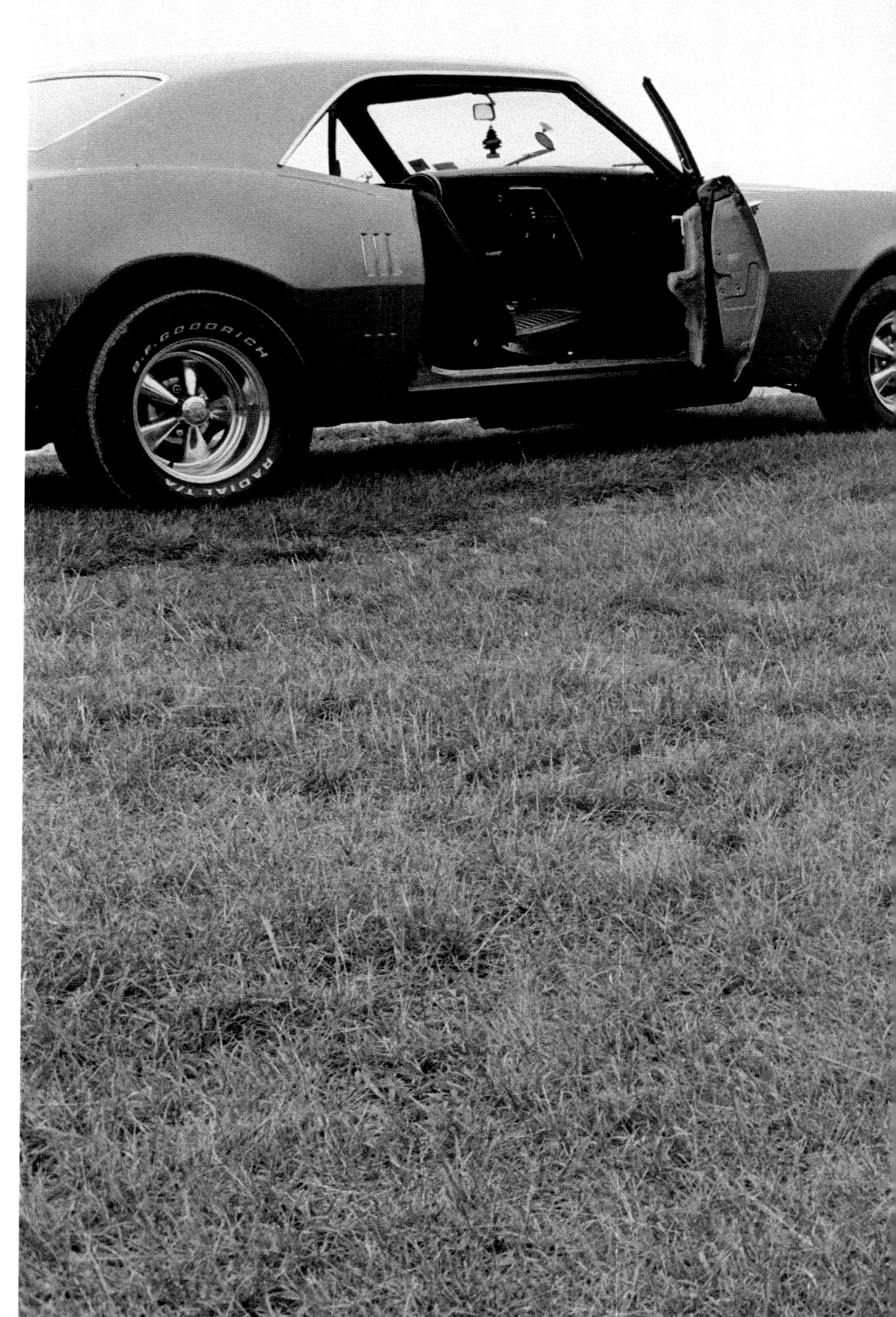

Kissing on the Highway, Queens
New York, 1980

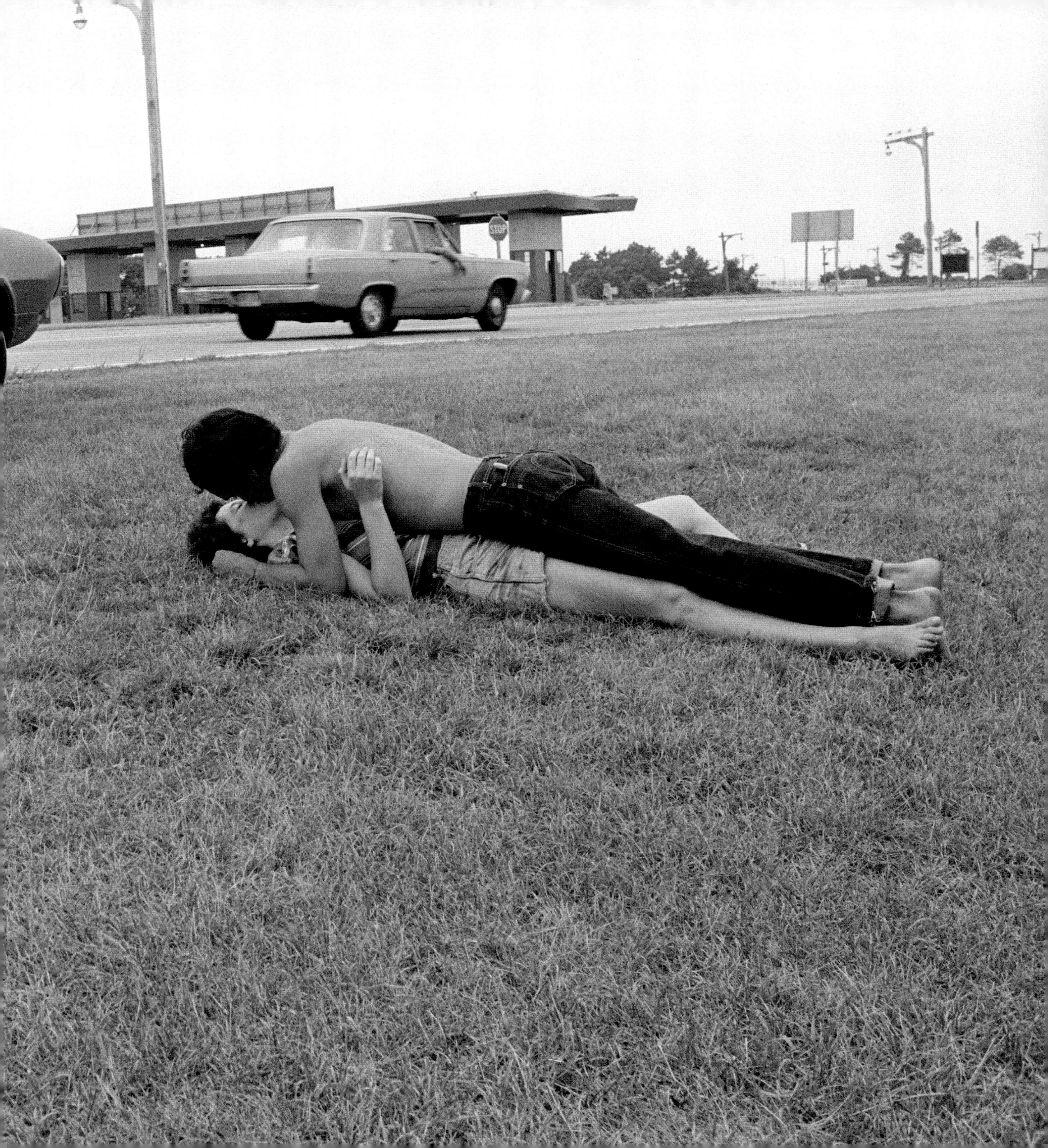
STOP

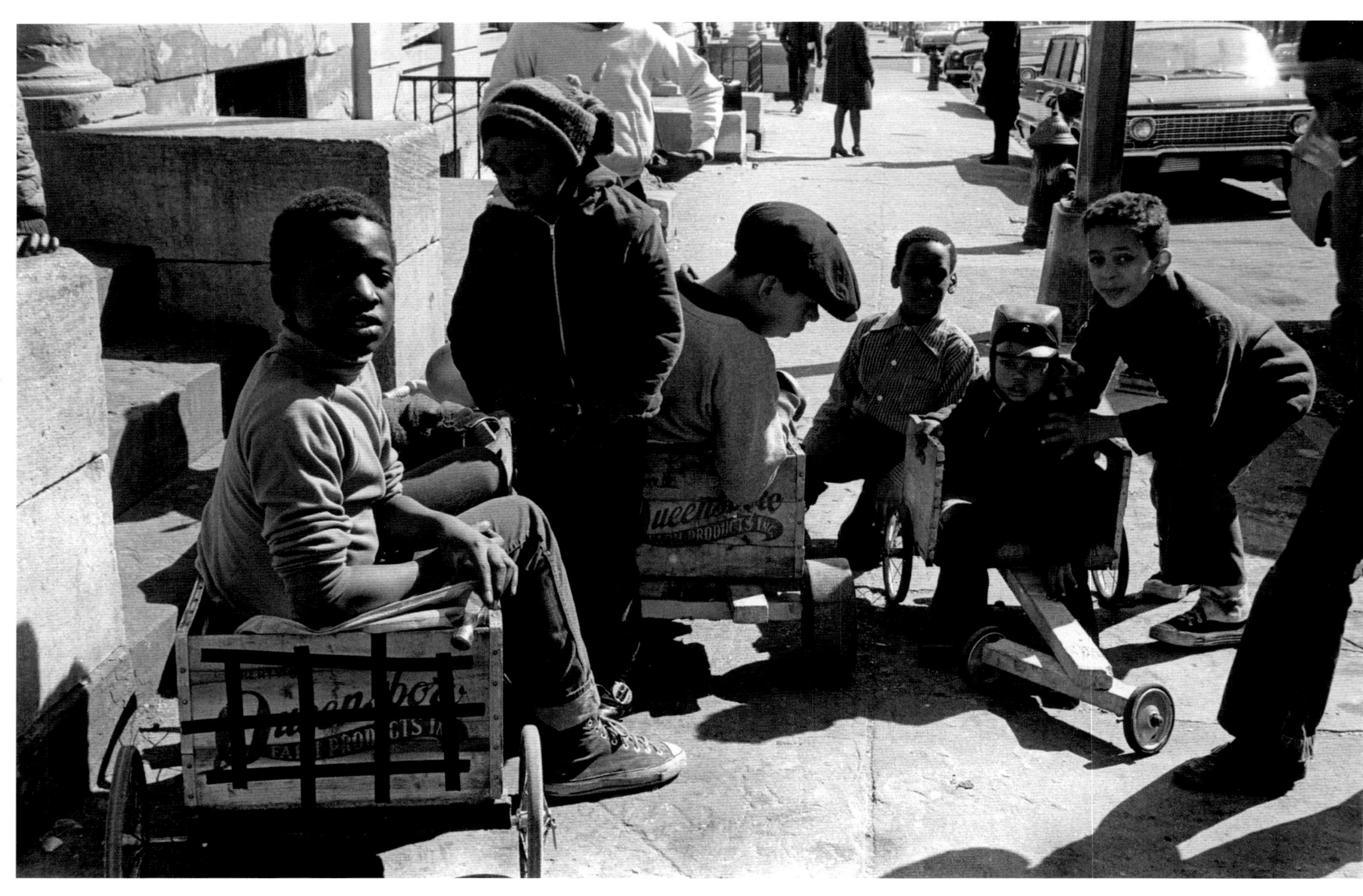

Scooters, Bedford-Stuyvesant
New York, 1970

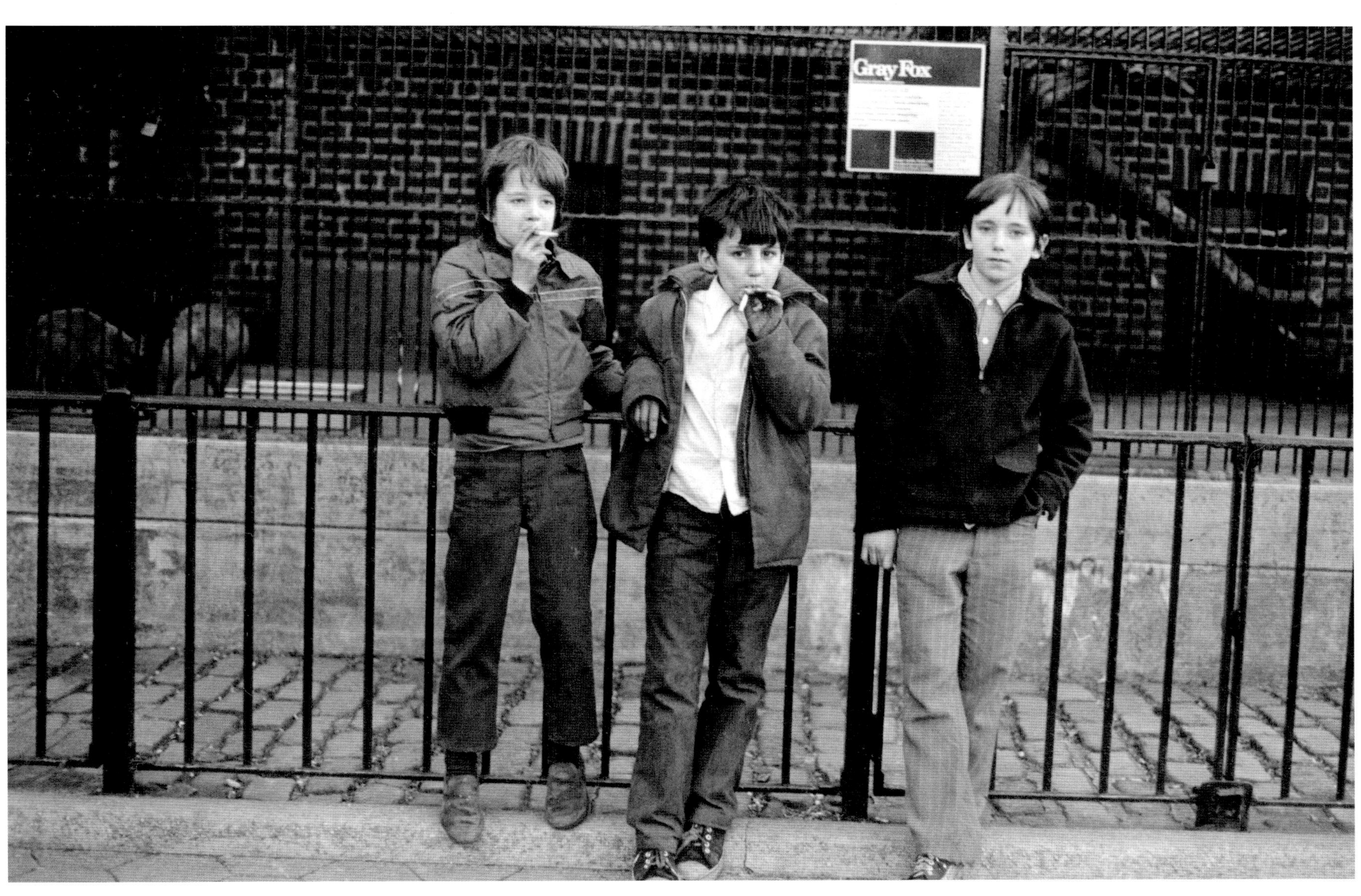

Central Park Zoo
New York, 1977

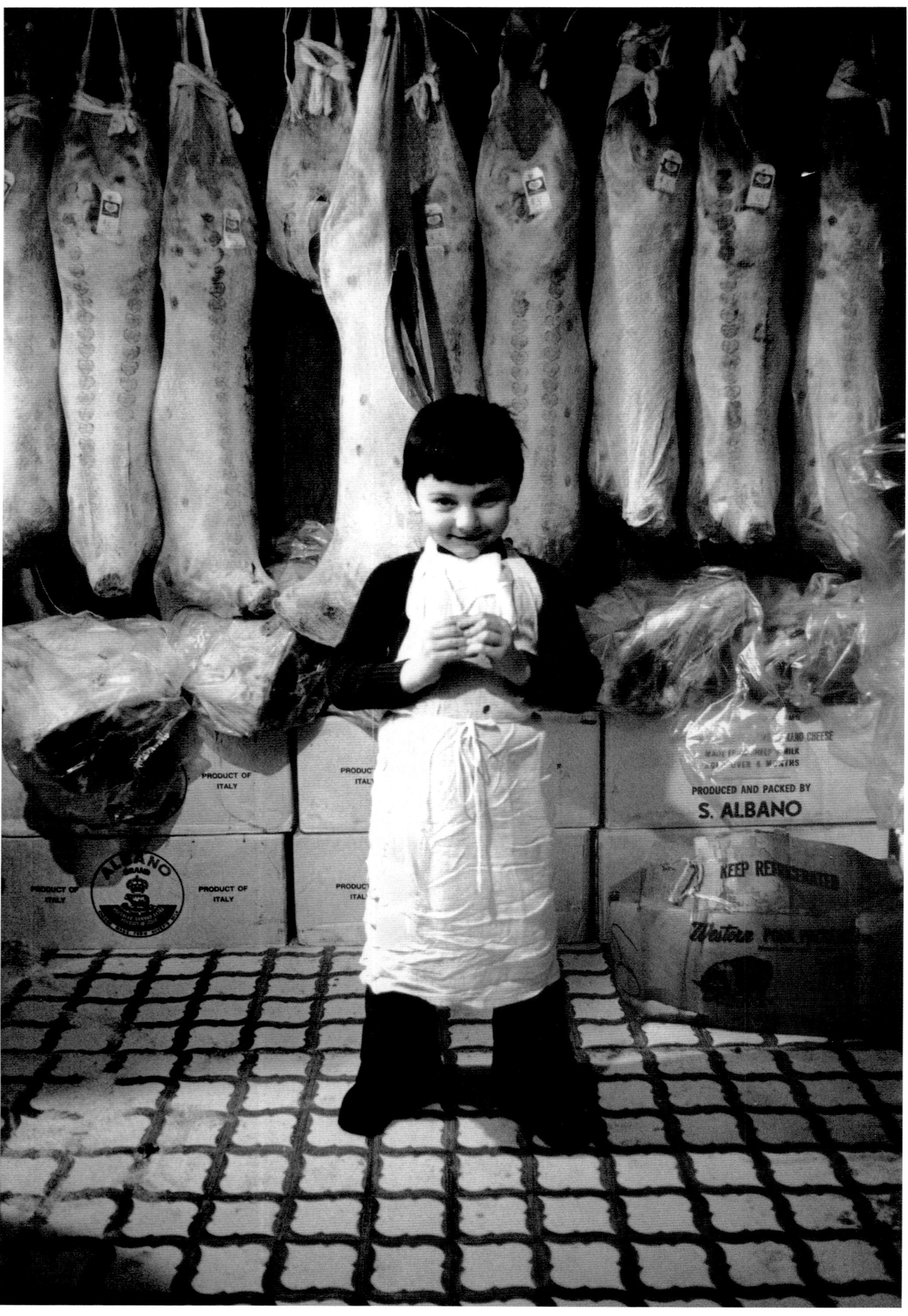

Butcher's Boy
Boston, 1975

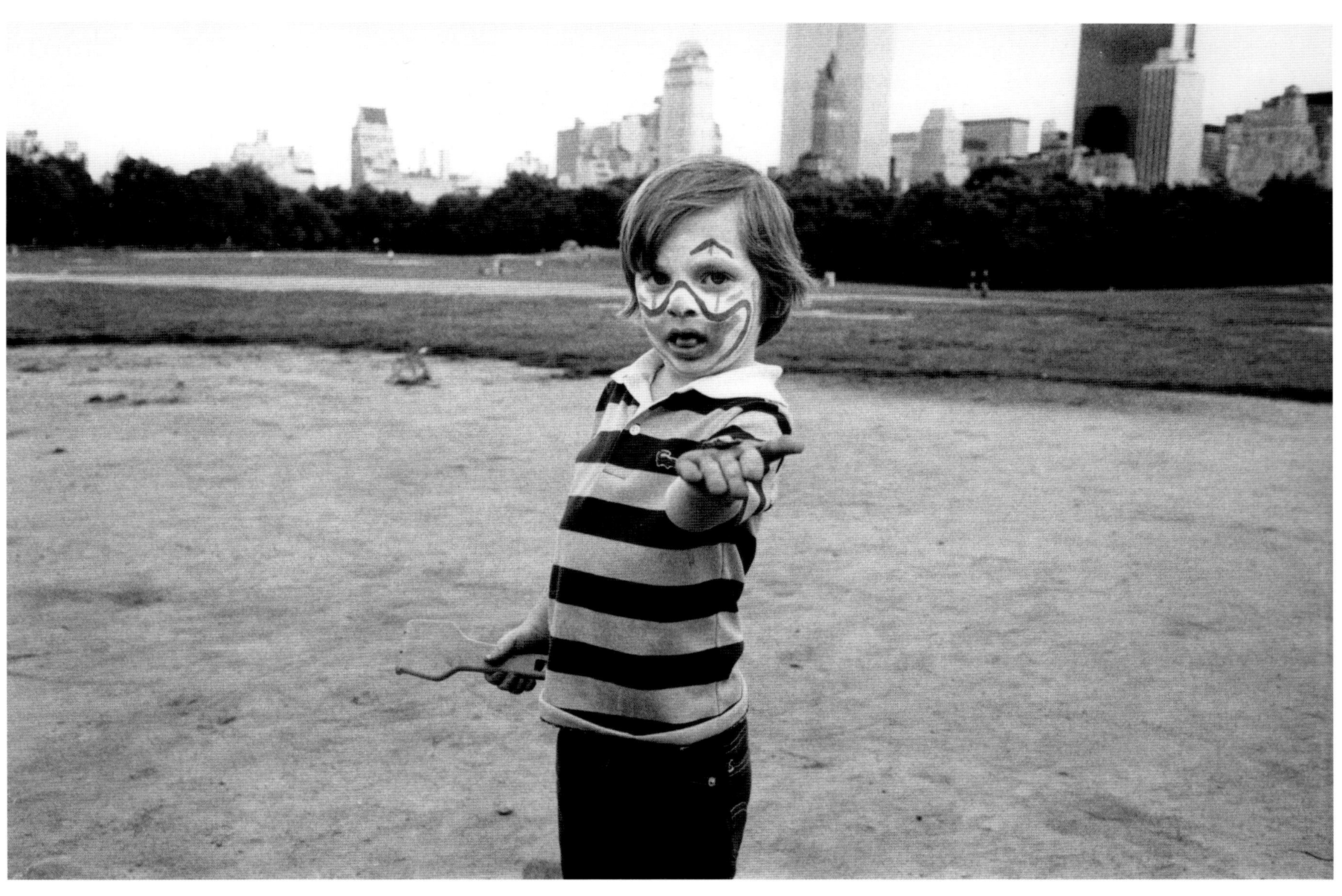

Central Park, Sheep's Meadow
New York, 1979

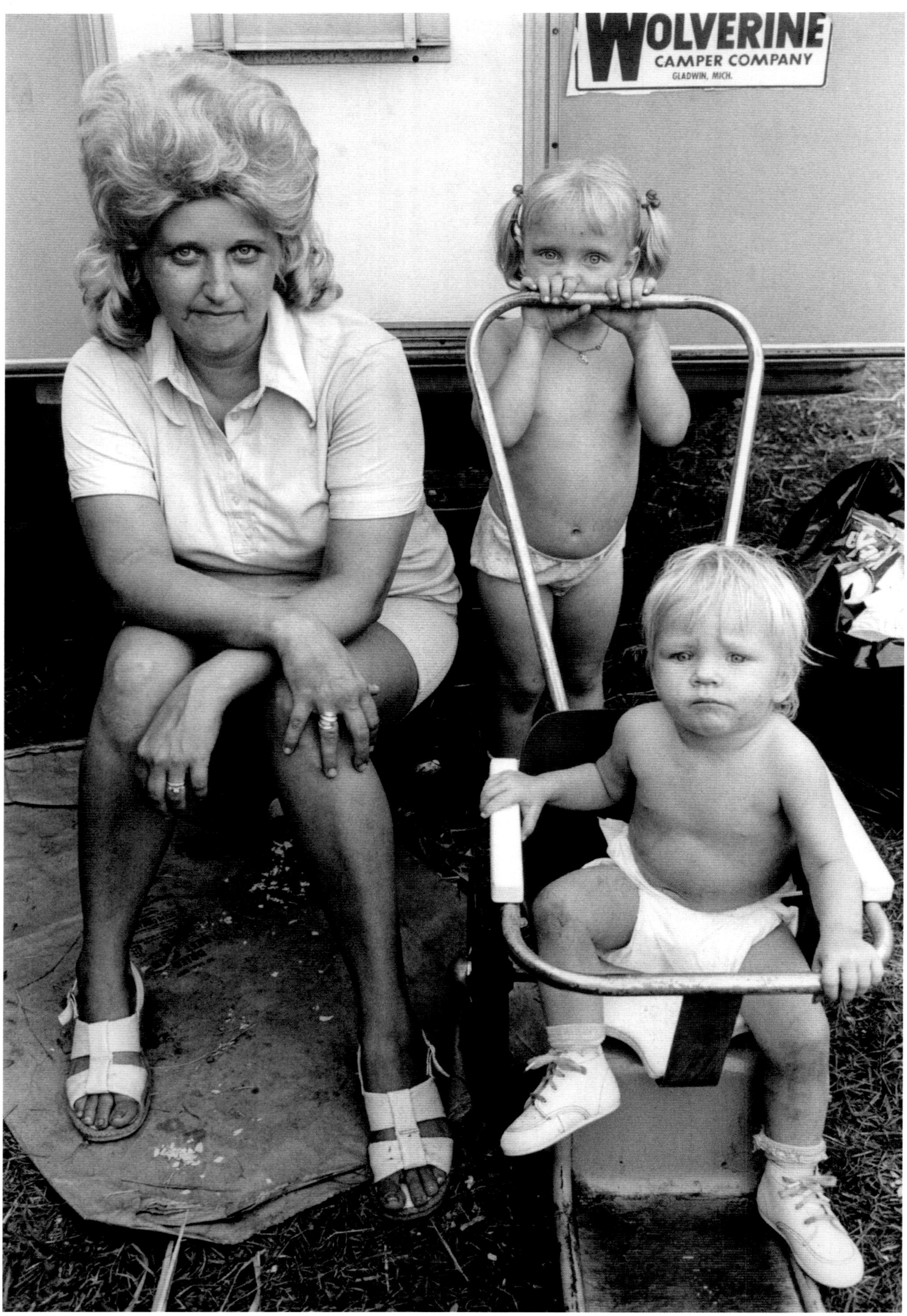
WOLVERINE
CAMPER COMPANY
GLADWIN, MICH.

Wolverine Camper, 1979

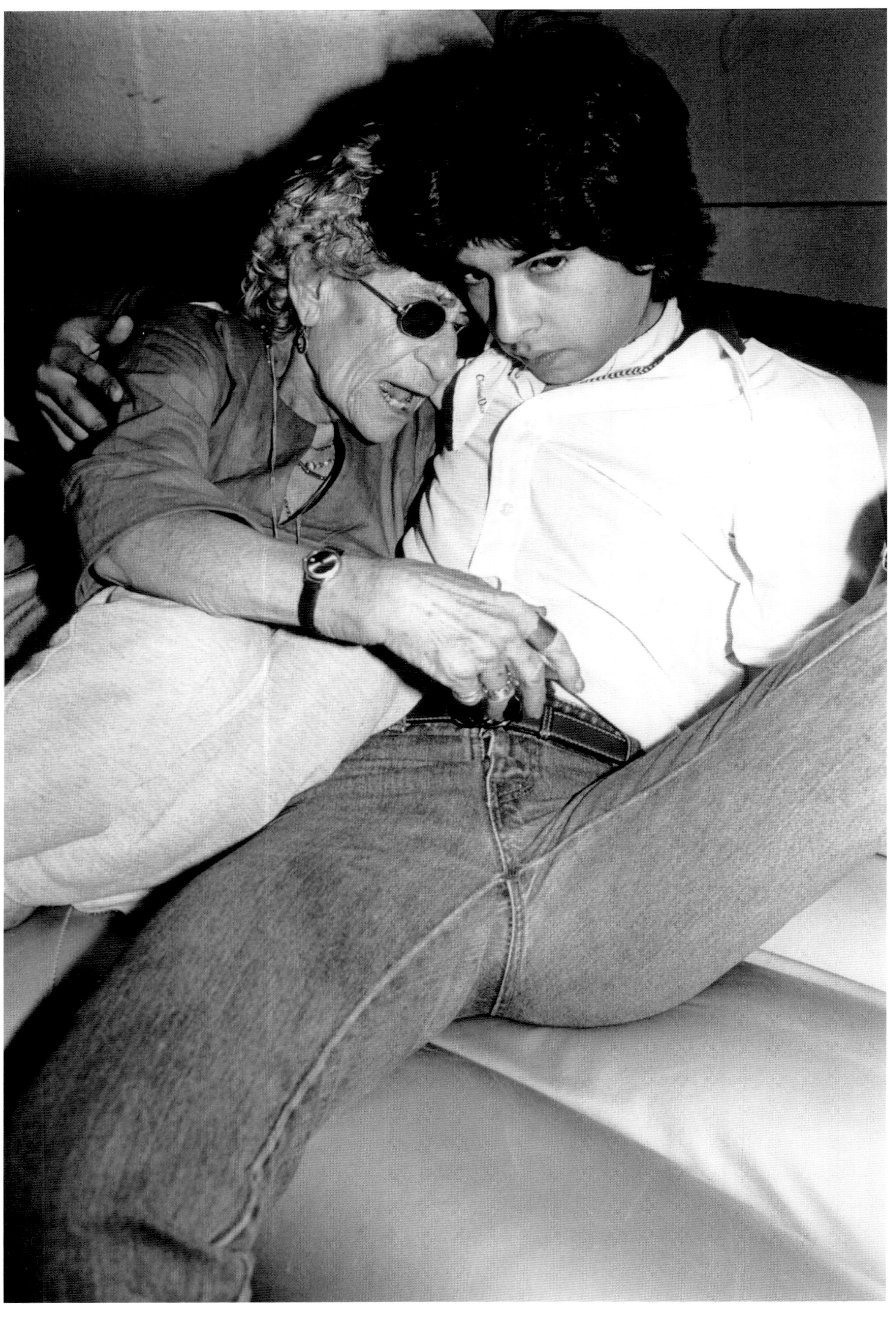

Disco Grannie at Studio 54
New York, 1979

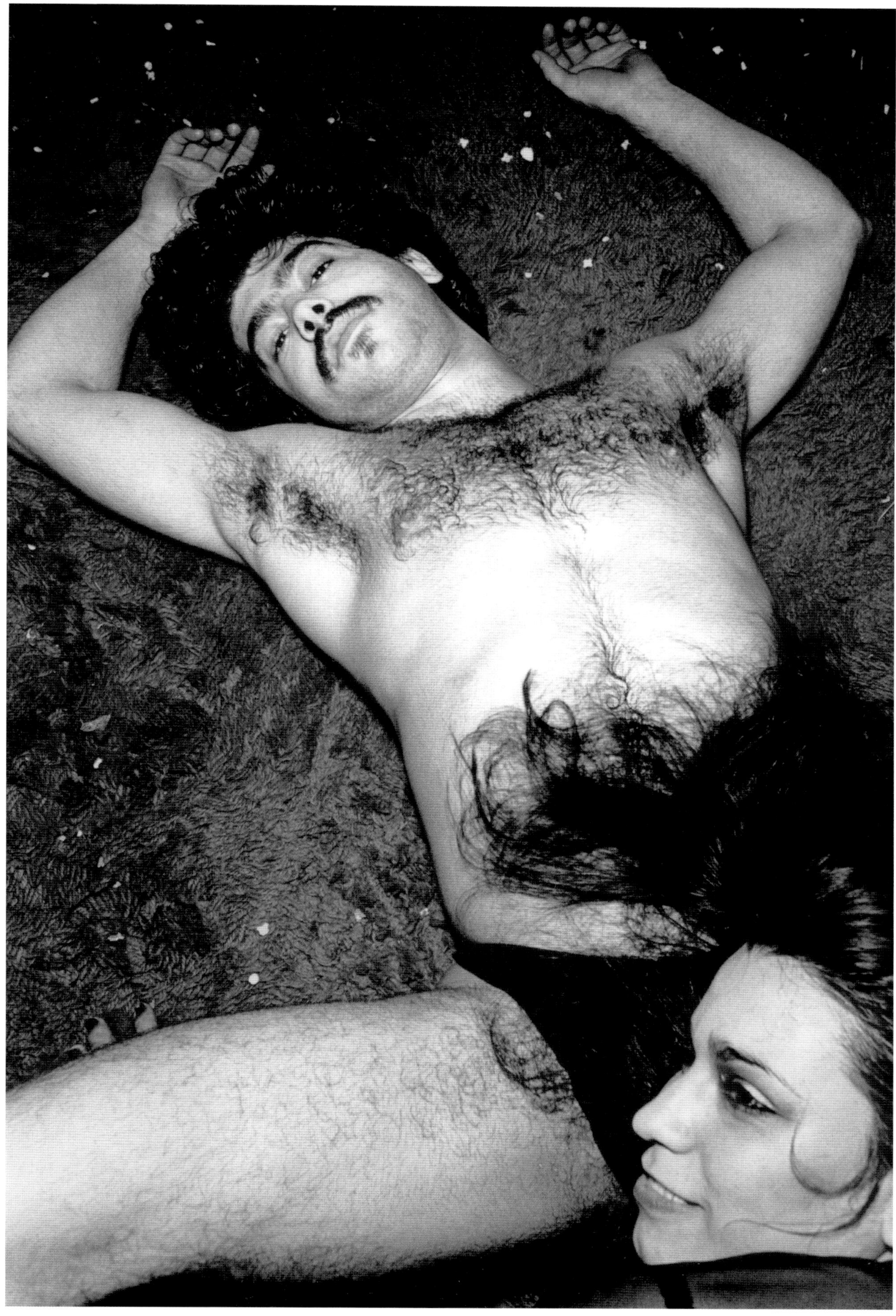

Trapeze Artists,
GG's Barnum Room,
Times Square
New York, 1979

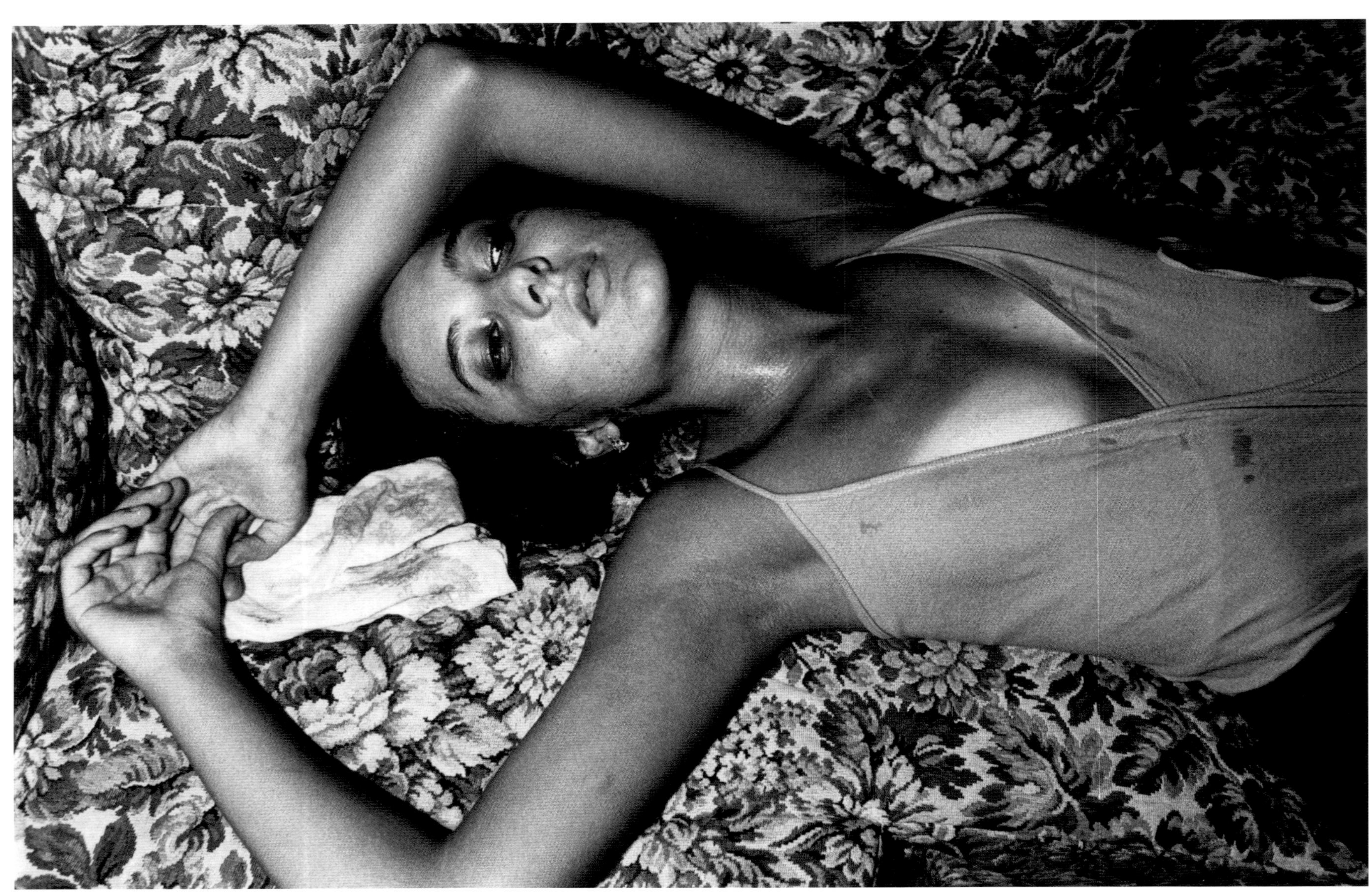

Pete's Sister-in-Law, 1981

Baby Paper Bag Hat,
Staten Island
New York, 1974

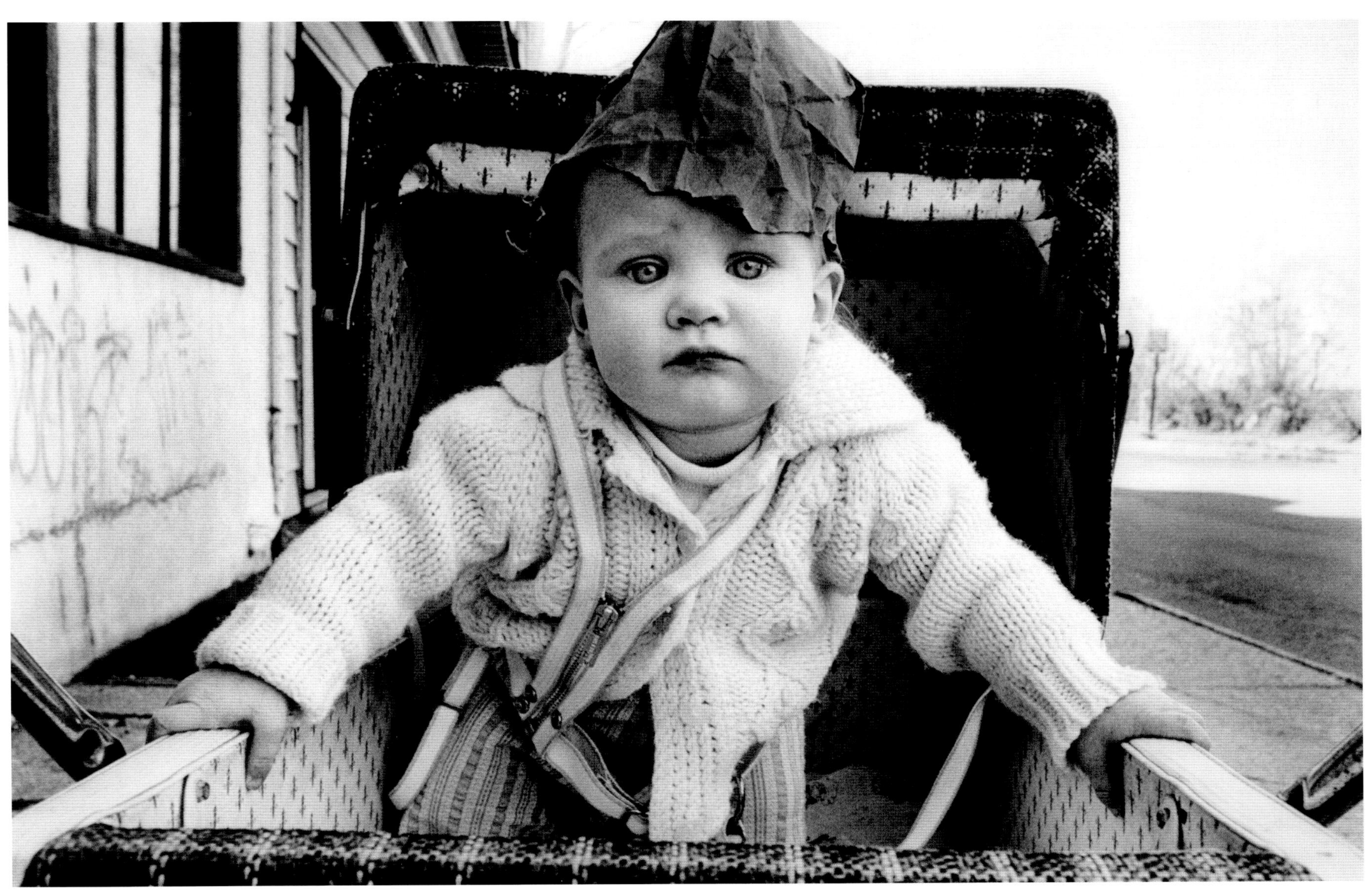

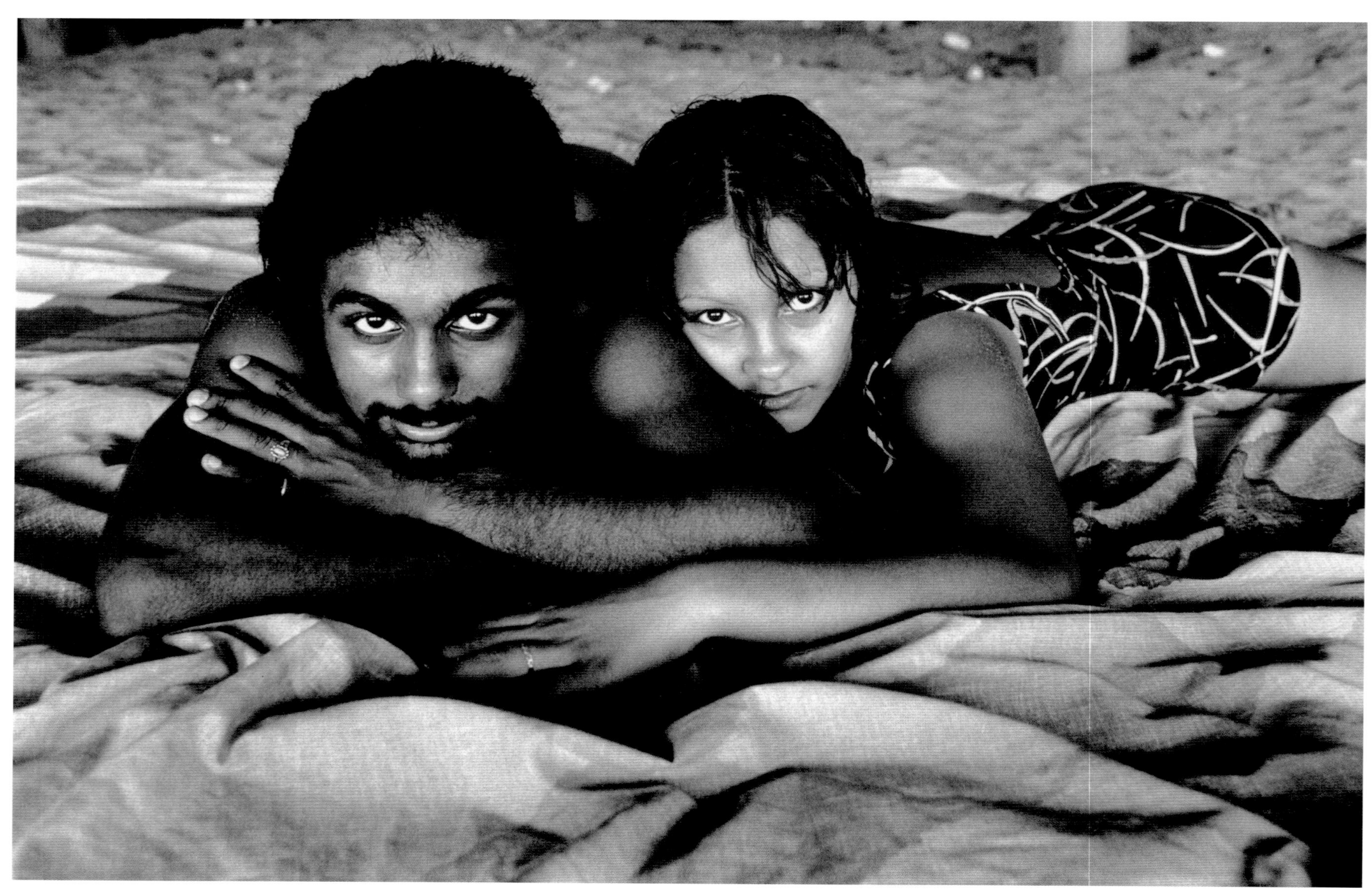

Under the Boardwalk,
Coney Island
New York, 1976

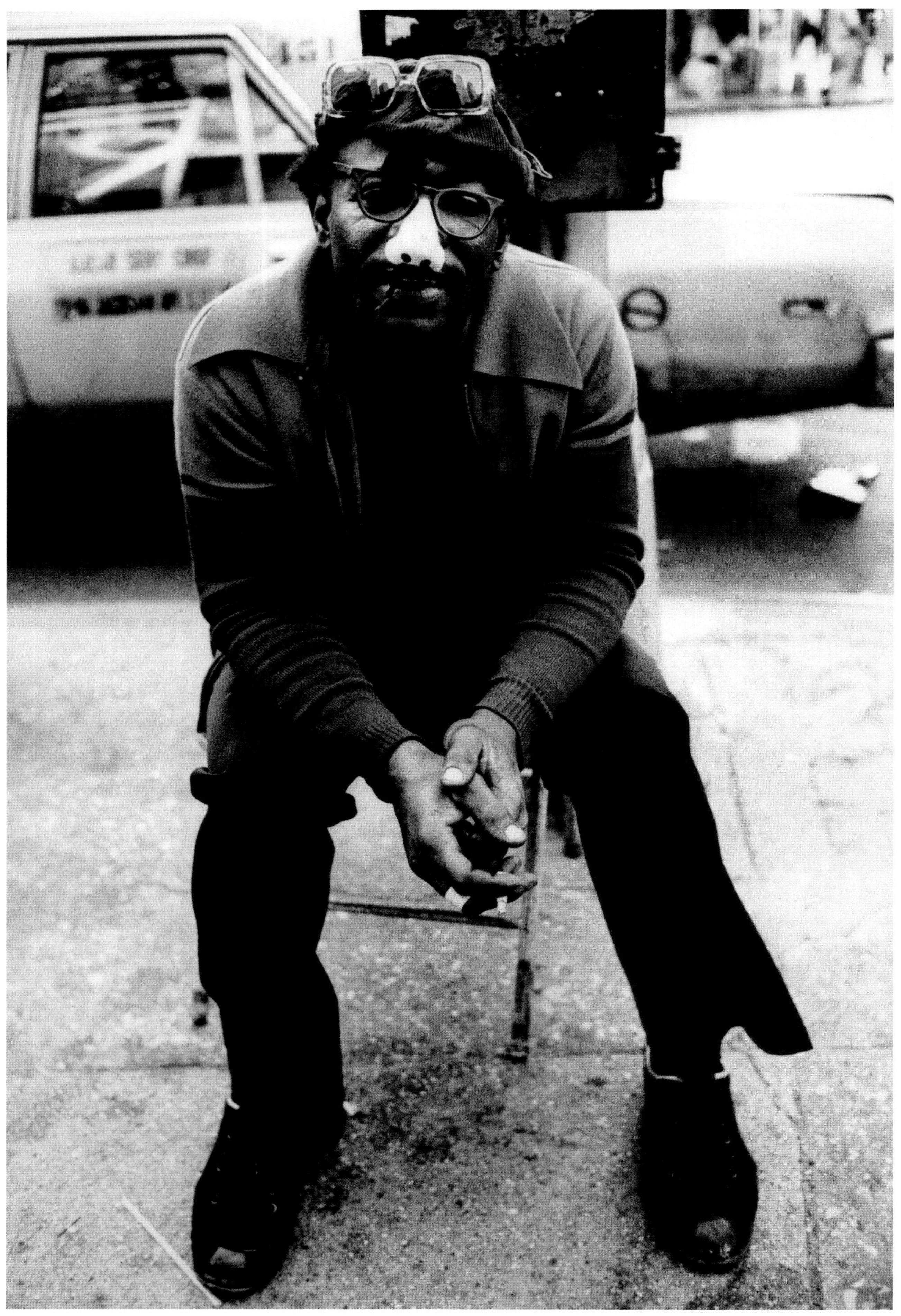

Black Man Wearing White Nose
in Times Square
New York, 1980

Upside Down,
Fire Island
New York, 1980

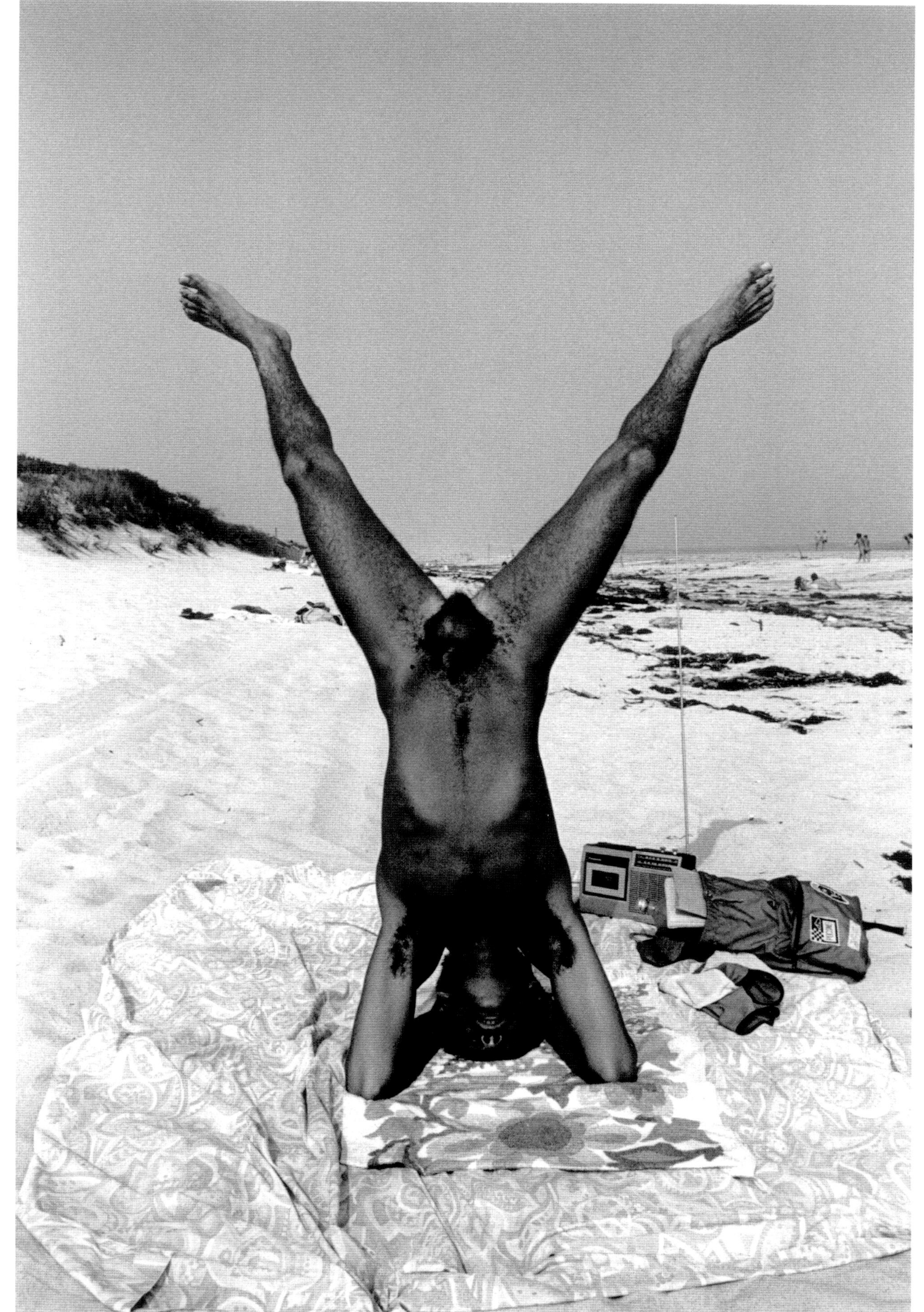

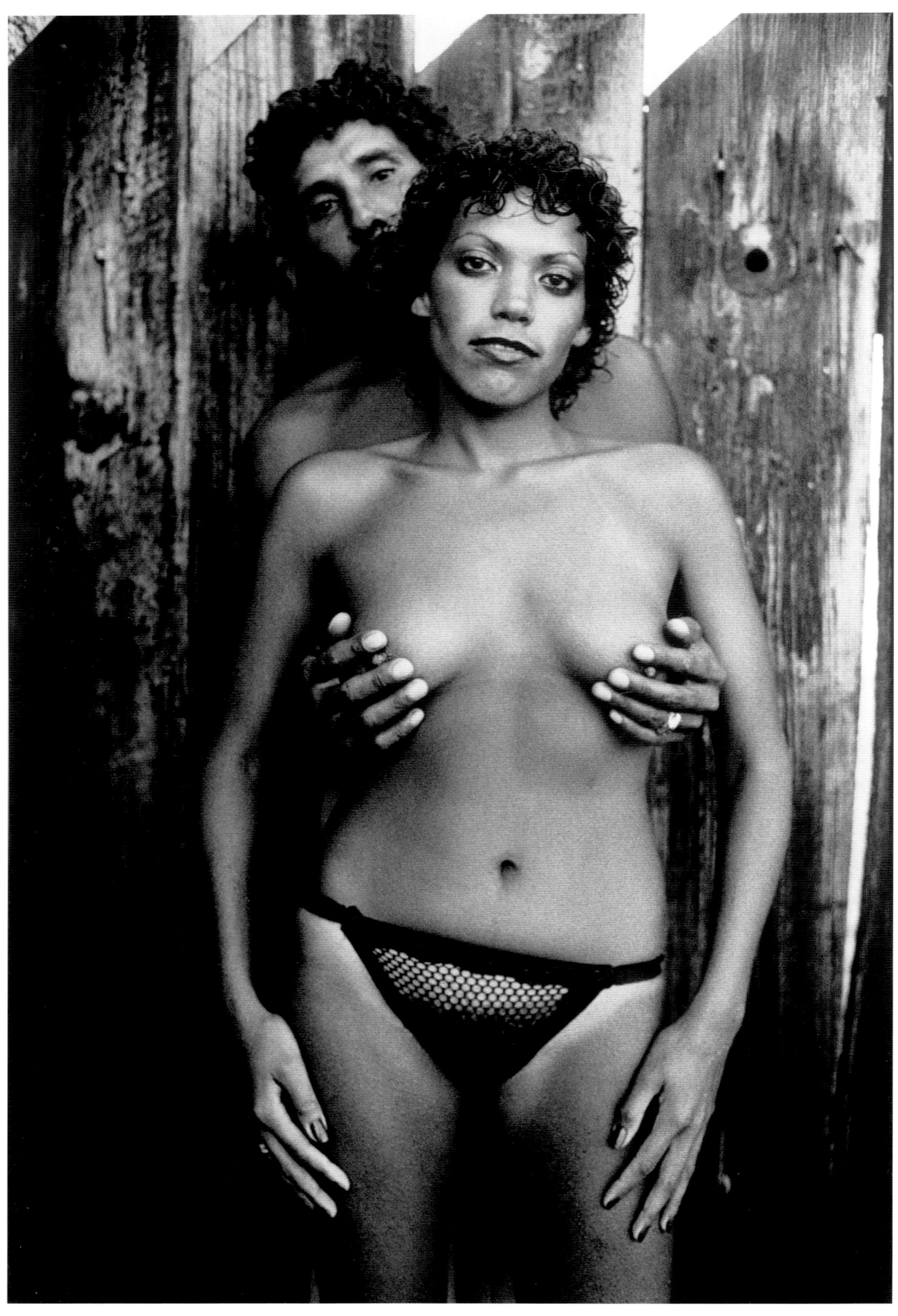

Vivian, Riis Beach
New York, 1980

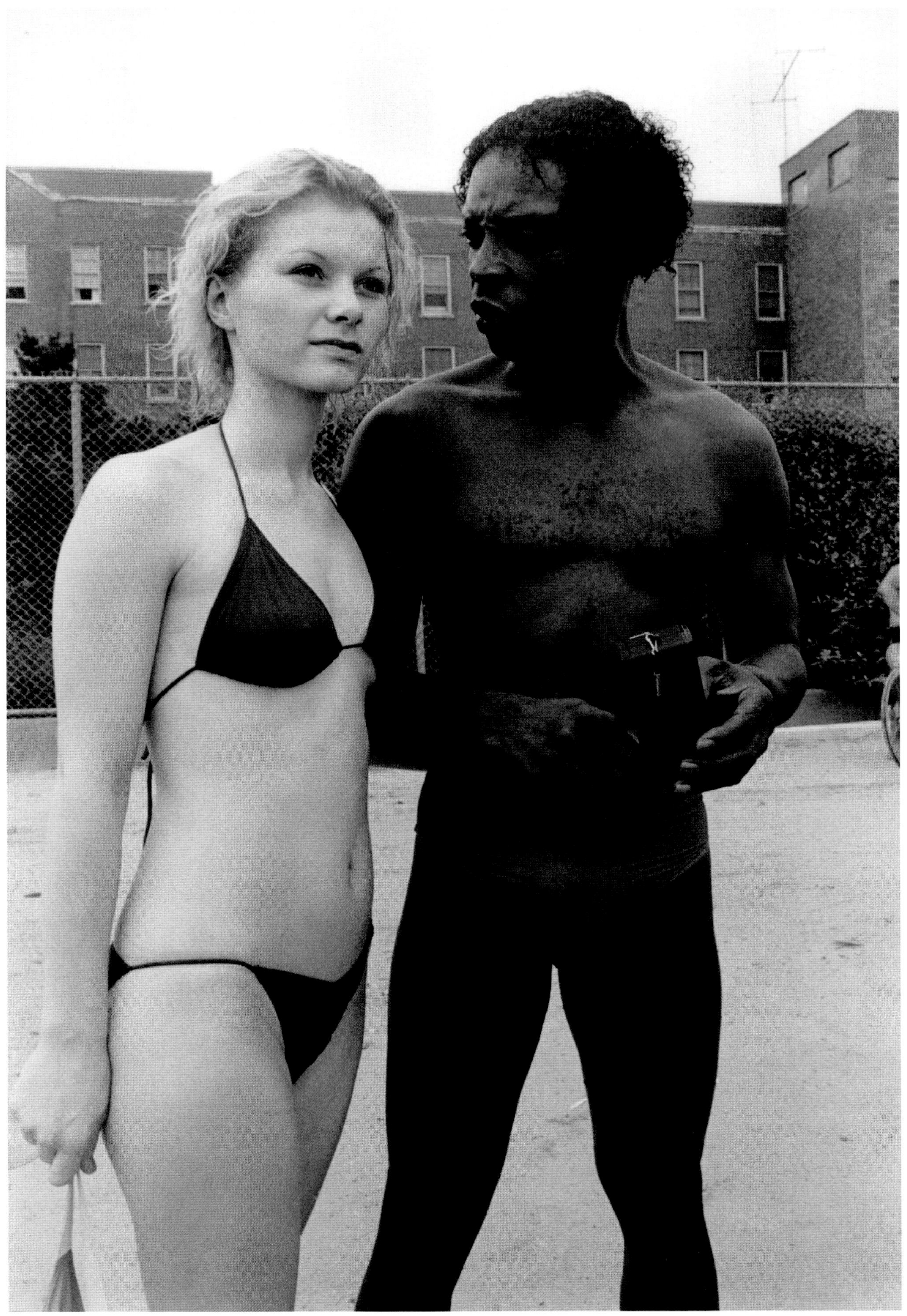

Argument on Riis Beach
New York, 1985

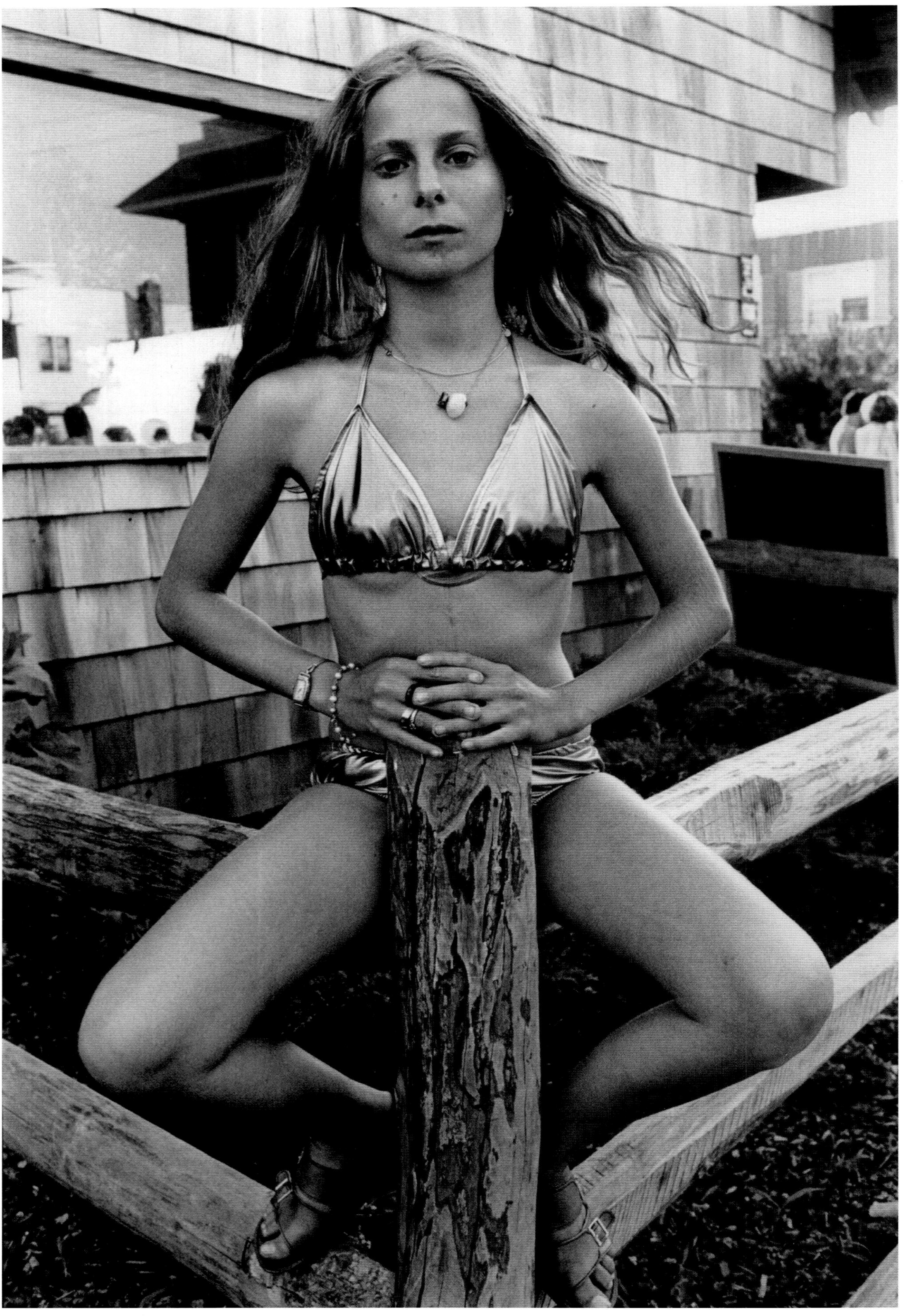

**Botticelli Girl,
Fire Island
New York, 1977**

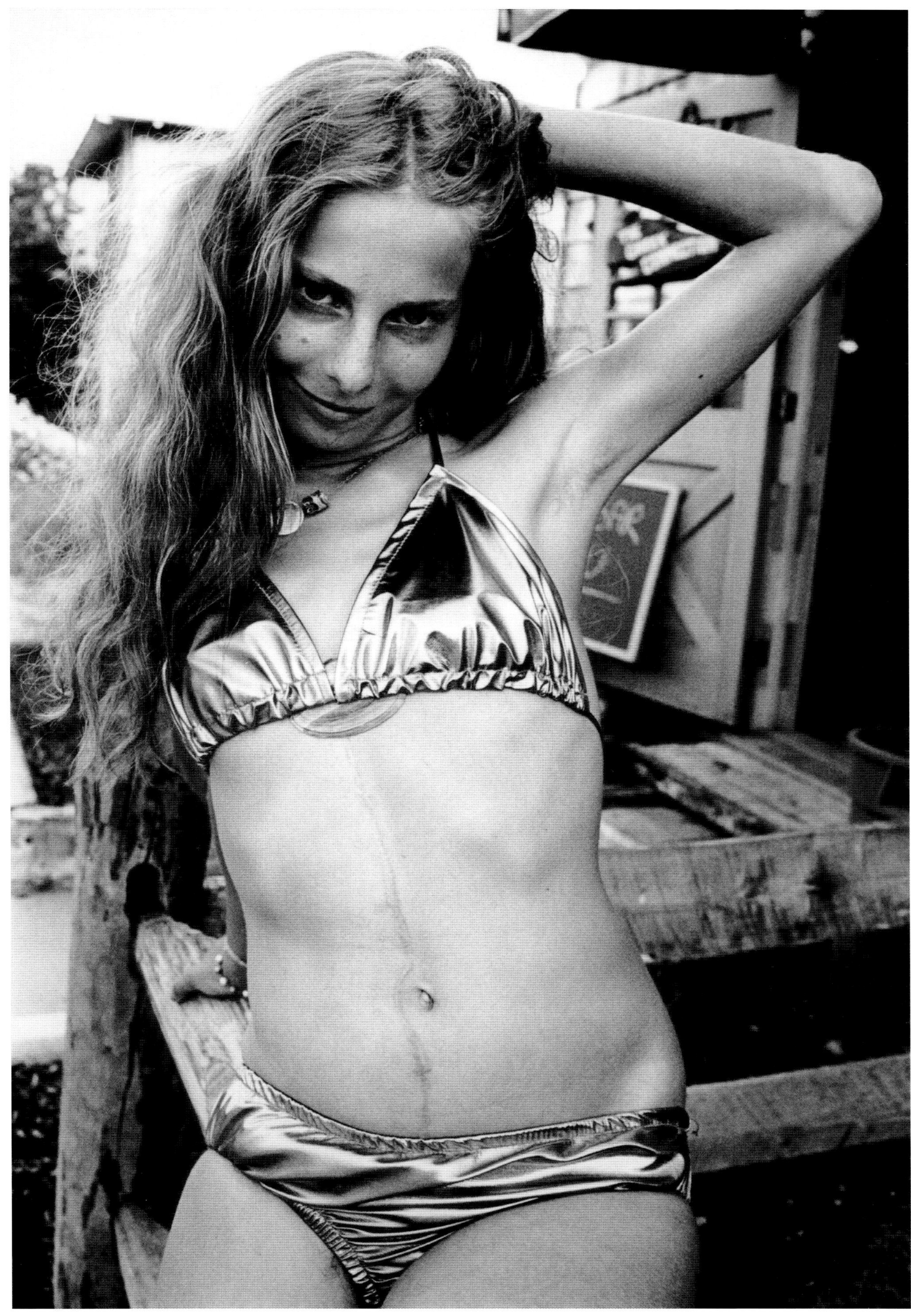

Her Other Side,
Fire Island
New York, 1977

Diamond Lil's
New York, 1982

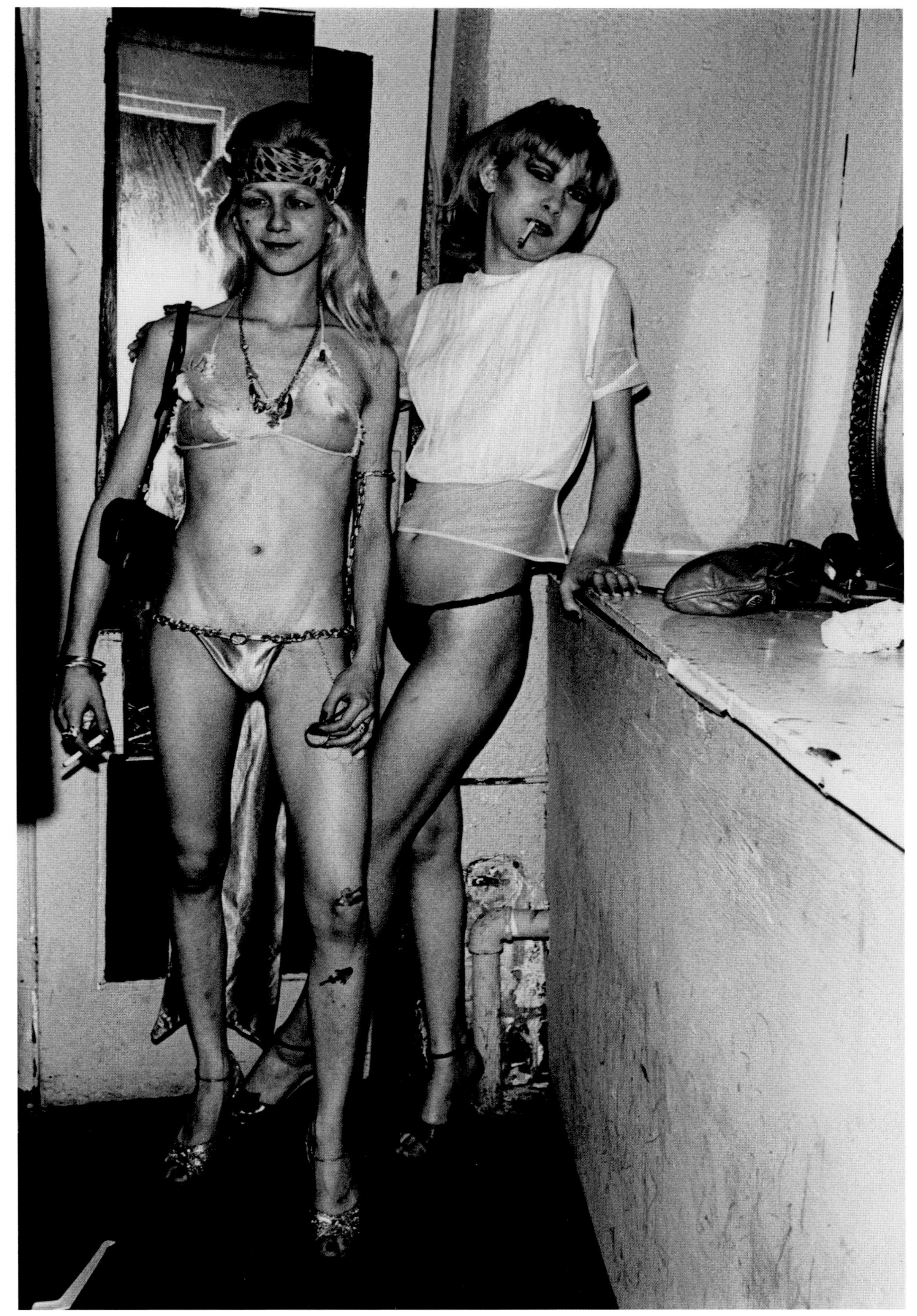

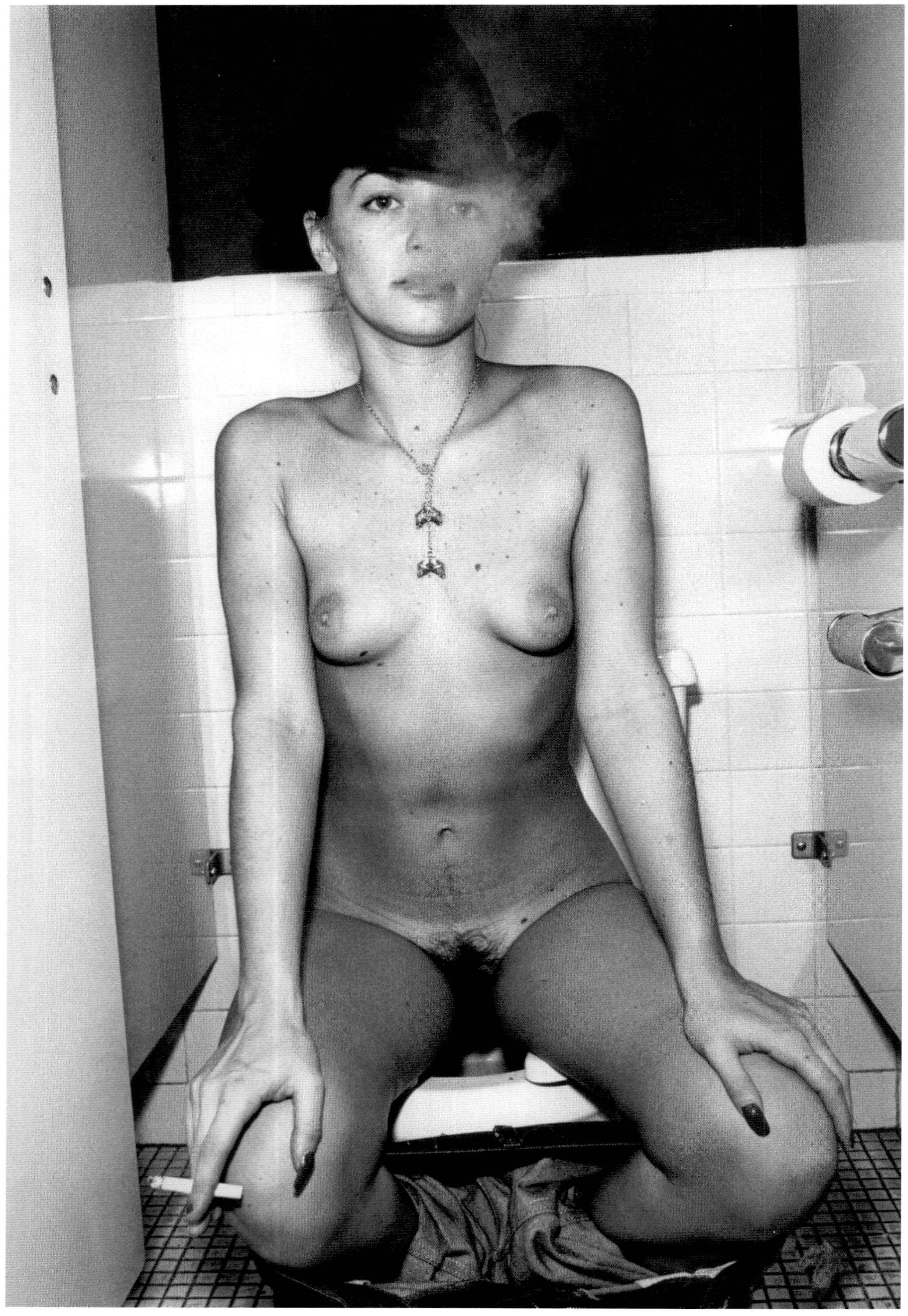

Paradise Garage
New York, 1979

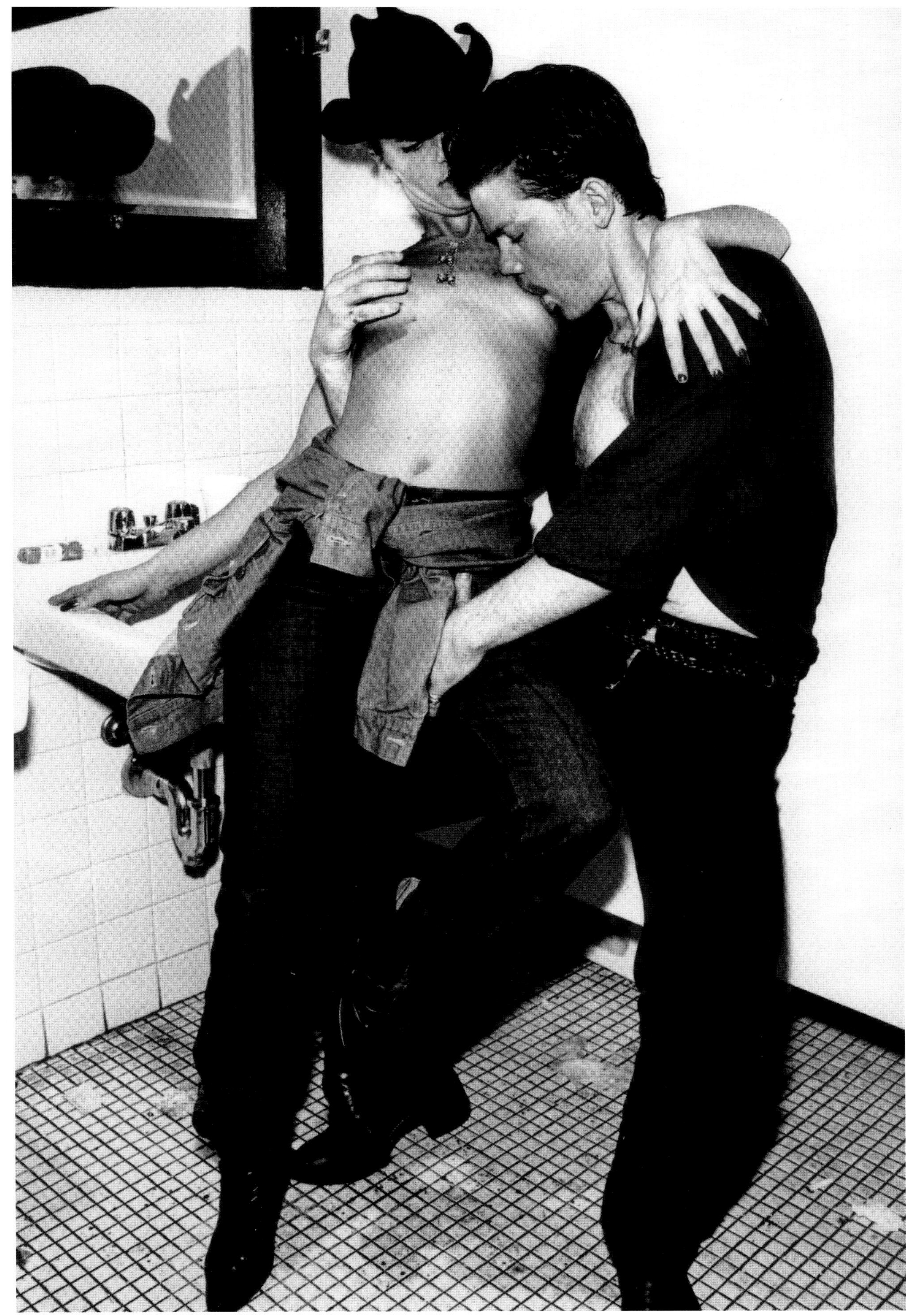

**Paradise Garage
New York, 1979**

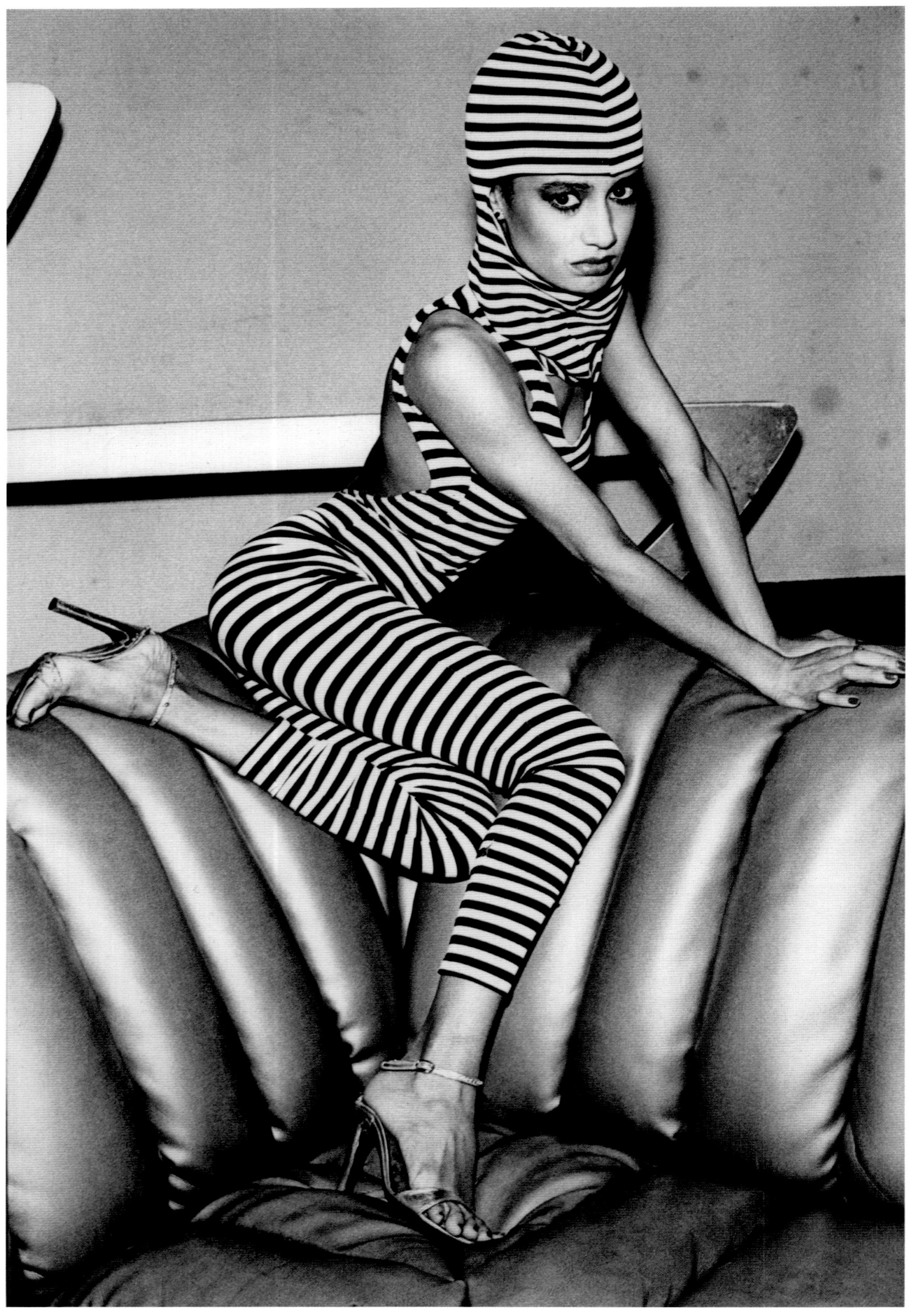

Striped Woman at Studio 54
New York, 1979

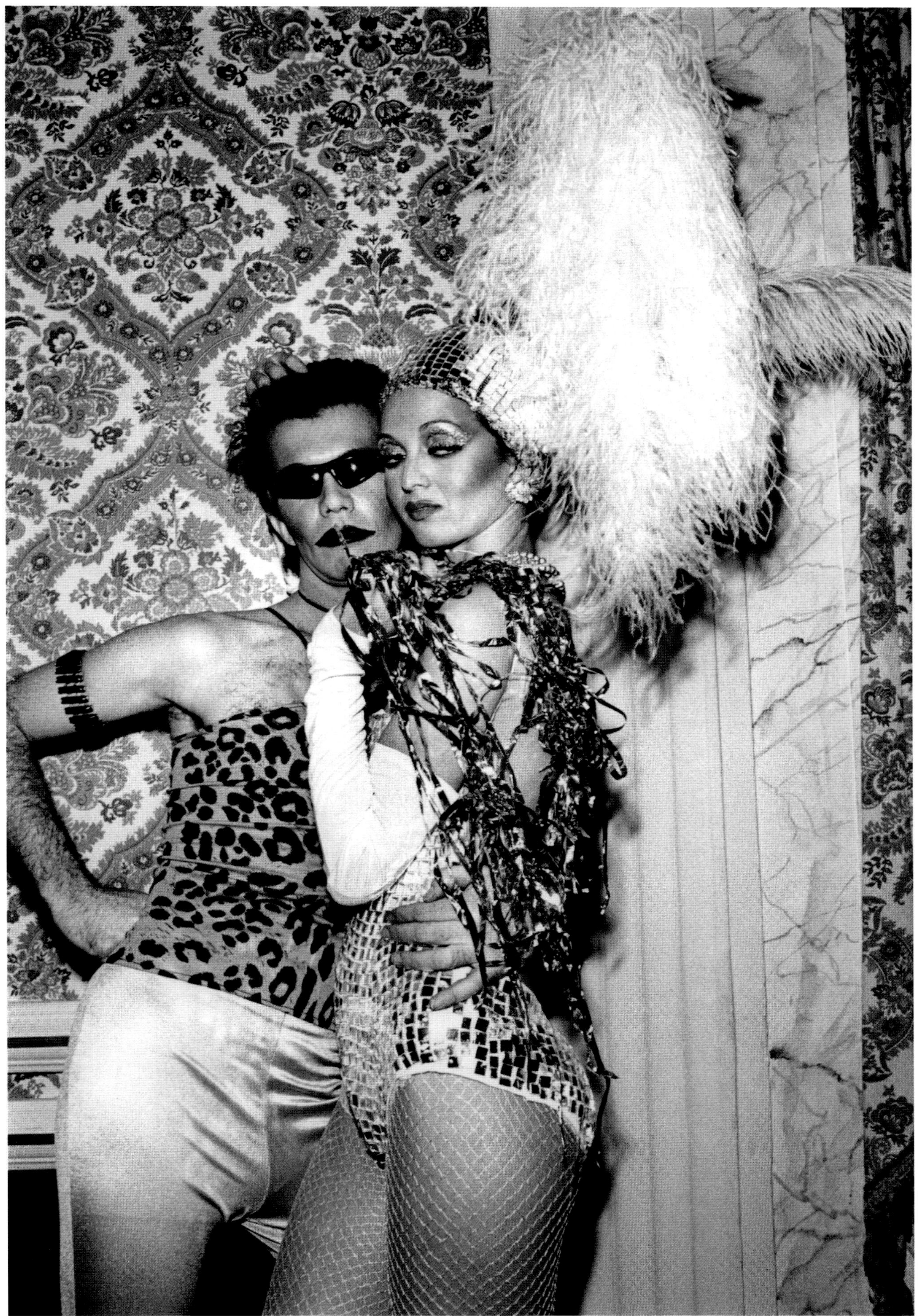

Brazilian Carnival,
Waldorf-Astoria
New York, 1979

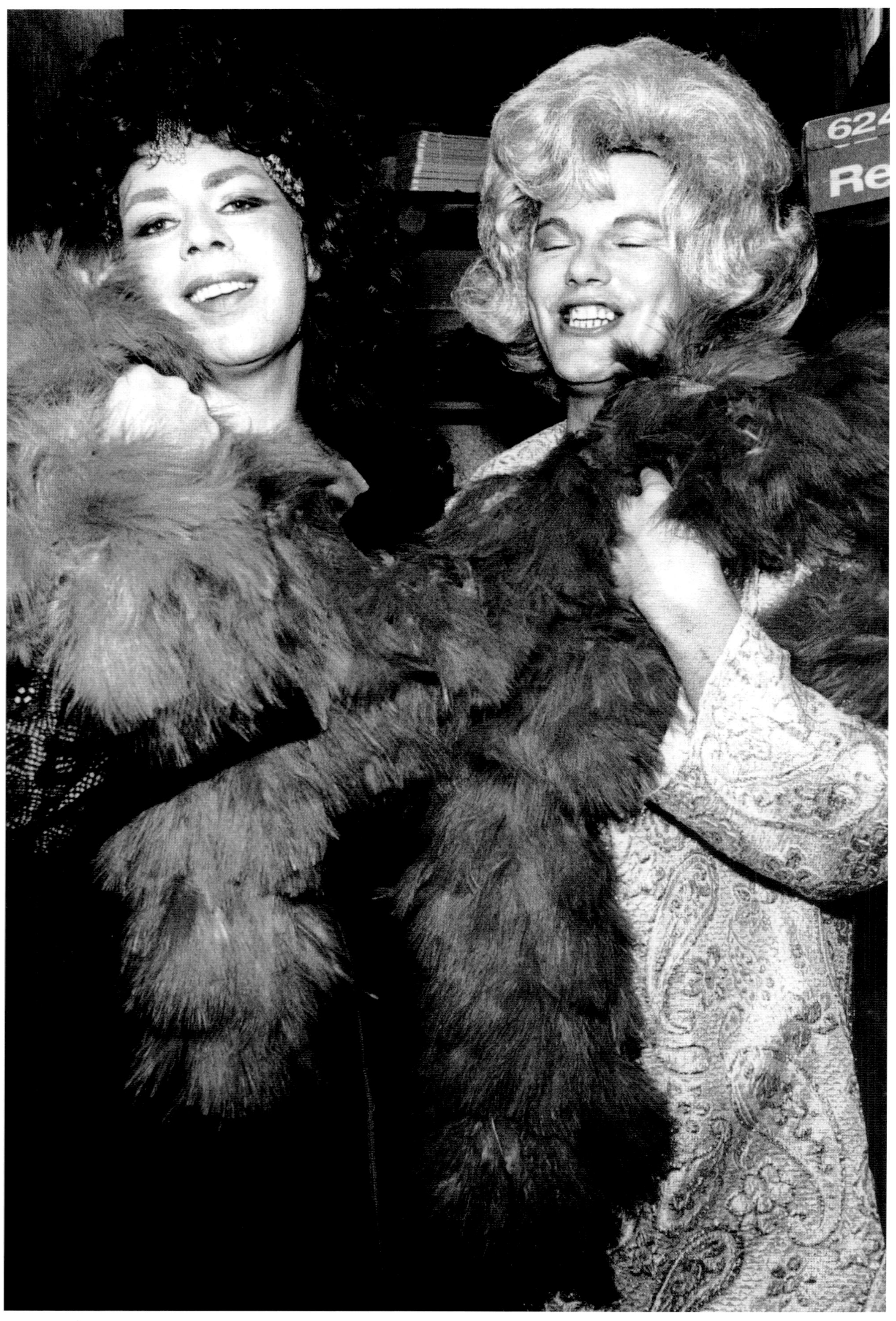

Drag Show in Restaurant,
Staten Island
New York, 1980

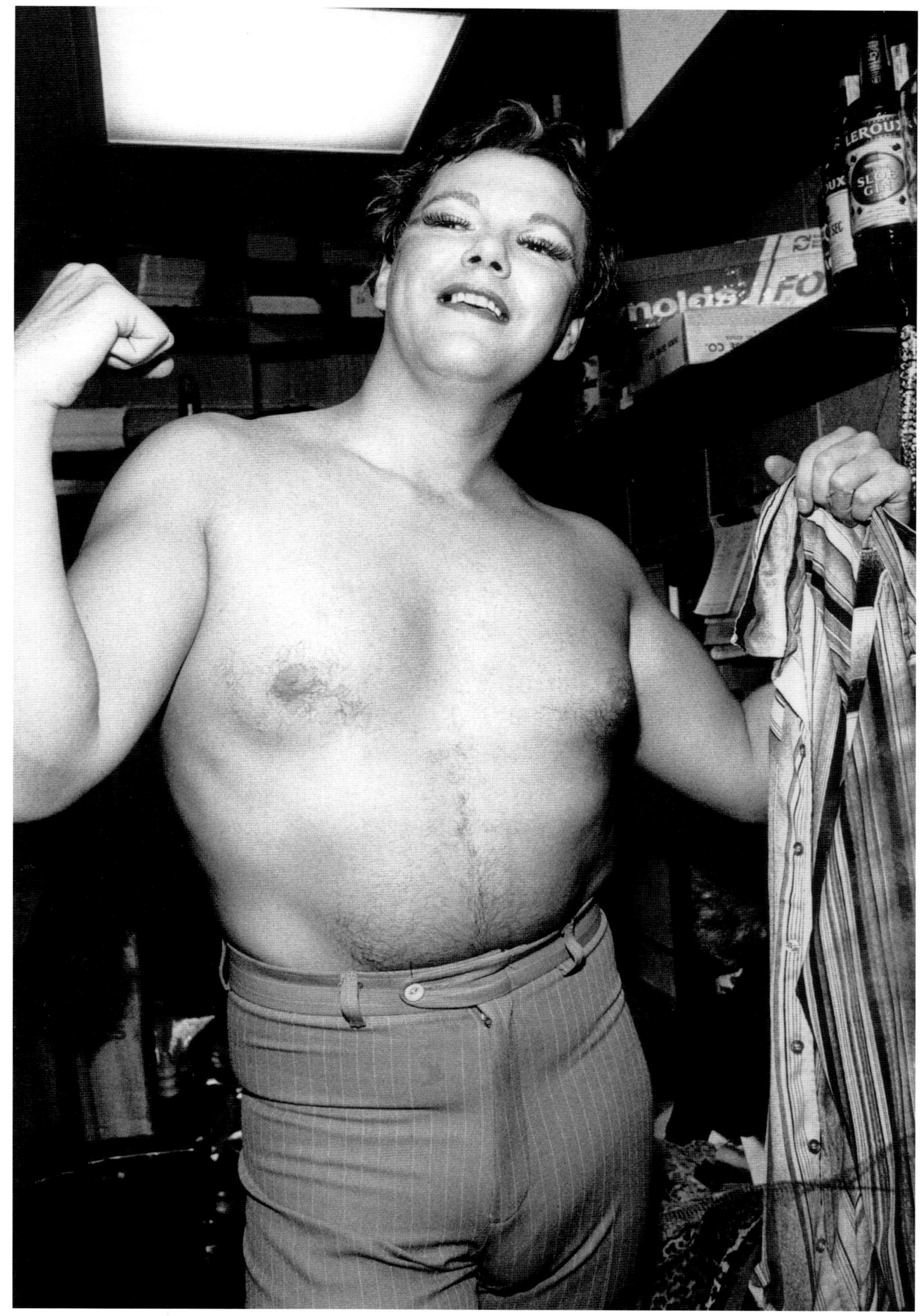

After the Show,
Staten Island
New York, 1980

After Hours
New York, 1979

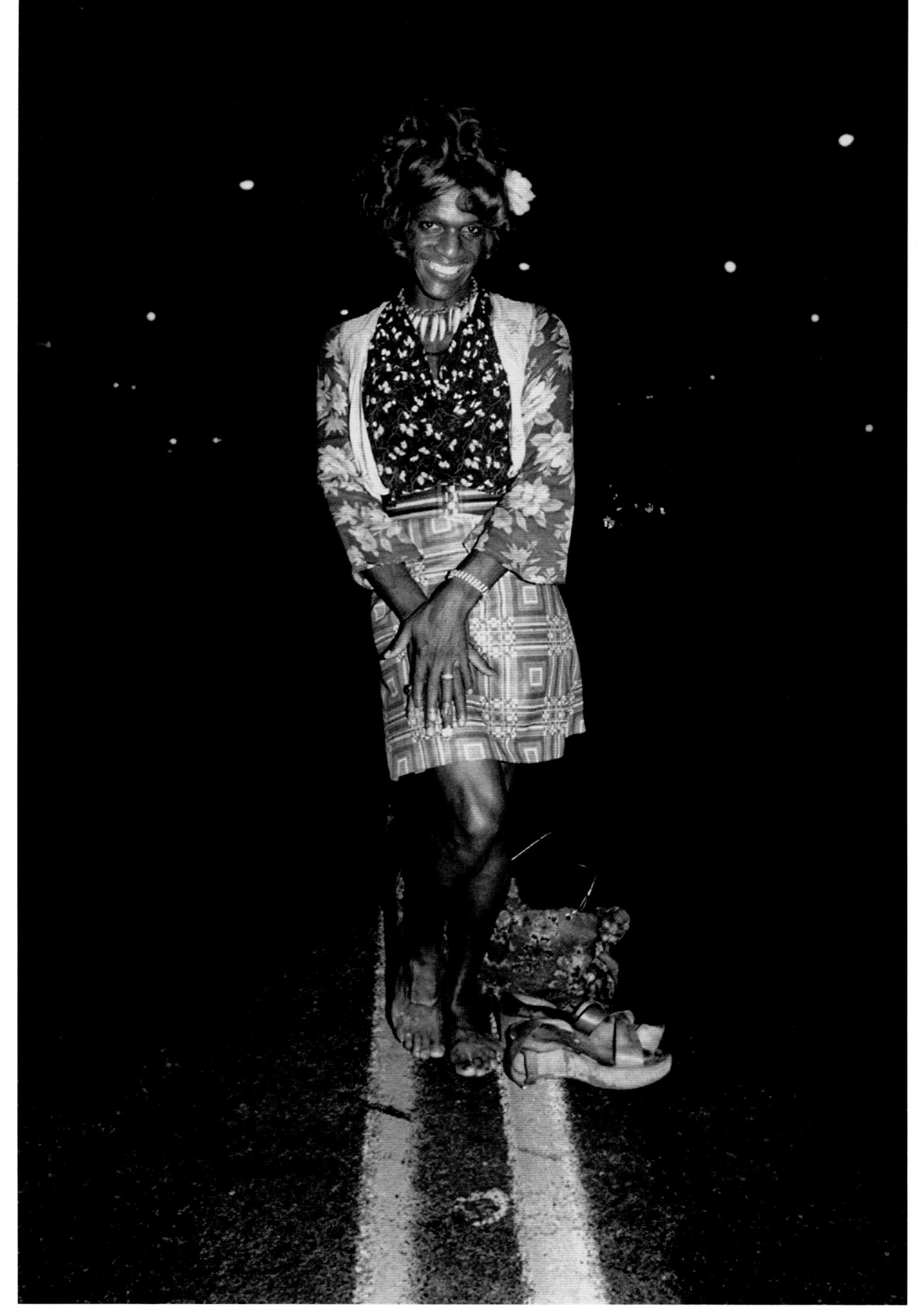

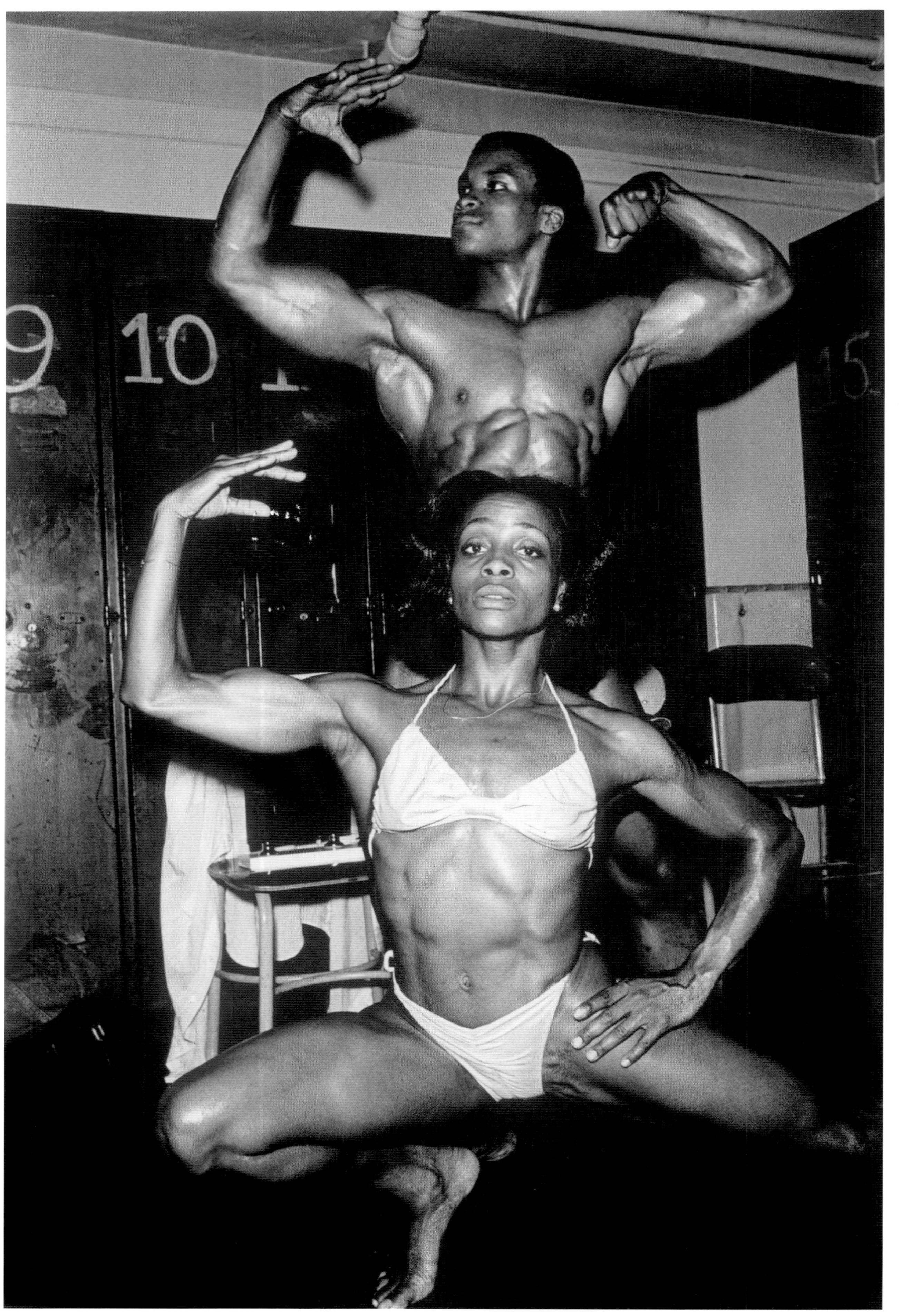
9
10
15

Bodybuilding Competition at
Washington Irving High School
New York, 1980

Bubble Dancer
New York, 1980

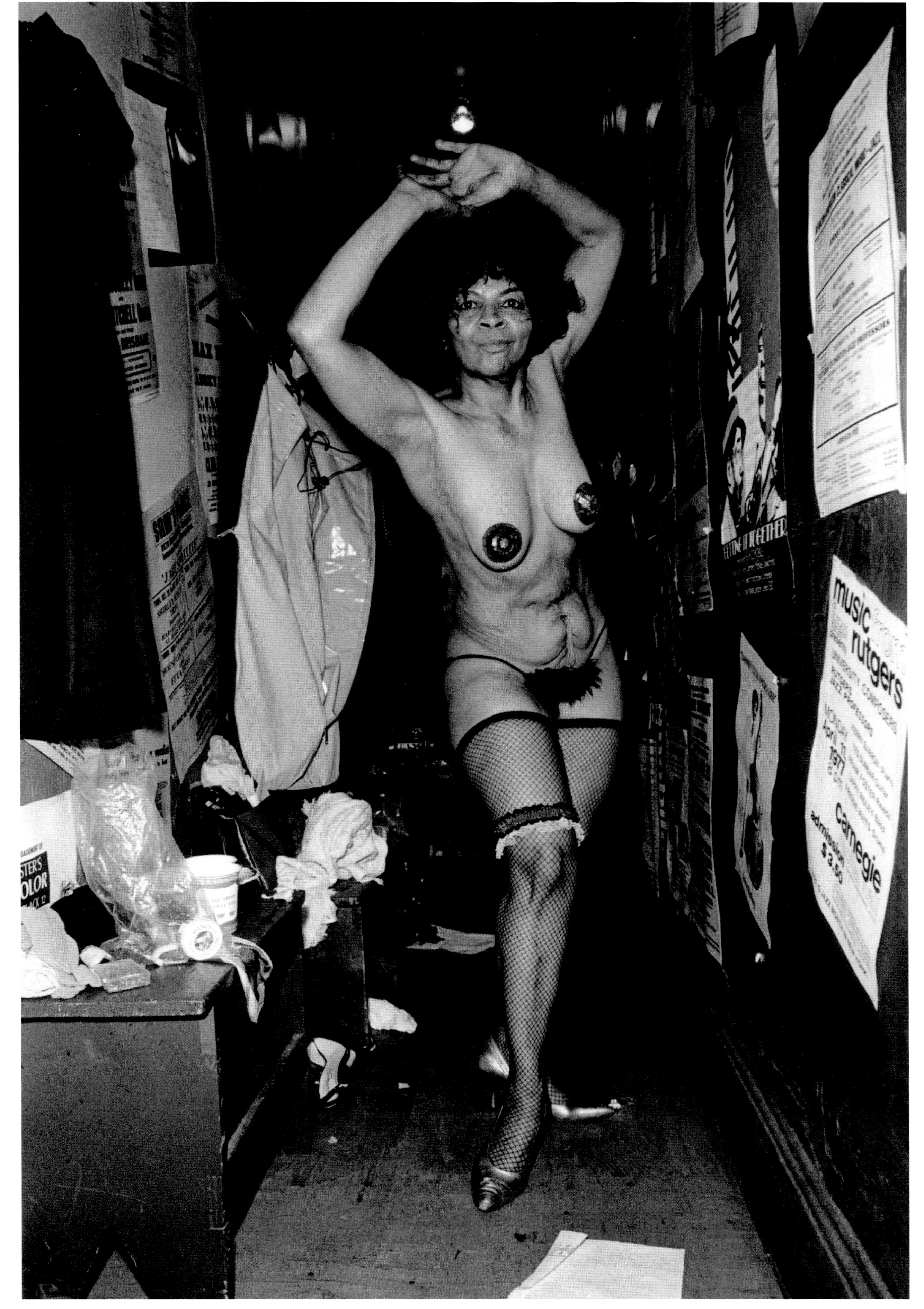
music
rutgers
1977
carnegie
admission
$3.50

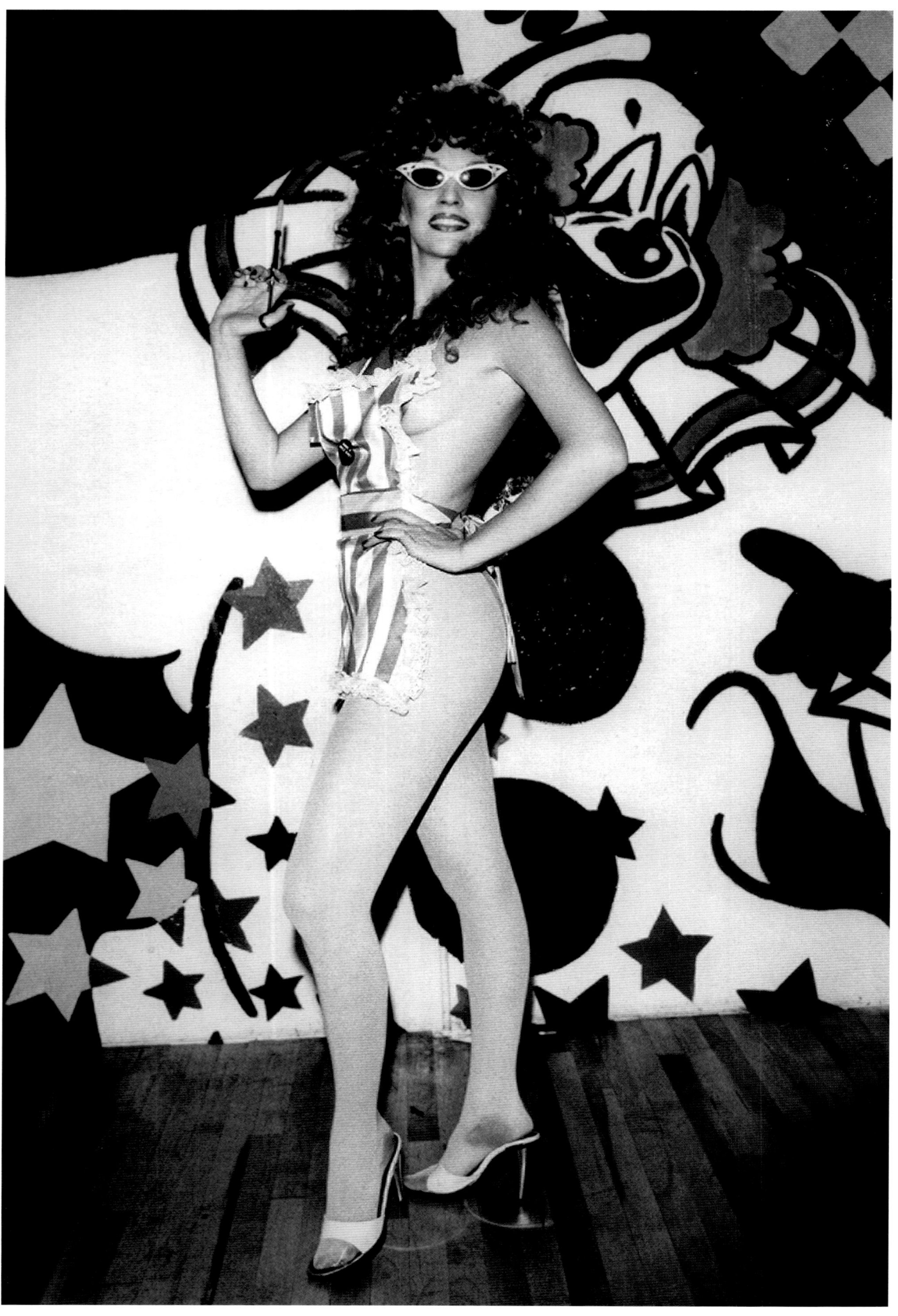

Disco Nurse, Le Clique
New York, 1979

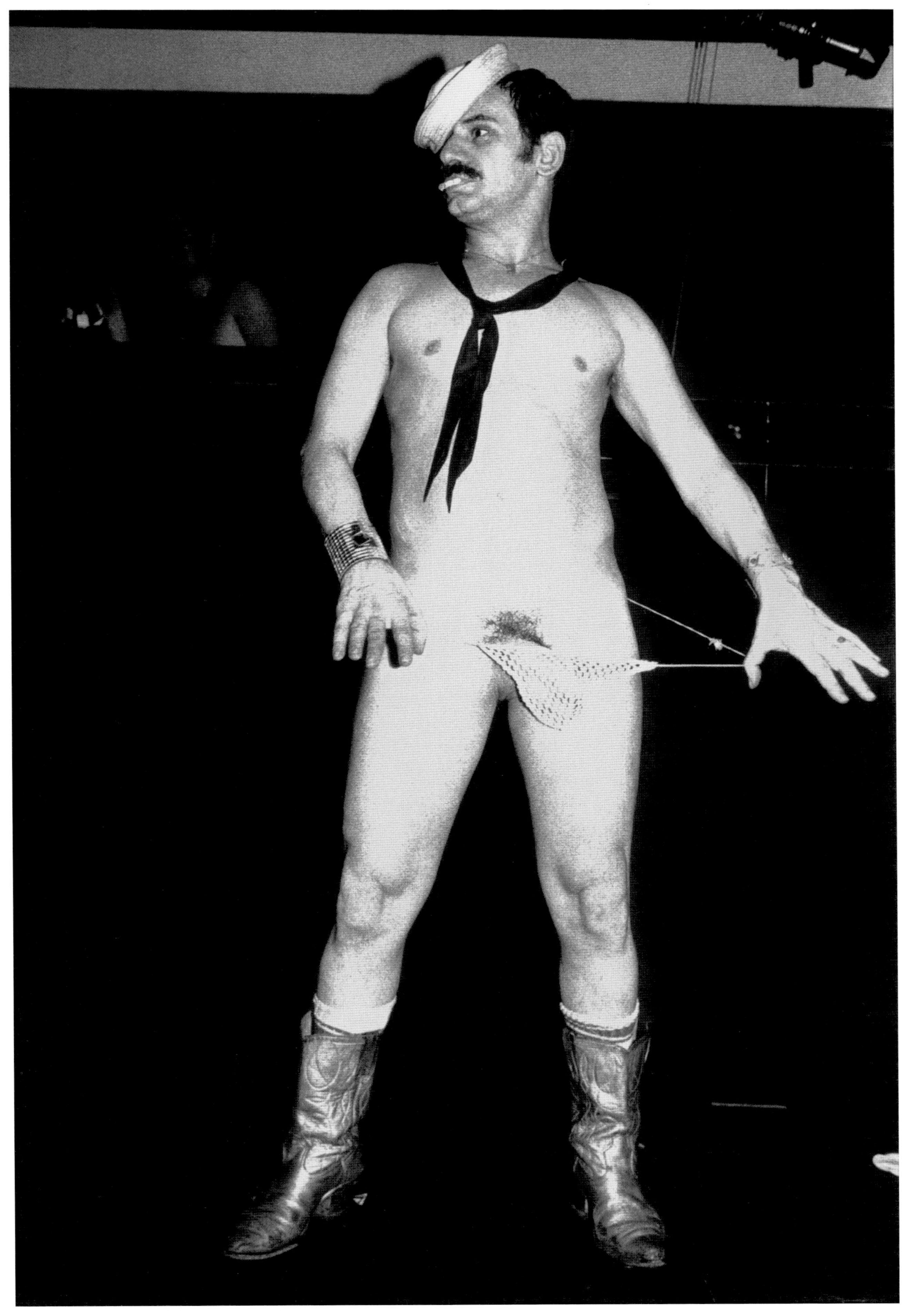

Disco Sailor, Les Mouches
New York, 1978

Giant Dildo, Les Mouches Party
New York, 1979

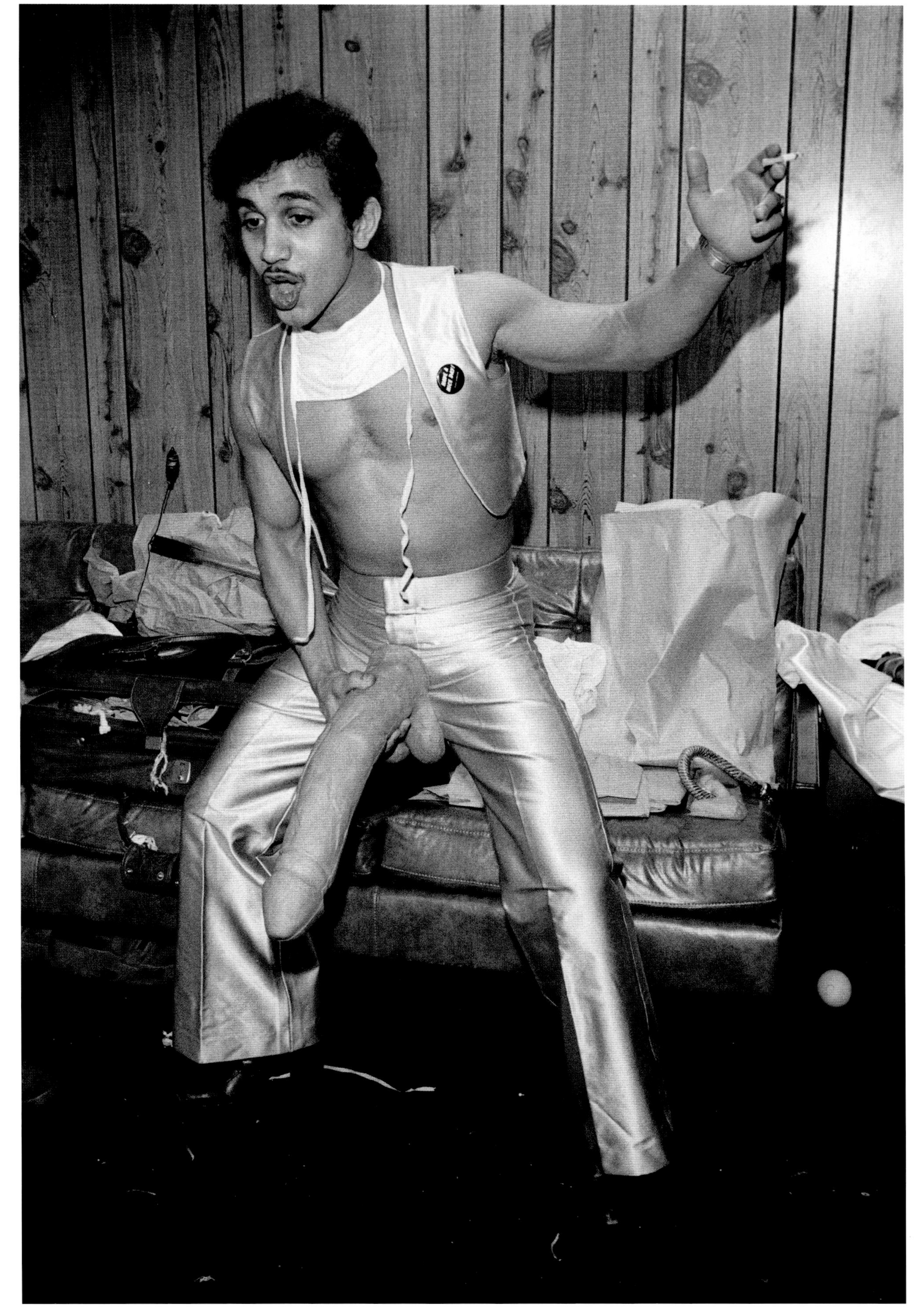

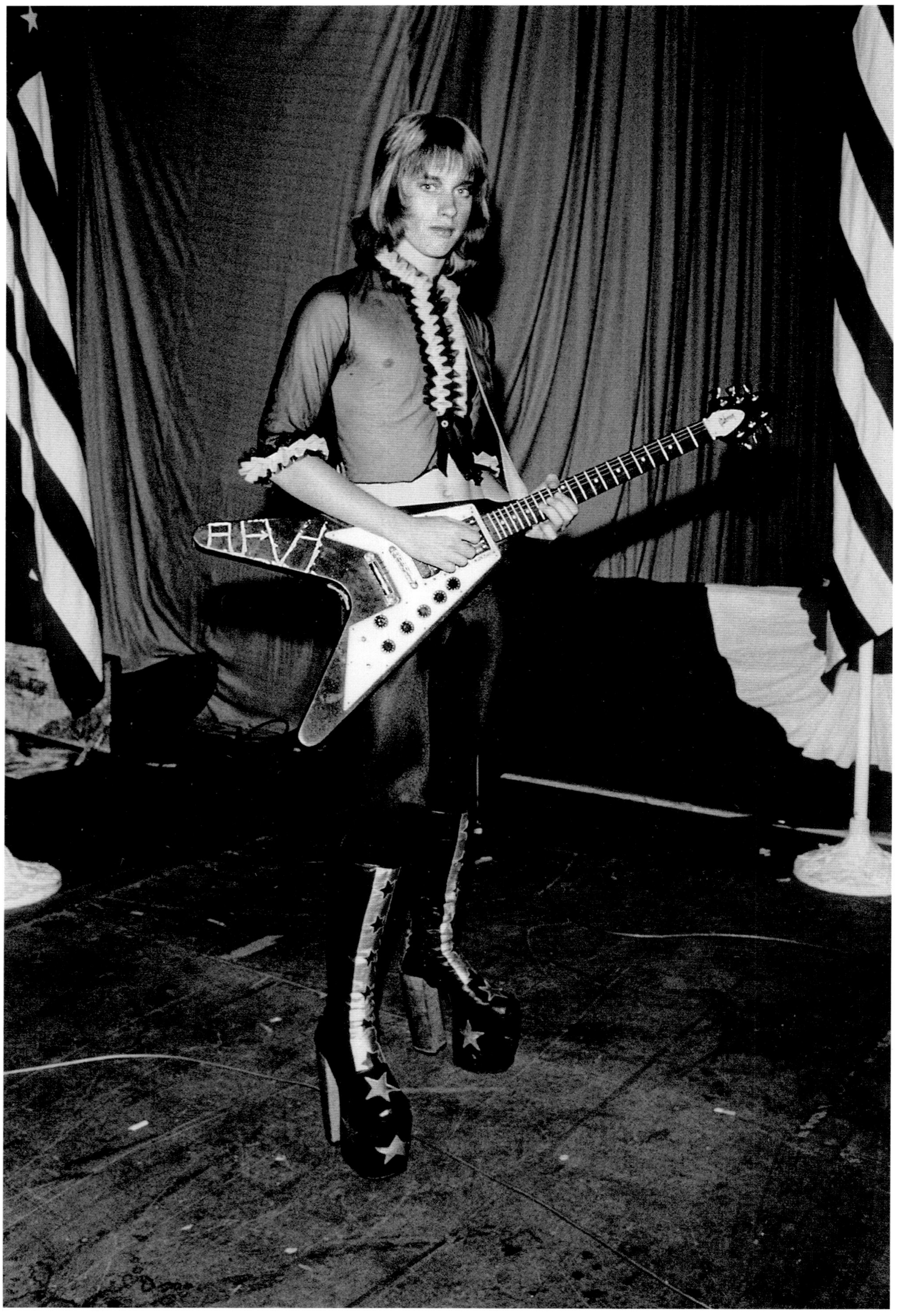

Platform Boots,
Madison Square Garden
New York, 1977

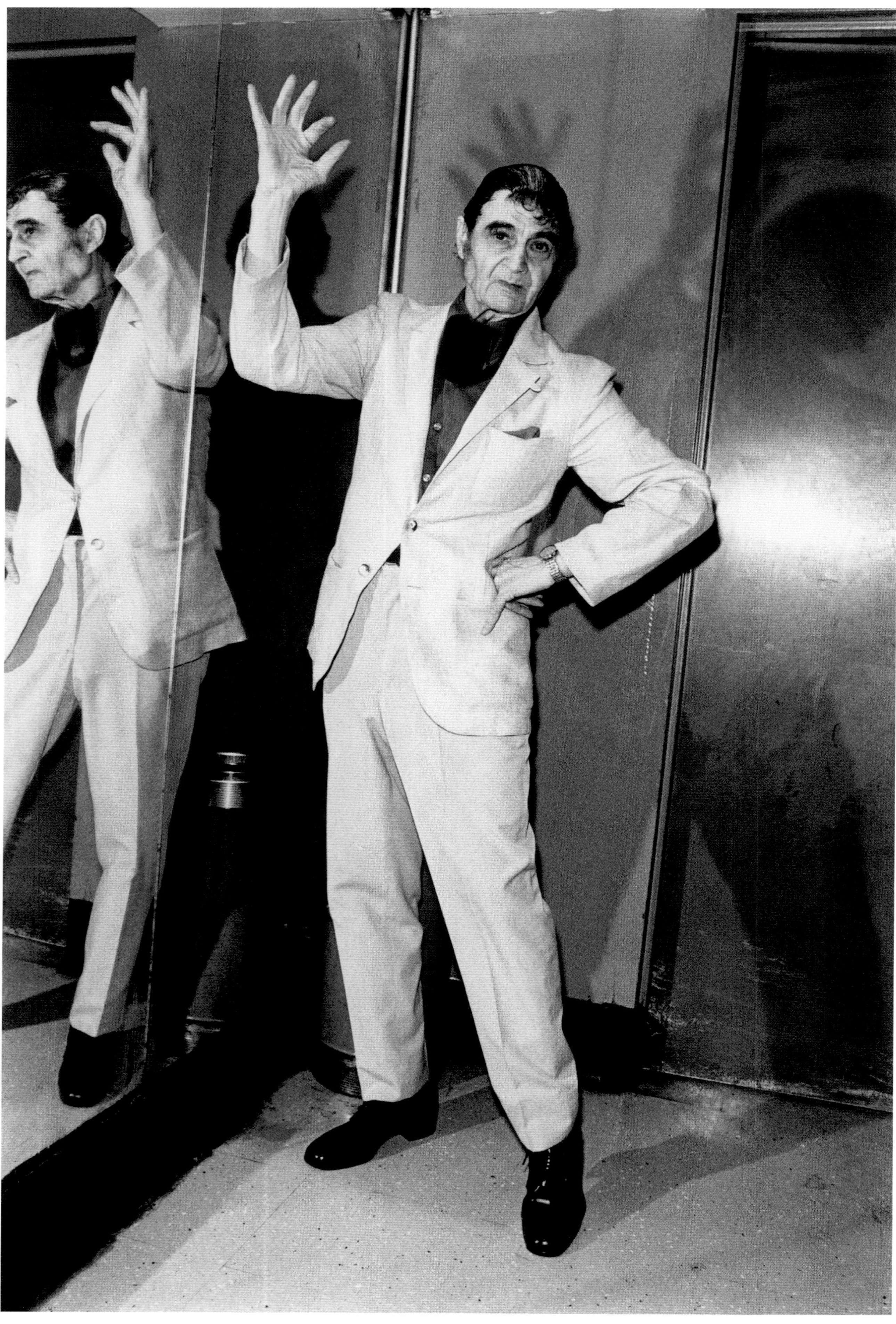

Roseland Ballroom
New York, 1980

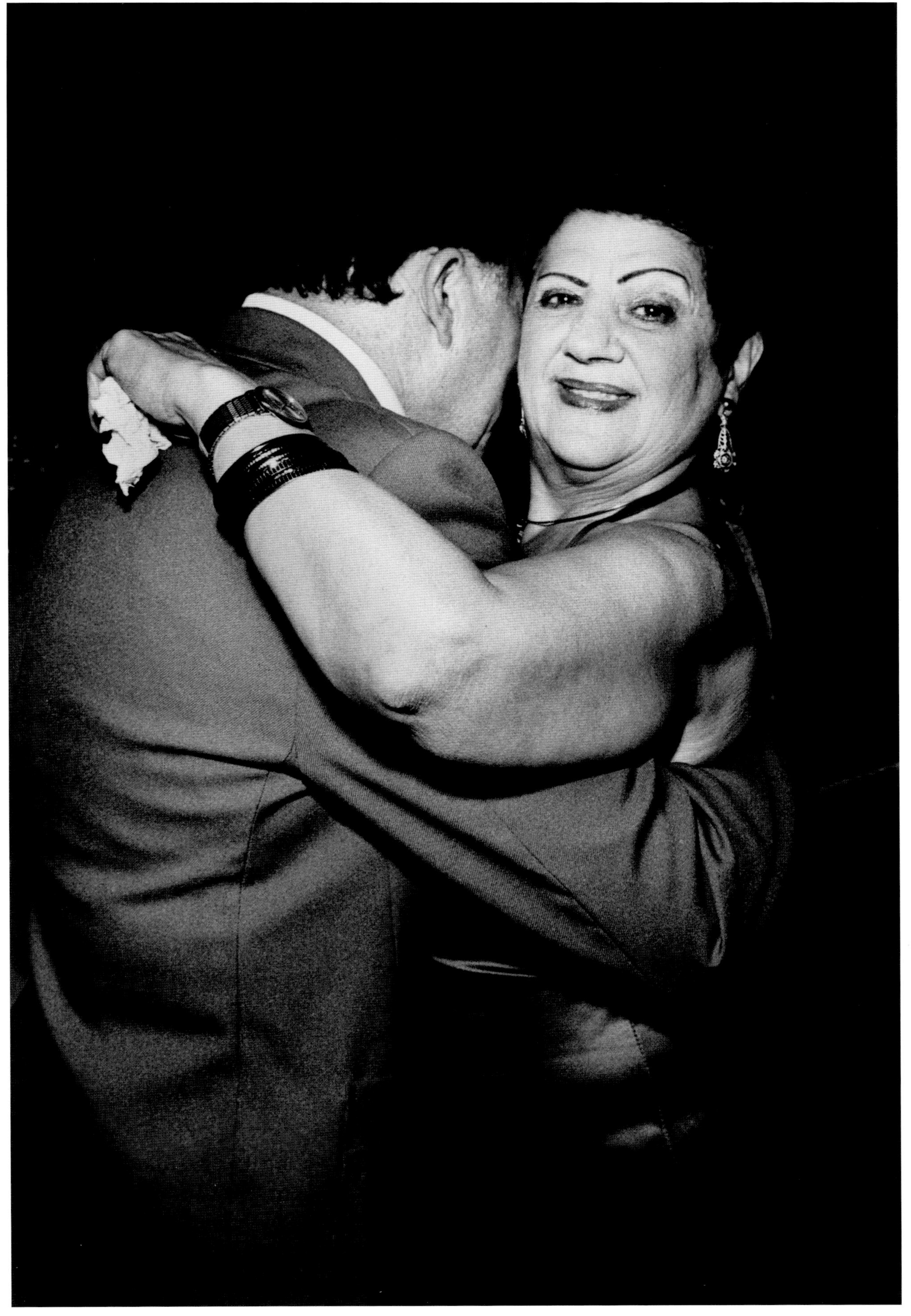

Roseland Ballroom
New York, 1980

Roseland Ballroom
New York, 1980

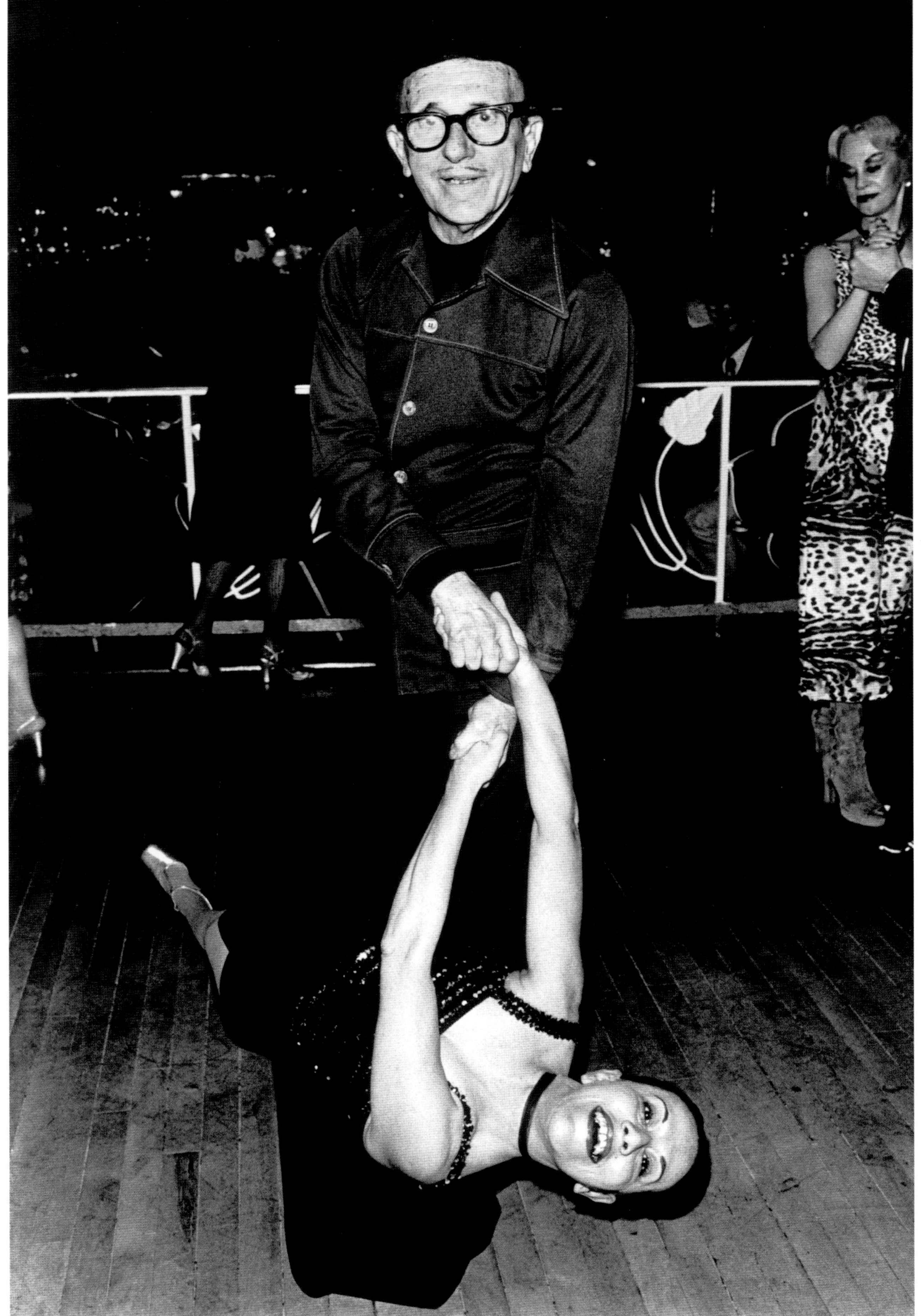

Roseland Ballroom
New York, 1980

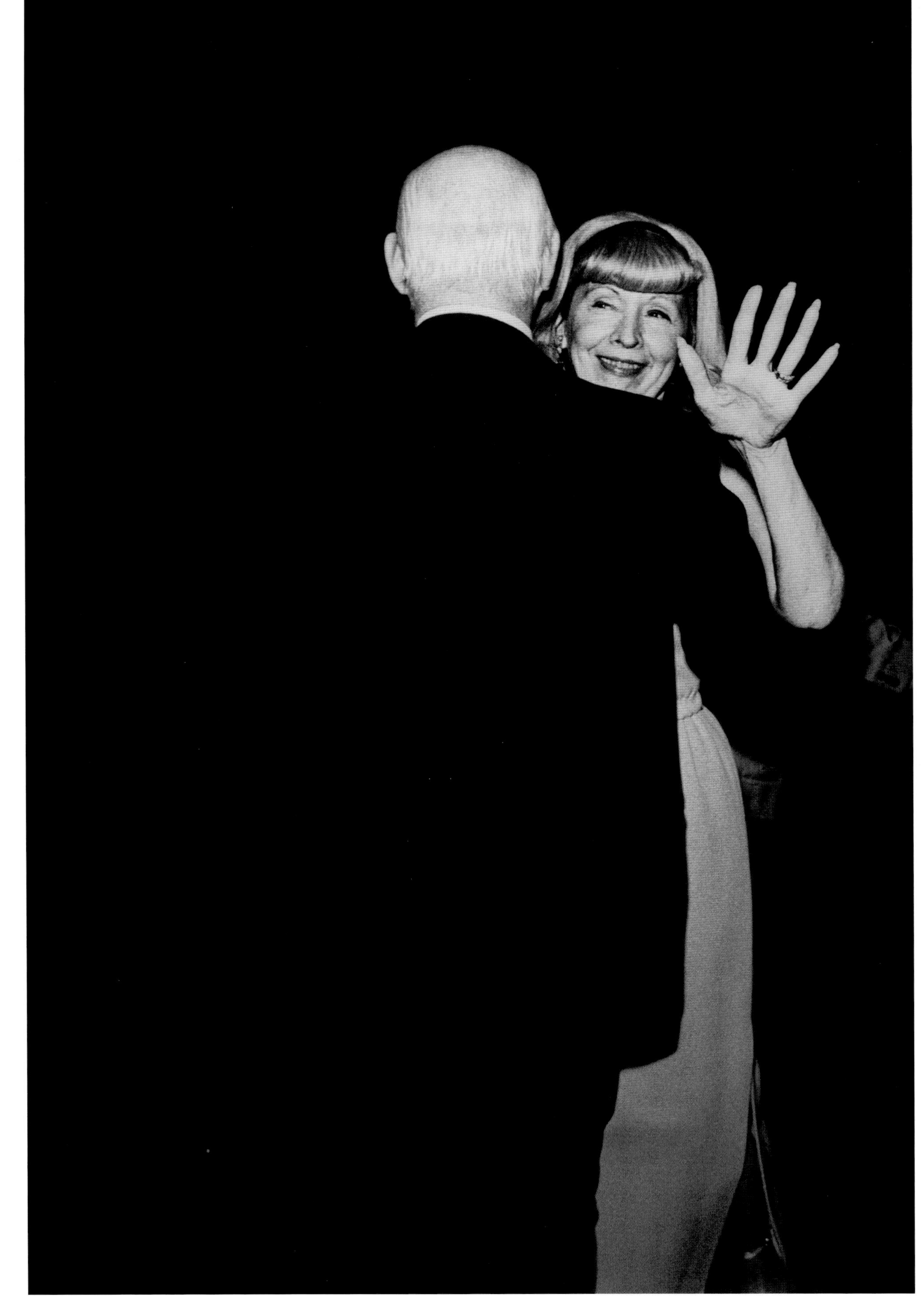

Sometimes Overwhelming

Hating high school, I graduated. My parents insisted I to go to college. I knew I would have to do something besides just sit in a classroom trying to pay attention, and it was my mother who looked through the college catalogue and asked if I would be interested in taking a class in art. At registration, I saw that there was a photography class listed.

One night a week, I left my typist job at in Manhattan at 5 PM and took the A train to High Street in Brooklyn, where the class was held in a factory building. The first time I entered the room full of all male students, I had to choke back the tears.

When I had gotten to know the guys a little, I was invited to a classmate's birthday party. A few weeks earlier, this student had taken a picture of me, but strangely, he had asked me to turn around and had photographed the back of my head. At the party, I asked to see the picture; he said he didn't have a print, but that I could look at the negative in the enlarger. When I saw the image of my long hair merging into my antique fur jacket, I realized why he had told me to turn around. That was a turning point for me; I knew then that photography could be a form of expression that spoke with a voice of its own. I began to consider the art more seriously, and decided to enroll in a two-year photography program at the Fashion Institute of Technology.

After graduating, I worked as an assistant for many photographers in their commercial studios, and also as a staff photographer at an advertising agency for several years. Even so, I was constantly photographing in my free time, after work and on weekends. Being a native New Yorker, I was always outside, where I felt most comfortable. I had grown up in Brooklyn, and so my first photographs were of life on the streets. I turned my camera on friends, relatives, and neighbors in my ethnically diverse area. Eventually, my photographs became instinctual, and I did not think about what to photograph or why.

It is clear to me now that these black-and-white photographs from the 1970s and 80s document a part of New York City that has disappeared. It was a rough and unpolished environment, and I always gravitated towards the individuals that had unique characteristics and large personalities. I went to festivals, block parties, and all the parades—Veterans Day, Easter, Puerto Rican Day, Gay Pride, St. Patrick's Day, and the especially charming and original early Halloween parade.

During the summers I returned to the beaches of my childhood, Coney Island and Brighton Beach. I have clear memories and strong attachments to these beaches, and still visit them. I photographed at Riis Beach's Bay One, the only nude bay in New York. When I was invited to clubs and discos I brought my camera; Studio 54, GG's Barnum Room, Le Clique, Les Mouches, Paradise Garage, and the roller disco Empire Rollerdrome had glamour, grit, sexual exhibitionism, and a sense of wild and free self-expression in a world before the AIDS epidemic. My photographs were like souvenirs; I liked to collect moments and remembrances of the people in the places that I visited. If I got great photographs out of them as well, that was the icing on the cake. When Radio City was going to be demolished, I joined those who were outraged by the loss, and decided to immortalize New York City's last great music hall by photographing the Rockettes. I photographed the dancers at Roseland Ballroom, who had started going there in the 1940s and 50s and still loved to dance.

The photographs in *Sometimes Overwhelming* are glimpses of an era and its people. Most of the people I photographed were aware of the camera, but I never told them to pose—it was a collaboration. The older people pictured, many of whom I know and love, didn't pay any attention to me, while the children acted completely out of their imaginations. Looking back at them, I am catapulted through time to each place and event, and to all those people I have had the pleasure of seeing along the way.

Arlene Gottfried

Acknowledgements

A very special thank you to Maria Mayer. Truly, without you, these photographs would still be mostly unseen. You ignited the spark that created *Sometimes Overwhelming*. Trips to the storage room, editing, scanning, and hours of making a book...you came to program my website, and used your magical powers to pull together years of photographs. I will always be grateful for your vision and friendship. Love You.... Reverend Arlene

powerHouse Books, for their enthusiasm for the photographs and for publishing *Sometimes Overwhelming*.

Mine Suda, for her gentleness and clarity.

Mets & Schilt Publishers, for bringing *Sometimes Overwhelming* across the ocean.

Isabel Croft, jumping rope because of Barry Cohen, my loyal supporter.

Solomon Roberts Jr., who brought me to Ben Fernandez's Minority Photographers workshop in the basement of the Public Theatre to see what a darkroom was all about.

Larry Siegel and Michael Spano, curators of the Midtown Y Gallery.

Helen Dubertein, for reading the afterword.

Karen Gottfried and a friend drove me out to Riis for some very memorable moments.

Pete Castagne, my music buddy from way back in the day.

Teri Castagne, for hanging out at Diamond Lil's, Roseland, the Nuyorican Poets Café, et cetera.

My soul brother Peter Hopson, who sent me to see brother Michael Hopson, who introduced me to Peg Leg Bates and invited me to photograph at the Granit Hotel for so many summers.

Steven Soloway, for running all around with me and cracking up laughing at the madness.

Julio Vega, who has been my sidekick and life preserver through many years, lighting, listening, and going on so many adventures...thank you.

David Chan, who has helped me endlessly.

Kish Manasse, we miss you so much.

Jim and Mary Marchese, for always showing up.

Colette Combader, for standing by over the years.

Lois Carlo, for witnessing the early prints and working on those early book maquettes.

Alex Coleman, director of Foto Gallery in the original SoHo, for my first one-woman show, *Coney Island*.

Monica Cipnic of *Popular Photography*'s gallery for the *People of Brooklyn* exhibit.

Carol Naggar, for her writing.

Kazuko Stone, for knowing in advance that the black-and-white photographs would be very timely now.

Jimmy Nicol, for the walks in Brooklyn with you and your camera, before all this began.

Sometimes Overwhelming

Published in the United States by powerHouse Books,
a division of powerHouse Cultural Entertainment, Inc.
32 Adams Street, Brooklyn, NY 11201-1021
www.powerHouseBooks.com

Second edition, 2018

Library of Congress Cataloging-in-Publication Data:

Gottfried, Arlene.
Sometimes overwhelming : photographs / by Arlene Gottfried.
p. cm.
ISBN 978-1-57687-371-7
1. Portrait photography--New York (State)--New York. 2. Street photography--New York (State)--New York. 3. Gottfried, Arlene. I. Title.
TR680.G6745 2007
779'.2092--dc22
2006048849

Paperback ISBN 978-1-57687-904-7

Printing and binding by Pimlico Book International, Hong Kong

Book design by Mine Suda

10 9 8 7 6 5 4 3 2 1

Printed and bound in China